WRITING THE FLESH

Medieval & Renaissance Literary Studies

Writing the Flesh

The Herbert Family Dialogue

by
Jeffrey Powers-Beck

DUQUESNE UNIVERSITY PRESS
Pittsburgh, Pennsylvania

Library of Congress Cataloging in Publication Data

Powers-Beck, Jeffrey P., 1964–
    Writing the flesh: the Herbert family dialogue / by Jeffrey
Powers-Beck.
        p.   cm. — (Medieval & Renaissance literary studies)
    Includes bibliographical references and index.

    ISBN 0–8207–0293–5 (acid-free paper)
    1. English literature—Early modern, 1500–1700—History and
criticism.   2. Authors, English—Early modern, 1500–1700—Family
relationships.   3. Herbert of Cherbury, Edward Herbert, Baron,
1583–1648—Family.   4. Danvers, Magdalen, Lady, 1567 or
8–1627—Family.   5. Family—Great Britain—History—17th
century.   6. Herbert, Henry, Sir, 1595–1673—Family.
7. Danvers, John, Sir, 1588?–1655—Family.   8. Herbert, Thomas,
1597–1642?—Family.   9. Herbert, George, 1593–1633—Family.
10. Herbert family.   I. Title.   II. Series: Medieval and Renaissance
literary studies
    PR431   .P69   1998
    820.9'004—ddc21

                                                                98–25499
                                                                    CIP

To my family, especially to my mother and father

"Listen now to something human."
—Li-Young Lee, "Always a Rose"

Contents

Illustrations

Acknowledgements

I am grateful to the National Endowment of the Humanities for granting an N.E.H. Summer Stipend to me in 1995, and to the East Tennessee State University Research Development Committee for awarding a Research Development Grant to me in 1996. Without their support, I would not have been able to conduct the archival research presented in this work. Similarly, I appreciate the research libraries and manuscript repositories that have contributed so much to my work. These institutions include the Bodleian Library, Oxford University; the British Library, London; the Guildford Muniment Room of the Surrey Record Office; the Folger Shakespeare Library, Washington, D.C.; the Huntington Library, San Marino, California; the Walter Clinton Jackson Library, University of North Carolina at Greensboro; the Magdalene College Library, Cambridge; the National Library of Wales, Aberystwyth; the Northamptonshire Record Office; the Public Record Office, London; the Westminster City Archives Center, London; and the Sherrod Library at East Tennessee State University. I also wish to acknowledge the kindness of John Herbert, Earl of Powis, and J. R. More-Molyneux of Loseley Park, Guildford, for allowing me to consult Herbert family papers in their possession. Likewise, Father Anthony M. Hurst, O.S.B., Rector of St. Nicholas Church, Montgomery, has been very kind in allowing me to publish my photograph of the tomb of Richard Herbert, Esq.

Without the guidance and encouragement of other scholars, I could not have begun nor have completed this project.

These scholars include: Judith H. Anderson, Indiana University; David R. Ransome, Rhode Island School of Design; Michael C. Schoenfeldt, University of Michigan-Ann Arbor; Claude Summers and Ted-Larry Pebworth, University of Michigan-Dearborn; Christopher Hodgkins, University of North Carolina-Greensboro; Cristina Malcolmson, Bates College; Eugene D. Hill, Mount Holyoke College; Elena Levy-Navarro, University of Wisconsin-Whitewater; Sidney Gottlieb, Sacred Heart University; N. W. Bawcutt, University of Liverpool; Susan Anne Dawson; Daniel Doerksen, University of New Brunswick; Chauncey Wood, McMaster University; Douglas Swartz, Indiana University Northwest; and John Shawcross, University of Kentucky. The chair of the Department of English at East Tennessee State University, Professor Styron Harris, and the dean of the College of Arts and Sciences, Donald Johnson, have been very kind in supporting my work, as have all of my colleagues, especially Professors Anne LeCroy, Barbara A. Johnson (formerly of E.T.S.U.), Kevin O'Donnell, Ernest (Jack) Branscomb, Thomas Alan Holmes, and Theresa Lloyd. I must also acknowledge the help of several persons who have assisted me in translating Greek, Latin, Italian, and French texts. They are Professor Betty Rose Nagle, Indiana University; Professor Kenneth Lloyd-Jones, Trinity College; Professor Glenn Steinberg, College of New Jersey, Trenton; and Anne Powers-Beck. Professor Nagle, especially, spent many hours correcting my Latin translations.

I wish to acknowledge the kindness of two publishers in granting me the permission to use portions of two published essays in this book. First, I wish to thank Professor Arthur F. Kinney, executive editor of *English Literary Renaissance*, for allowing me to print large portions of the following essay in this book: "'Proudly Mounted on the Oceans Backe:' The Myth and Emblematical Method of Thomas Herbert," *English Literary Renaissance* 28, no. 2 (May 1998).

Second, I wish to thank the Southeastern Renaissance

Conference, and particularly its Secretary-Treasurer Professor John N. Wall, for allowing me to print large portions of the following essay in this book: "'Slack Time' and the 'Uncessant Minutes': Time in 'The Two Herberts.'" *Renaissance Papers*, 113–124. Edited by George Walton Williams and Philip Rollinson. Raleigh, N.C.: Southeastern Renaissance Conference, 1997.

I also wish to acknowledge those scholarly libraries and museums that have permitted me to publish photographs of books and manuscripts as illustrations for this work. Those institutions are: the Walter Clinton Jackson Library, Greensboro, N.C.; the Cambridge University Library, Cambridge; the National Portrait Gallery, London; the Folger Shakespeare Library, Washington, D.C.; the Houghton Library, Harvard University; and the Bodleian Library, Oxford.

In the editing of this work, Susan Wadsworth-Booth of Duquesne University Press has been a constant and invaluable guide. My graduate assistant, Karen Daniel, has also been of great service in proofreading the manuscript. I thank them both very gratefully.

Finally, I would be remiss not to mention the generous support of my own family, especially that of my wife, Anne; my daughters Emily and Eleanor; my father and mother, Arnold J. Beck and Jacqueline R. Beck; my brothers, especially my twin brother, Brian J. Beck; and my father-in-law and mother-in-law, James B. Powers and Katherine R. Powers. Simple thanks do not suffice to express my deep gratitude to them.

Abbreviations

The following frequently mentioned works will be cited parenthetically throughout the text using these abbreviations:

KJV *Holy Bible. King James Authorized Version.* Edited by C. I. Scofield. New York: Oxford University Press, 1967. Cited by book, chapter, and verse.

OED Simpson, J. A., and E. S. C. Weimer, eds. *The Oxford English Dictionary.* 2d. ed. 20 vols. Oxford: Oxford University Press, 1989. Cited by term and entry number.

OLD Glare, P. G. W., ed. *Oxford Latin Dictionary.* Oxford: Oxford University Press, 1983. Cited by term and entry number.

STC Pollard, Alfred W. and G. R. Redgrave. *A Short-Title Catalogue of Books Printed in England, Scotland, & Ireland . . ., 1475–1640.* 2d ed. London: Bibliographical Society, 1976–1991.

Wing STC Wing, Donald G. *Short-Title Catalogue of Books Printed in England, Scotland, Ireland, Wales, and British America . . ., 1641–1700.* 2d ed. New York: Modern Language Association, 1972–1988.

Works Herbert, George. *The Works of George Herbert.* Edited by F. E. Hutchinson. Oxford: Oxford University Press, 1945.

Portrait of George Herbert. Robert White's engraving for *The Life of Mr. George Herbert* by Izaak Walton, 1670. By permission of the George Herbert Collection in the Special Collections Division, Walter Clinton Jackson Library, University of North Carolina at Greensboro.

1 Writing the Flesh

ða

The Herbert Family Dialogue

Fiction is like a spider's web, attached ever so lightly perhaps, but still attached to life at all four corners. Often the
attachment is scarcely perceptible; Shakespeare's plays, for
instance, seem to hang there complete by themselves. But
when the web is pulled askew, hooked up at the edge, torn in
the middle, one remembers that these webs are not spun in
midair by incorporeal creatures, but are the work of suffering
human beings, and are attached to grossly material things,
like health and money and the houses we live in.

Virginia Woolf, *A Room of One's Own*

This Authour, *MR. G. HERBERT*, was extracted out of a Generous, Noble, and Ancient Family. . . . His Mother . . . was so
good and godly a mother; She had ten children . . .; for whose
education she went and dwelt in the University, to recompence
the losse of their Father, in giving them two Mothers. . . . The
Obsequious *Parentalia*, he made and printed in her [Magdalen
Herbert's] memory: which though they be good, very good,
yet (to speak freely even of this man I so much honour) they
be dull or dead in comparison of his *Temple Poems*. And no
marvel. . . . In those he writ Flesh and Blood: A fraile earthly
Woman, though a MOTHER, but in these he praysed his Heavenly FATHER. . . .

Barnabas Oley, *George Herbert: The Critical Heritage*

Although there is no household equal to the Brontës in early modern English literature, critics, impelled by feminist historical scholarship, have recently discovered the writings of a handful of intriguing literary families. The late sixteenth and early seventeenth centuries in England feature a number of distinguished, often aristocratic, literary families: the secular poet Isabella Whitney and her emblematist brother Geoffrey; the courtly trio of Sir Philip Sidney, the Countess of Pembroke, Mary Sidney, and Sir Robert Sidney; the Spenserean poets Giles and Phineas Fletcher; the accomplished sonneteer Lady Mary Wroth and her cousin and lover William Herbert, Third Earl of Pembroke; the devotional and elegiac writers Henry King, Bishop of Chichester, John King, the Oxford University Orator, and Anne King; the sister dramatists Lady Jane Cavendish and Lady Elizabeth Brackley; and the Welsh twins Henry and Thomas Vaughan. And like the Brontës' great novels, the best of this writing sometimes takes family conflict itself as its subject, portraying the domestic scene as a locus of natural and supernatural crisis.[1]

As numerous and prolific as any of these early modern literary families were the Herberts of Montgomery and London. The family included the admired patroness Magdalen Herbert, Lady Danvers (circa 1561–1627), her second husband, Sir John Danvers (circa 1588–1655), a leading member of the Virginia Company and one of the first exponents of Italian gardening in England, and Magdalen's literary sons, the poet-priest George Herbert (1593–1633), the poet-philosopher Edward, Lord Herbert of Cherbury (circa 1581–1648), the Master of the Revels Sir Henry Herbert (1594–1673), the Oxford scholar Charles Herbert (circa 1592–1617), and the obscure sailor-poet Thomas Herbert (1597–before 1643). John Donne sometimes visited the Danvers House in Chelsea, where, in a letter dated 12 June 1625, he said "I make up my Tusculan" (Kempe *The Loseley Manuscripts*, 347), alluding to Tusculan retreats of Cicero and Maecenas. Donne also corresponded with

members of the Herbert and Danvers families, wrote verses
for Magdalen, exchanged verses with George and Edward,
and ultimately preached Magdalen's funeral sermon on 1 July
1627 (Charles, *A Life*, 118–19, 132). Nourished by this family milieu, George Herbert wrote his own Latin elegies for
Magdalen's death, *Memoriae Matris Sacrum*, and his virtuoso
lyrics of divine grace and courtly supplication in *The Temple*.

This study of the Herberts begins with the assumption,
stated famously by Virginia Woolf, that the imaginative work
of poetry and fiction is attached, however subtly, to "grossly
material things," like money and houses, and these things
deserve the consideration of literary critics. The social structures of families, which were closely allied with money and
houses in the seventeenth century, are such material things,
the subjects and sites of symbolic activity. The richness of
an imaginative work, Woolf argued persuasively, in no way
belies the social conditions and life experiences of the artist.
Indeed, George Herbert's poems, such as "Affliction 1," are
often insistently autobiographical, and invite the reader to
examine his family and career: "Wheareas my birth and
spirit rather took/The way that takes the town" (*Works*, 47,
ll. 37–38). Throughout *The Temple*, one is struck by the myriad
attachments between the material and symbolic dimensions
of families—the conflations of God and the household master,
of Christ and the family's sons and servants, and of Mother
Church and the lady of the household.

In studying the family as a material reality and a symbolic
construction in George Herbert's poetry, I also seek to extend the work of New Historicist scholars such as Arthur F.
Marrotti, Cristina Malcolmson, Marion White Singleton, and
Michael C. Schoenfeldt, who have demonstrated the manifold connections between courtly supplication, coterie groups,
and manuscript poetry in the early seventeenth century.[2]
The poetry of *The Temple*, I would add, takes readers not only
to the banqueting chambers of the great, as they received

petitioners or read commendatory verses, but also to the household chambers of gentry, as they addressed parents, children,
and servants in matters that were both personal and public.
The relations of masters, servants, fathers, mothers, children,
kin, and friends are persistent subjects of George Herbert's
verse. In "The Odour," for example, he asks, "*My Master*, shall
I speak? O that to thee/*My servant* were a little so [sweet-
sounding],/As flesh may be" (*Works*, 175, ll. 11–13). The sweetness of "flesh" in this poetry invokes not just the Church's
sacraments and theology, but also the material realities of
family rank, inheritance, and kin patronage and clientage.

Certainly, the Herberts have been discussed before, in biog-
raphies by Amy M. Charles and Mario M. Rossi, as well as in
important studies of George Herbert's poetry by Cristina
Malcolmson, Robert N. Watson, E. Pearlman, Anna K. Nardo,
George Held, Leah S. Marcus, Deborah Rubin, and Joan K.
Costello. Yet no critic has written a book-length study of the
Herbert family, nor has any critic thoroughly investigated
the family dialogue that occurs between the Herberts' poems,
letters, treatises, and other documents. How do George Herbert's lyrics converse with other family members' writings
and what do they say about family matters? As early as 1846,
the American essayist Margaret Fuller recognized that the
poetry of George Herbert formed a dialogue with his brother
Edward's poetry, a dialogue concerning Christian faith and
natural theology. Recently, Malcolmson has proposed that
George and Edward participated in a Herbert family literary
coterie, rivaling and sometimes parodying each other's verse.
This dialogue, furthermore, included other members of George
Herbert's family and also involved the family matters of service, inheritance, vocation, patronage, mediation, and frater-
nal support and rivalry that are at the center of the speaker's
conflicts in *The Temple*.

In his biographical account of George Herbert in 1652,
Barnabas Oley observed that the poet "writ Flesh and Blood"

in his Latin verses for his mother, but that his English poems were "Inspirations propheticall . . . distilled from above" (Patrides, *George Herbert: The Critical Heritage*, 77). Oley's remark serves as a title for this book because Oley was among the first to recognize Herbert's expression of "the motions of Nature," the domestic relationships and conflicts inherent in the poetry. Yet it is also the purpose of this book to correct Oley's opinion, one that is shared by some modern critics of *The Temple*, that the religious devotions of Herbert's English poetry somehow transcend the domestic concerns of his Latin poems. Oley's preference for the supernatural father over the natural mother is unfortunately misogynistic and shortsighted. In *The Temple*, the natural and supernatural are conjoined inextricably, as spiritual conflicts are constantly imagined in domestic situations. In "Longing," Herbert states, "Mothers are kinde, because thou art, . . . / Their infants, them; and they suck thee/More free" (*Works*, 148–49, ll. 14, 17–18); in "The Sonne," "How neatly doe we give one onely name/To parents issue and the sunnes bright starre!" (168, ll. 5–6); and in "The Collar," "Me thoughts I heard one calling, *Child!*/And I reply'd, *My Lord.*" (154, ll. 35–36). George Herbert is a powerful devotional poet not because he avoids worldly matters nor because he is absorbed in theological speculation of the how-many-angels-fit-on-the-head-of-a-pin variety. Rather, his poetry is powerful because it enacts a dialogue with a God who is at once a personal and a public figure, a father and a magistrate of his time, a lord, a brother, a mother, and a servant.

But what might "family" have meant to George Herbert, the fifth son and seventh child of ten children, born to noble parents in Montgomery, Wales, in the spring of 1593? It meant neither the modern English nuclear family, with parents and children co-resident in a household through adolescence, nor the modern extended family, with a large kin group co-resident in a stable household for many years. The Herbert family was larger than modern nuclear families, because of the presence of many servants and dependents, and it was a more labile group than modern extended families because of factors of mortality (Richard Herbert, the family patriarch, died in 1597), boarding of children with relatives and schoolmasters, and travel between multiple households. In *The Family, Sex and Marriage in England, 1500–1800*, Lawrence Stone popularized the term "extended stem family" to account for the aristocratic English family of the early modern period, in which the eldest son and his bride often lived together with his parents for a time before setting up an independent household or before inheriting the family manor house. Noting the dynamic nature of early modern families, Stone described them as expanding and contracting "like a concertina, moving from the extended stem family to the nuclear and back again, as it passed through various stages" (*The Family, Sex and Marriage*, 24).

The Herbert household certainly waxed and waned in this fashion. The eldest son Edward Herbert brought his bride Mary to live with his mother and brothers in Oxford in 1598 and then to the family's Charing Cross house in 1600, before he established his own household at Montgomery Castle. Then his siblings also left home to pursue their fortunes and set up their own houses. In fact, the movement of aristocratic family members was not simply a part of the gradual lifecycle of the family, but it was also a constant requirement for families with political ambitions and kinship ties both in London and in their local counties. The opening pages of Edward, Lord Herbert's autobiography, the kitchen account book of Magdalen Herbert in 1601, and George Herbert's *Country Parson* all illustrate a family in perpetual motion: the children are frequently committed to schoolmasters in distant parts; the eldest son travels abroad or attends the Assizes or Parliament; servants come from and go to other kin; and the bulk of the family departs the London house, enroute to Eyton, Shropshire, seat of Magdalen's Newport kin, or Montgomery, seat of the late Richard Herbert's estate, to visit relatives and family allies.

Like his friend John Donne, Edward Herbert became practiced at valedictions, as he left his pregant wife Mary and two children in Montgomery in 1608 for the first of many European travels. Like Donne, Edward sought his fortune abroad, and like Sir Henry Wotton, he found it there, becoming French Ambassador in 1619. Edward Herbert wrote his Donnean lyric "I must depart" in May, 1608, and "Another" soon after, both possibly directed to his wife. His "Another" begins:

> Dear, when I did from you remove,
> I left my Joy, but not my Love,
>   That never can depart,
> It neither higher can ascend
>   Nor lower bend,
> Fixt in the center of my heart.
>   (*Poems*, 19, ll. 1–6)

Edward traveled again in Europe in 1610 and from 1614 to 1616, frequently accompanied by his younger brothers. In fact, all of the Herbert brothers but George—Edward, Richard, William, Charles, Henry, and Thomas—traveled to the continent, and Thomas sailed to the East Indies and throughout the Mediterranean. In this context, the opening exclamation of "The Collar," "I struck the board, and cry'd, No more./I will abroad" seems less a blustering threat than a family routine of departing from the household. The Herberts often did "abroad."

Apart from the lability and itineracy of the early modern aristocratic family—its movements from house to house and its amoebic expansions and divisions—a second feature that distinguished it clearly from modern English and American familes was its employment of a large retinue of servants. According to Rosemary O'Day, the cast of servants clearly expanded families in this period beyond the nuclear parent-child group: "Though early modern (or *ancien-régime*) households were larger than today's, the difference is accounted for by the presence of servants in earlier households and their absence in modern. Even the very large early modern households were very large chiefly because they were prosperous households with many servants" (*The Family and Family Relationships*, 101). Similarly, Stone wrote: "In the Early Modern period, living-in servants were not the rarity that they are today, but a normal component of all but the poorest households. From the time of the first censuses in the early sixteenth century to the mid-nineteenth century, about one third or more of all households contained living-in servants" (*The Family, Sex and Marriage*, 27–28). Such was certainly the case for the Herbert households.

On the title page of her kitchen account book of 1601, Magdalen Herbert listed four "Nurses & Chambermayds" and eight "Seruingmen" among "the names and nomber of my howsehoulde." Other servants from the Herbert family estates in Montgomery and Monmouthshire also appear in the lists of table guests in the *Kitchin Booke* (see appendix A). Sir John Danvers's Chelsea house, with its ornamental Italian garden, must have also required a formidable cast of servants. John Aubrey recalled the elegant Danvers house, visited by Donne and Sir Francis Bacon, in a humorous anecdote involving servants. While touring Danvers's garden, Bacon suddenly swooned, and upon reviving, apologized wittily to Lady Danvers: "Madam, I am no good footman" (*Aubrey's Brief Lives*, 12). More prosaically, in his will of 1633, George mentioned his six servants at the Bemerton Rectory by name as "Elizabeth," "Ann," "Margeret," "William," "John," and "Sara," to whom he gave various monetary gifts (*Works*, 382).

As French Ambassador and Baron of Cherbury, Edward Herbert also employed large staffs of servants. In suing for the surrender of Montgomery Castle in September 1644, the parliamentarian Lieutenant-Colonel James Till proposed that Lord Herbert be allowed to retain "half a dozen men-servants within the castle to do his business and three or four maids to attend his daughter" (Smith, *Herbert Correspondence*, 115). And in his will of 1 January 1673, Sir Henry directed that all of his servants at his Ribbesford house be paid their wages and given suits of mourning, and singled out his longtime servant Walter Vaughan for a special gift. In his *Country Parson*, George gave advice about the management of household servants, as did Edward in his "Praecepta & consilia," addressed to his grandsons.

As a skilled classicist, George Herbert would have recognized that the English word *family* derived from the Latin *famulus*, meaning servant. Peer and gentry families of the period maintained large companies of servants as a mark of social distinction, as a gesture of *noblesse oblige* to relatives and tenants, and as a labor force for agricultural and domestic tasks. Thus, a writer in 1631 describes an English household: "His family were himself and his wife and daughters, two mayds and a man" (qtd. in Williams, *Keywords*, 132). "The very fact that the domestic servants were considered members of the family in these households," says Joan K. Costello, "is an indication of their unusual role by today's standards" ("True Child," 40). In many cases, adolescent servants were equated with the family's children: "The child, like the servant, had to learn to serve—a traditional form of education—before being able to establish himself and become, in his turn, 'the father of the family'" (Flandrin, *Families in Former Times*, 64). As he discussed the discipline of children and servants in his *Country Parson*, George Herbert collapsed the distinction between them even as he made it: "To his Children he shewes more love then terrour, to his servants more terrour then love; but an old good servant boards [i.e., takes the place of] a child" (*Works*, 241). Obedient children and servants were often considered interchangeable, and George Herbert took on both roles in his poems.

Given the presence of numerous servants, the social structure of the seventeenth century family tended to be more hierarchical and less private than that of modern families. In

George Herbert's "The Familie," the speaker expresses greater
concern about the behavior of servants than that of children.
The poem begins with a rhetorical question that leads to a
series of prescriptions typifying an ideal, orderly, and godly
family. The speaker asks:

> What doth this noise of thoughts within my heart,
>> As if they had a part?
> What do these loud complaints and puling fears,
>> As if there were no rule or eares?
>
> But, Lord, the house and familie are thine,
>> Though some of them repine.
> Turn out these wranglers, which defile thy seat:
>> For where thou dwellest all is neat.
>
> First Peace and Silence all disputes controll,
>> Then Order plaies the soul;
> And giving all things their set forms and houres,
>> Makes of wilde woods sweet walks and bowres.
>
> Humble Obedience neare the doore doth stand,
>> Expecting a command:
> Then whom in waiting nothing seems more slow,
>> Nothing more quick when she doth go.
>
> Joyes oft are there, and griefs as oft as joyes;
>> But griefs without a noise:
> Yet speak they louder then distemper'd fears.
>> What is so shrill as silent tears?
>
> This is thy house, with these it doth abound:
>> And where these are not found,
> Perhaps thou com'st sometimes, and for a day;
>> But not to make a constant stay.
>>> (*Works*, 136–37, ll. 1–24)

The lord of the house represents at once three forms of authority: the patriarchal authority of the father, the social authority

of noble landowner, and the divine authority of Christ and his ministers over the church. The servants are expected implicitly to obey the lord's authority. The lord has the power to expel unruly servants, giving commands and anticipating their speedy fulfillment. He commands agricultural laborers who are at work on timber land and gardens, domestic laborers who keep the house "neat," and messengers like "Humble Obedience," who stand ready at the door.

While the disciplinary order of "The Familie" is patriarchal, it is eased somewhat by the fifth stanza, which assures the reader that there is joy in the house and that the lord responds to the "silent tears" of his servants. Louis L. Martz cites this stanza as a quintessential example of the poet's struggles to maintain strict emotional control "both in himself and in the larger family of the Christian community." "The phrase 'silent tears,'" says Martz, "suggests a basic concept of expressive control that lies at the center of Herbert's poetic—and, no doubt, at the center of his conception of the Christian life" (*From Renaissance*, 45). Furthermore, the poet suggests that such expressive control begins at home, where patriarchal, social, and religious authority are all exercised. In fact, in "Sinne I" he stipulates that such control is instilled by a succession of paternal authorities: "Lord, with what care hast thou begirt us round!/Parents first season us: then schoolmasters/Deliver us to laws; they send us bound/To rules of reasons, holy messengers,/Pulpits and Sundayes . . ." (*Works*, 45, ll. 1–5).

Modern critics, as Claude J. Summers and Ted-Larry Pebworth have suggested, have often been troubled by "The Familie," finding in it an individual's uncertain attempt to regain his spiritual equilibrium. Summers and Pebworth's political interpretation of the poem—as a reproof to noisy Puritans who were disturbing the order of the Church of England—resolves the uncertainties of these earlier readings ("The Politics of *The Temple*," 1–15). In this political reading, the "set forms and houres," the ceremonies and offices of the Church of England, are kept by the obedient servants of God, the faithful priests, but are disputed by the Puritans within the church and by the Indepedents outside it. To such undisciplined children and servants, God comes "sometimes, and for a day;/But not to make a constant stay." Apart from its insistence upon restraint and ceremony both at home and at church, Herbert's "The Familie" indicates just how multivalent the categories of parent, child, and servant were in seventeenth century thought. The micro-political structure of the home was remarkably transferable to the larger structures of the church and the commonwealth, and these three realms of authority were endlessly commingled. Hence, Robert Cleaver and John Dod's oft-quoted maxim "A Householde is as it were a little common-wealth" was a commonplace among advice writers, whatever their religious persuasion (*A Godlie Forme*, 13).

Conflating the authorities of father, ruler, and God, George Herbert's country parson schools his children. "His children," Herbert writes, "he first makes Christians, and then Commonwealths-men; the one he owes to his heavenly Countrey, the other to his earthly, having no title to either, except he do good to both" (*Works*, 239). As rector at Bemerton, Herbert stressed his status as "Father" to his parish, writing:

> The Countrey Parson is not only a father to his flock, but also professeth himselfe throughly of the opinion, carrying it about with him as fully, as if he had begot his whole Parish. And of this he makes great use. For by this means, when any sinns, he hateth him not as an officer, but pityes him as a Father. . . . (*Works*, 250)

This passage of *The Country Parson* is striking not only for the surprisingly bawdy jest ("as if he had begot his whole Parish"), but also for the parson's candid admission of how he used paternalism to superintend his parish. In this concept of the parish, says Douglas J. Swartz, "Private life and public life, government and self-government, are completely conjoined" ("Discourse and Direction," 199). The early modern concept of family is not that of a wholly private group or of a personal refuge from state and religious authority; rather, it is the foundation of all institutions in the authority of the lord and master.[3]

A third characteristic of the early modern family, and particularly of the Herberts, is that of clan cohesiveness—its participation in a network of kin, family allies, patrons, and clients. Patronage was not excusively, or even most frequently, a benevolence given to an unknown and unrelated suitor by a flattered lord or lady. Recently, historians have reconsidered the importance of kin networks for patronage in the period. Based upon his study of family letters, David Cressy has argued that kin interaction, often across great distances, was vital throughout the seventeenth century and, *contra* Lawrence Stone, that it did not erode during the period. Seen as a resource rather than a concrete set of obligations, kinship ties were often instrumental in securing employment, consolidating political alliances, securing legal assistance, and offering emotional comfort. Cressy writes:

> Kinship, once established, permitted intimacy, and intimacy invited favours. Kinship carried "clout", or at least opened doors that might otherwise have remained closed. ("Kinship and Kin Interaction," 47)

Similarly, based on his study of British autobiographies from 1600 to 1750, Michael Mascuch has stressed the role of kinship ties in securing employment and patronage:

> Close family and effective kin operated as the decisive asset in making and maintaining a career. Certainly other forms of property . . . were important factors in rendering some opportunities viable to the individual. However the network cultivated by one's family constituted the framework without which a person of the middle sort in pursuit of a career could not fully

> realize the potential value of whatever other assets he possessed.
> ("Continuity and Change," 187)

In the parlance of the period, one required the offices of "friends"—and kin and family allies were foremost among the "friends."

"He quits his place well," says George Herbert's *Outlandish Proverb*, "that leaves his friend there" (*Works*, 350, no. 875). This meaning of "friend," as a family ally or kinsman, recurs throughout the Herberts' poems and letters, and is quite distinct from modern uses of the word. Miriam Slater discovered the same usage of "friend" by the Verneys of Claydon House. She writes:

> In the correspondence, "friend" is repeatedly and almost exclusively used to refer to someone who can be helpful in advancing one's career or prospects, and is never used to describe someone freely chosen on the basis of mutual psychological attraction. A friend was a person who was important to one's interest; he was not necessarily likeable or personally attractive, though he was often related by blood or marriage. As Lady Verney put it . . ., "it was friends which did all." (*Family Life*, 34–35)

Likewise, when Sir John Danvers wrote to his stepson Edward Herbert on 8 April 1615, informing him of his assistance in settling his debts, Danvers referred to both family members and family allies as "friends." Danvers accented his loyalty to Edward: "For I am soe sencible of my *frends* wants beyond seas, as I was willing to offer my self, and if it had not servd, to haue procured other of my *frends* to have given" (Herbert Family, PRO 30/53/10; my emphasis). George Herbert spoke similarly of his "friends." In "Affliction I," he referred to the death of friends: "Thus thinne and lean without a fence or *friend*,/I was blown through with ev'ry storm and winde" (*Works*, 47, ll. 35–36). Thus, Herbert may have alluded either to the deaths of his brothers Charles and William in 1617, as Amy Charles has argued, or to the deaths of close family patrons, the Duke of Lennox, Ludowick Stuart, in 1624, and the Marquis James Hamilton in 1625, as Izaak Walton suggested (Charles, *Williams Ms.*, xxv–xxvii; Walton, *Lives*, 276). The implication that such "friends" also served as "fences," or patrons, makes the Walton's identification of these "friends" as powerful family allies more likely.

As a family seeking places in the Stuart court, the Herberts frequently depended on "friends." When George sought to procure the office of Cambridge University Orator, he wrote to Danvers in 1619, asking him to deliver a message to the former orator, Sir Francis Nethersole, on his behalf (*Works*, 369). He also mentioned his plan to write to "my Lord," probably his powerful cousin, William Herbert, the third Earl of Pembroke, to obtain his support for his candidacy (*Works*, 370, n. 581). In 1623, Pembroke's support was decisive in securing the position of Master of the Revels for Sir Henry Herbert. Richard Dutton says that Sir Henry "attached himself to Pembroke at court, and the biographical details of his office book consistently reflect the Lord Chamberlain's patronage." Sir Henry was knighted by King James at Pembroke's Wilton estate with the sword of Marquis Hamilton on 7 August 1623. Dutton asserts that "the Lord Chamberlain's hand [was] behind all this business. He not only encouraged it: he engineered it," seeking to promote a political and family ally to the position at court (*Mastering the Revels*, 228). Later, as rector at Bemerton, George Herbert solicited funds from Lady Anne Clifford, the Countess of Pembroke, for the reconstruction of the Leighton Bromswold Church in Huntingdonshire, and sought his brother Sir Henry's help in obtaining further contributions from the Duchess of Lennox, the Earl of Manchester, and the Earl of Bolingbroke (*Works*, 376–79). Aubrey also reported that while at Bemerton George served as chaplain to Philip Herbert, the fourth Earl of Pembroke (*Aubrey's Brief Lives*, 137).

In *The Temple*, letters, and proverbs, George Herbert uses

the words *friend* and *friends* more than 30 times, usually in the sense of "a kinsman or near relation" or the sense of "a sympathiser, favourer, helper, patron, or supporter" (OED, friend, 3, 5a), and he frequently combines the two meanings. Proverbs like "When a friend askes, there is no to morrow" (*Works*, 322, no. 32) and "Life without a friend is death without a witnesse" (334, no. 385) are not simple expressions of affection and generosity, but are considered judgments about the strategic value of powerful kin and family supporters. The second of these proverbs, for example, refers to the offices of friends as witnesses to a last testament. Without friends' support of one's estate, one could expect to die intestate, penniless, without property or bequests to one's children. The "Deare Friend," who serves as a counsellor in "Love unknown" and "The Holdfast" is a confidant of the speaker's household chamber, who gives him candid advice about his lord's love and favors. The known love of the friend enables the speaker to recognize the lord's "love unknown": "*Truly, Friend,/For ought I heare, your Master shows to you/More favour then you wot of. Mark the end*" (*Works*, 130, ll. 61–63). This advice is as politic as it is personal, coming from a family ally who mediates between the unhappy speaker and the mysterious master. Ends, favor, and love are worldy categories of politic friendship.

Indeed, George Herbert considered Jesus Christ himself as such a "friend," one who procures unmerited favors from his Father for his beloved petitioners. In "The Bag," Christ, the ultimate friend, carries his friends' letters or petitions within his wounded side to his Father: "Or if hereafter any of my *friends*/Will use me in this kinde, the doore/Shall still be open; what he sends/I will present, and somewhat more,/Not to his hurt" (*Works*, 152, ll. 37–41; my emphasis). The bitter pun on "kinde" indicates that Christ will serve his human family with maximum generosity, even when they treat him most unkindly.

Exactly what favors might a family member wish a friend

to perform? In "Unkindnesse," George Herbert presents his most compelling analysis of the family-friend relationship. The poem provides an incisive summary, contrasting the speaker's success as a "friend" to his lesser kin with his failure as a "friend" to his divine Lord. The speaker addresses his Lord:

> Lord, make me coy and tender to offend:
> In friendship, first I think, if that agree,
> > Which I intend,
> Unto my friends intent and end.
> I would not use a friend, as I use Thee.
>
> If any touch my friend, or his good name,
> It is my honour and my love to free
> > His blasted fame
> From the least spot or thought of blame.
> I could not use a friend, as I use Thee.
>
> My friend may spit upon my curious floore:
> Would he have gold? I lend it instantly;
> > But let the poore,
> And thou within them, starve at doore.
> I cannot use a friend, as I use Thee.
>
> When that my friend pretendeth to a place,
> I quit my interest, and leave it free:
> > But when thy grace
> Sues for my heart, I thee displace,
> Nor would I use a friend, as I use Thee.
>
> Yet can a friend what thou hast done fulfill?
> O write in brasse, *My God upon a tree*
> > *His bloud did spill*
> *Onely to purchase my good-will.*
> Yet use I not my foes, as I use Thee.
>
> > (*Works*, 93–94, ll. 1–25)

The "friends" of the poem are the opposite of "foes": they are vital supporters of the speaker's estate and career. So the speaker eagerly reciprocates his friends' favors: he offers to them unlimited hospitality in his house (l. 11), loans of money (l. 12), protection of their persons and their reputation (ll. 6–9), assistance in obtaining desired posts (ll. 16–17), and overall support of their political and career objectives (ll. 1–4). In this period, a friend's favors were favors indeed.

Cementing the reciprocal favors between kin was the quasinatural bond of "kindnesse." Kindness meant not just generosity, but "kinship; near relation; natural affection arising from this" (OED, kindness, 1). A partiality toward one's kin in all one's affairs was assumed natural, and the speaker of "Unkindnesse" professes to uphold the bond of kindness almost perfectly. Yet, throughout the poem, the speaker points out a glaring exception to this rule—his remarkable betrayal of his Lord, his greatest "friend," whom he neglects, starves, spurns, and displaces at every turn. The divine "friend" has shed his blood "to purchase my goodwill," but the speaker has withheld even this meager favor. The overriding irony of the poem is not that the kinship bond of kindness is wrong in any sense, but rather that it is transcendentally right, subsumed in the divine bond of love between the Lord and his creature. The speaker has not been offering too much kindness to too many kin, but too little to too few. Or as Schoenfeldt says of the poem: "The conduct of God is seen as the epitome rather than the repudiation of friendship" (*Prayer and Power*, 83).

A fourth and final characteristic of early modern noble families, and of the Herbert family in particular, is a reverence for paternal authority, a reverence nigh to ancestor worship. In the period, there was an insistent homology, reinforced by gospel parables, between God the Father and the father of a human family. Indeed, Stone argued that "The growth of patriarchy was deliberately encouraged by the new Renaissance state on the traditional grounds that the subordination of the family to its head is analogous to, and also a direct contributory cause of, subordination of subjects to the sovereign" (*The Family, Sex and Marriage*, 152). In a time when age was equated with wisdom, when obedience towards parents was a cardinal biblical tenet, and when wealth was often attained by inheritance, the family patriarch was accorded paramount authority in the household. The father was customarily the family's dispenser of goods, manager of estates, constable, judge, matchmaker, and vocational counsellor. In "Providence," George Herbert describes God as such a heavenly householder: "For either thy command or thy permission/Lay hands on all"; "Thy cupboard serves the world"; "And as thy house is full, so I adore/Thy curious art in marshalling thy goods" (*Works*, 117–19, ll. 33–34, 49, 93–94).

As patriarchs were revered, ancestors were also cherished eagerly in genealogies, and their legends haunted their families for generations. Many high-born families of the time had, as O'Day puts it, "an obsession with the family name, coat of arms, and memorials" (68–69). When George Herbert wrote in "Affliction I," for instance, that "my birth and spirit rather took/The way that takes the town" (*Works*, 37, ll. 37–38), he was referring not just to the military careers of his brothers Richard and William, but also to a family martial tradition that stretched back for at least four generations. In the same vein, Edward Herbert says more in his autobiography of his great-great grandfather, Sir Richard Herbert (a hero at the battle of Edgecote field in 1469), than he does of most of his brothers and sisters.

Part of this obsession with ancestors derived from the inheritance of property and the maintenance of kinship alliances, and part from the dispossessed child's idealization of lost parents. Hamlet's words undoubtedly had great resonance in a time when many children lost their parents at an early age: "So excellent a king, that was to this/Hyperion to a satyr" (I.ii.139–40). In fact, William Kerrigan has speculated that because George Herbert's father Richard died when he was

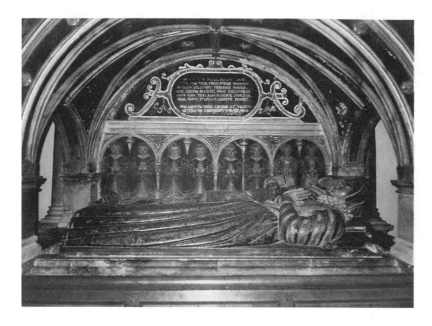

Figure 1

Herbert Family Tomb. St. Nicholas Church, Montgomery,
Wales. Photograph by Jeffrey Powers-Beck. By permission of
Fr. Anthony M. Hirst, O.S.B., Rector.

yet three years of age, the poet "inherited from his father the
deep bruise of an unfinished mourning. . . . His devotional
poems yearn for, but never attain, once-and-for-all evidence
of fatherly affection" ("Ritual Man," 72).

Whatever the underlying reasons, the patriarch and ancestors formed the core identity of the noble family as a cohesive
group. It was proverbial among the Herberts that "In the house
of a Fidler, all fiddle" (*Works*, 328, no. 223), and "One father is
enough to governe one hundred sons, but not a hundred sons
one father" (335, no. 404). This characteristic of upper-class
families is manifested concretely in the tomb of Richard
Herbert, esquire, in St. Nicholas Church, Montgomery. The
canopied tomb (see figures 1 and 2) is in the south transept or
"Lymore chapel" of the parish church, a chapel long regarded

"as the property . . . of the Herbert family as Lords of the Manor" (Lloyd, "A Guide Book"; Lloyd, "The Herbert Tomb," 101–02). The lavish tomb of Richard, erected by his widow Magdalen in 1600, presents an idealized vision of the entire Herbert family: life-size effigies of Richard and Magdalen lie side-by-side, their eyes directed toward heaven, their hands folded in prayer; and in four recessed niches, the figures of six boys and two girls kneel in prayer. Beside the tomb lie two medieval effigies of knights in full suits of armor, one of whom was a Herbert family ancestor, most probably Sir Richard Herbert (d. 1534), the great-grandfather of George and Edward, Lord Herbert of Cherbury.

In the canopied tomb, the central effigies of Richard and Magdalen depict them as the living rulers of the house: Richard appears, like his medieval forebears, in full armor, his head resting on his plumed casque, a gauntlet at his side and a spaniel at his feet; and Magdalen appears as the elegant lady of the house, dressed in a florid gown, a ruff, and cap, her head resting on tasselled pillows. A second effigy of Richard, his gaunt corpse wrapped in a winding sheet, his face and feet exposed, lies directly below the effigies of the living couple. Richard Herbert in his two bodies is at once dead and yet still alive to his family. The presence of the patriarch, who is still one flesh with his widow and whose piety and courage the children still emulate, haunts the family, as the effigies of his ancestors apparently haunted him.

At the back of the tomb, the figures of the praying children have usually been taken as representing Richard and Magdalen's "numerous progeny," or "their six sons and two daughters." Yet, there were ten Herbert children in all, and there is very little in these stylized figures that would enable one to distinguish them as children of different ages and identities—one as George, one as Henry, and so on. Their cheeks rouged identically by a Victorian restorer, the boys appear as pious miniatures of Richard and the girls as pious miniatures

This Plate is presented by the Earl of Powis to the Powys-Land Club.

MONT. COLL. VOL. VI. P.109.   MONUMENT TO RICHARD HERBERT ESQ: IN MONTGOMERY CHURCH.

Figure 2

Herbert Family Tomb. M. Underwood's engraving from
Montgomery Collections, vol. 6. By permission of the Syndics of
Cambridge University Library, Cambridge.

of Magdalen. The figures are rigid and uniform, but charming, like marble Pinocchios praying for animation—or perhaps, rather, praying to please the lord and lady of the house. Once again, as the proverb says, "In the house of a Fidler, all fiddle." Since Magdalen also included relatives and many servants in the list of her Charing Cross household, one might conclude that the background figures of the tomb do not represent any of her children in particular. They represent, rather, the entire Herbert clan of children, relatives, and servants— all of the obedient youths who honored the memory of the late patriarch and the example of his surviving widow.

This sense of the family's group identity, centered around the patriarch and ancestors, pervades *The Temple*. The obeisance of "This is thy house" is addressed both to God and to the family patriarch. If "Childhood is health," as in "H. Baptisme II," it is because the child is expected to be "soft and supple to thy will," obedient to the father and subject to loving correction. Many critics have observed how frequently George Herbert speaks as a child in his lyrics, but have neglected an equally important point. In even his most distressed lyrics, the poet speaks not just as a child but as an aggrieved family member, one seeking reproachment, correction, or a vital favor. And in his great lyric "The Crosse," he speaks as a *paterfamilias*, who has dedicated his entire family to God's household service. He complains that though the lord has finally yielded a long-sought place to him, the lord has also taken away his bodily ability to do service, making him "a weak disabled thing." In confronting this contradiction, the speaker enacts almost every role in an early modern family— of father, master, servant, friend, and son.

In the family drama of "The Crosse," George Herbert reverses the rhetoric of natural obligation in "Unkindnesse." In this case, it is God's "crosse actions" that are unnatural:

> What is this strange and uncouth thing?
> To make me sigh, and seek, and faint, and die,

Untill I had some place, where I might sing,
        And serve thee; and not onely I,
But all my wealth and familie might combine
To set thy honour up, as our designe.

        And then when after much delay,
Much wrastling, many a combate, this deare end,
So much desir'd, is giv'n, to take away
        My power to serve thee; to unbend
All my abilities, my designes confound,
And lay my threatnings bleeding on the ground.

                *   *   *   *

        Ah my deare Father, ease my smart!
These contrarieties crush me: these crosse actions
Do winde a rope about, and cut my heart:
        And yet since these thy contradictions
Are properly a crosse felt by thy Sonne,
With but foure words, my words, *Thy will be done.*

                        (*Works*, 164–65, ll. 1–12, 31–36)

The angry speaker resents the "crosse" as "uncouth," an alien and unfamiliar way to treat a loyal servant and his kin. He has offered his family, honor, and the "threatnings" of kindness to his lord, only to find the gifts spurned (OED, threaten, 6). Family members, he suggests, should not "crosse" one another's "designes," but should seek to advance them. The speaker feels, as he puts it graphically, double-crossed. His response to the lord, however, is not to repudiate him, but to claim a deeper kinship. By joining his suffering to Christ's and by asking for a father's favor to his son, he, in a sense, crosses his double-crossing lord. The deft closing of line 36 does not simply capitulate to the master, but coopts Christ's words as "my words" and stakes a claim to Christ's reward. The overall argument of "The Crosse" resembles somewhat that of Milton's famous sonnet, "When I consider how my light is spent." Yet while Milton's poem is the drama of an isolated individual, who receives a sudden, astounding revelation, Herbert's poem is a family drama, in which an angry servant gains a paradoxical satisfaction from his lord.

This, then, is the social structure of the Herbert family: a dynamically shifting but cohesive patriarchal group, united by kinship, friendship, and servitude to one another and a wider social network, and dependent upon one another for property, employment, service, and patronage. While formally ordered, it was by no means what Stone has called a "low-affect" family.[4] Grateful and guilty love, remonstrance, fear, remorse, silent tears, and fits of choler: they are all part of the Herberts' family poems. Furthermore, the Herberts' surviving letters and literary works engage in a vigorous family dialogue, including both coterie literary exchange and the transaction of family business. While George Herbert's poetry most fully "writ the flesh," his mother and brothers also did so in their writings. The following chapters will demonstrate how his poetry joins in dialogue with the writings of Magdalen, Henry, Edward, Thomas, and Sir John Danvers and the Virginia Company.

The second chapter discusses Magdalen Herbert's wide-ranging influence upon George's poetry, politics, and religion. In his own words, she "united contrary realms," acting frequently as a social and family intermediary, providing a maternal symbol for the poet's *via media*. The recent work of women historians, such as Barbara J. Harris and Caroline Bowden, has emphasized the significant roles that noble women played in this period in resolving social disputes and managing family affairs. Magdalen's own letters and kitchen account book showed that she played such a mediative role, often intervening on behalf of her friends and family, and reinforcing bonds between Herberts, Newports, and Danvers kin. Her boldness in mediation, her "lepos severos," is described in *Memoriae Matris Sacrum* and is dramatized in the eucharistic invitations of *The Temple*. The speaker of "The Invitation" and "The Banquet" welcomes all Christians to his Father's table within his Mother Church. These invitations, characterized by what Louis L. Martz calls "generous ambiguity," bespeak a mediator's attempt to bring together worshippers of different theologies into the "Familie" of the British church (*From Renaissance*, 64).

The third chapter demonstrates the Herberts' investment in the literature of domestic advice—displayed in proverbs, sententious letters, and advice poems, "The Church-porch," in particular. As individuals and as a family unit, the Herberts were vitally concerned with matters of vocation and employment. While modern critics have attacked "The Church-porch" as an early, tedious, and morally dubious poem, it clearly reflected the Herberts' engagement in secular employment as a religious and family duty. George Herbert shared the energetic pursuit of courtly self-advancement with his brothers Edward and Henry, who gave much the same advice in their own writings. Far from repudiating the prudential concerns of "The Church-porch" in his later writings, he repeated them in his *Country Parson* and *Outlandish Proverbs*. Furthermore, the search for "brave employments" that so occupies *The Temple* was not simply the quest of an isolated individual, but a family initiative, occuring within a network of kin and friends.

The fourth chapter examines the relationship of George and his closest brother, Sir Henry Herbert—the family's most successful courtier—and the writings that resulted from it. It is tempting to think, as Amy Charles did, that Henry Herbert wrote two devotional books—*The Broken Heart* and *Herbert's Golden Harpe*—characterized by the affliction themes and biblical resonances of *The Temple*. Yet manuscript and documentary evidence recommend against this attribution (see appendix B). Sir Henry's successful pursuit of a career at court—with the help of his Pembroke kin—does, however, make a fascinating parallel to George Herbert's poetry. New Historicist critics have demonstrated convincingly how persistently patronage figures in George's lyrics, but have said remarkably little about his courtier brother, Sir Henry. Preserved in the Public Record Office and British Library, Sir Henry Herbert's news-at-court letters to Lord Scudamore reveal his mastery of what George in "The Forerunners" called "Lovely enchanting language, sugar-cane,/Hony of roses," the witty artificial style of courtly writing (*Works*, 176, ll. 19–20). The letters also suggest that in taking a rural parish George Herbert did not—indeed, could not—entirely reject the political maneuverings that preoccupied his family.

The fifth chapter attends to the vibrant dialogue, first noticed by Margaret Fuller, between the "brother poets," George Herbert and Edward, Lord Herbert of Cherbury. Their poetry, like their relationship as brothers, is characterized by both emulation and rivalry. They used similar imagery in some of their poems, and even echoed each other in their echo poems. Yet the younger brother, George, wrote a poetry of the suffering son Christ and his Church, while the elder brother, Edward, wrote a poetry of the free soul liberated from filial obligations to church and priest. The ritual sacrifices that George celebrated as the "liquor sweet and most divine" of God's family, Edward reviled as "no better than a butchery." While the younger, dependent brother could not, even in the pique of "The Collar" flee from the "board" of the church, the elder, independent brother could not brook remaining there. George's vision of heaven in "Love III" is of an intimate communion with Christ, who serves him without regard to rank or merit; Edward's vision of heaven in "De Vita Coelesti" is of a single soul's attainment of unlimited freedom, merit, and pleasure by his earthly works. The religious differences between George and Edward Herbert, I maintain, are not merely those between Calvinism and Arminianism, or even those between Christian orthodoxy and natural religion, but those between the theology of a younger brother and the theology of an elder brother.

The sixth chapter discusses the youngest Herbert son, Thomas, a well-traveled sea captain, whose maritime career Edward recounted with ostentatious pride in his autobiography. Despite the family pride in Thomas, very little is known of his life as a writer: various political tracts, circa 1639, have been freely attributed to him, but it is clear from an inspection of those tracts that George's brother Thomas had a hand in few or none of them. The one literary work that can be attributed to him with reasonable certainty is a manuscript poem in the National Library of Wales entitled "The Storme . . . from Plimmouth." The poem dramatizes an Atlantic storm in the Bay of Biscay with a Protestant faith in God's protection of the English crew, and with a sailor's keen attention to the condition and navigation of his ship. The poem employs classical literary allusions, Donnean cosmological conflict, and a sacred emblem, and it bears a fascinating comparison to poems by George Herbert, such as "The Storm" and "The Bag." While George often recorded stormy "inner-weather" in his poems, his brother Thomas wrote about stormy "outer-weather," the geographical, meteorological, and political conditions of English sailors in the period. The difference in their poetic registers, which evoked similar images for divergent effects, is as striking as is the family dialogue in their poems. Storms were the triumphs of both brothers' arts.

The seventh chapter explores the active participation of Sir John Danvers (Magdalen Herbert's second husband) in the Virginia Company, and it relates the government of the company by Sir Edwin Sandys, Nicholas and John Ferrar, and Danvers to George Herbert's missionary vision in "The Church Militant." Danvers recruited adventurers from his family members and servants for the Virginian voyages of the early 1620s. Recent historical research on the Ferrar papers and the Virginian migrations suggests that "The Church Militant" was almost certainly written during the administration of the Company by Sandys and the Ferrars, the only period during

George Herbert's lifetime when "Religion" stood "tip-toe in our land,/Readie to passe to the American strand" (ll. 235–36). George Herbert's sharing of his poetic manuscripts with the Ferrars and Nicholas Ferrar's insistence upon the publication of *The Temple* without censorship of "The Church Militant" suggest that Herbert wrote the poem in support of his family allies in the Company. If the poem seems an appendix to *The Temple*, as critics have termed it, it is an appendix that documented a crucial turning point, circa 1623, in the poet's career and that corresponded with important reversals in the political careers of his family. The poem also suggests that the Herberts' dialogue extended well beyond the immediate circle of the family, to political and religious allies such as the Ferrars.

Because of the paucity of surviving materials related to George's brothers Charles, Richard (circa 1587–1622), and William (1590–circa 1617), and to his sisters Elizabeth (born 1583), Frances (born circa 1595), and Margaret (circa 1585–1623), this study will not discuss all of the siblings at length. It is worth observing, however, that they too must have joined in some fashion in the Herbert family's literary dialogue. Edward wrote of his brother Charles that he "was fellow of New College in Oxford, where he died young, after he had given great hopes of himself every way" (*Autobiography*, 11). The one vestige of those "great hopes" is a Latin commendatory verse, which was written in 1613 for the publication of Richard Zouch's *The Dove: or Passages of Cosmography*. The four-line verse, like so many of George Herbert's Latin poems, devotes skillful elegiac couplets to a sacred theme:

> Aspice; non veneri est deuota Columba; mouetur
> Illius, auspicijs, penna, Minerua, tuis.
> Ergo Deae noctis studiosae Noctua cedat,
> Dum tu gaudentem luce tueris auém.

Car. Herbert, N. C.
(Zouch, *The Dove*, ll. 1–4)

> Behold, this Dove is not pledged to Venus, but flies
>   Upon your wings, Minerva, by your decrees.
> Therefore, let your owl retire, eager for Night,
>   While you gaze on a bird that rejoices in light.
>
> (My translation)[5]

In its transformation of the Venusian dove into a sacred symbol, Charles's poem recalls one of the English sonnets that George Herbert wrote from Cambridge to his mother in 1610: "Cannot thy *Dove*/Out-strip their *Cupid* easily in flight" (*Works*, 206, ll. 8–9). Both younger Herbert brothers were skilled Latinists who wrote sacred parodies of the kind of Petrarchan love lyrics that their elder brother Edward and their Pembroke cousins wrote:

> Why dost thou hate return instead of love?
>   And with such merciless despite,
>   My faith and hope requite?
> Oh! If th' affection cannot move,
>   Learn Innocence yet of the Dove . . .
>
> (Edward Herbert, *Poems*, 56, ll. 1–5)

So even in Charles Herbert's lone surviving lyric is the resonance of the family's literary dialogue.

It is a disheartening fact that while the Herbert brothers wrote dozens of literary works, the Herbert sisters, in spite of their mother's example as a patroness, appear to have written none at all. Although a great deal has been learned in recent decades about women writers of the early modern period, Virginia Woolf's pointed remark about women's exclusion from verse writing still seems apposite to the Herbert family: "For it is a perennial puzzle why no woman wrote a word of that extraordinary literature when every other man, it seemed, was capable of song or sonnet" (*A Room*, 43). Of course, women did write extraordinary words—Magdalen Herbert's few surviving letters and kitchen account book are remarkable documents, even though she was not accorded the same imaginative freedom enjoyed by her sons. Deborah Rubin refers to Magdalen as "a woman who has been silenced by the loss of almost all of her extensive correspondence" ("The Mourner," 14).

Of the three Herbert daughters, apparently only one proof of their literacy has survived: a letter written by Frances, Lady Browne, on 28 June 1647, to her brother Sir Henry Herbert. It is one of a series of letters she wrote to her brother in order to secure annuities for her self and her children. The letter reads in part:

> Good Brother
> I sent you a letter last terme by my so[nne] Estrourte wherein I did desyer your assistance & care of me & mine in your Joyninge wth Sr John Monson in seeinge of that small annuitie wch I am to haue well secured wch I doo earnestly desyer you to see donne before the writinges are pted withall. . . . I haue now likewise written to Sr John Monsone to the same purpose and I shall intreate you to doo the like for my younger children to take some care of them in seeinge theire portions & annuities wch they are to have vpon saile of the lease in y[ou]r marsh well secured[.] I understand by my sonne Estrourt that you are willinge to doo me & them any good you canne which kindnes of yours shall euer be most thankfully acknowledged by them & me that am your assured louing though poore sister Fr[ances] Browne (British Library, B.L. Add. Ms. 37,157)

Frances's letter provides ample testament to her literacy, intelligence, and involvement in the family patronage network, but it bespeaks more than one form of impoverishment. It is a letter written from a family's public room, not from "a room of one's own." During hard times, Frances was reduced to begging, but throughout her life she was also a "poore sister" in the circumscribed conditions of her writing. The Herberts' family dialogue, one must admit, was not nearly so rich or full as it might have been, had women's voices joined more equally in it.

In listening to that part of the Herbert family dialogue which is still audible, one recognizes the domestic and estate concerns in its members' literary works. Magdalen's mediative letters, Henry's courtly news, Edward's verses of departure and rarefied liberation, Thomas's stormy poem, and George's verses of divine fathers and suffering children are all of a piece with the family's structure and rank. This family, like so many other noble families, formed constellations of shared dependencies and interests with many kin and friends (Cressy, "Kinship and Kin Interaction," 67–68). The constellations radiated out from a household solar system of self and immediate kin and servants, and all the stars and planets exercised gravity upon one another.

If George Herbert's *The Temple* is a "Book of Starres," as one critic has called it, referring to the lyrics' interactions with one another and with readers, it is also a "Book of Starres" in this second domestic sense (White, "*This Book of Starres*," 165–66). The book reflects the literary movements of the starry Herberts, their attractions and repulsions, apogees and nadirs, and music as a family. The metaphysical sun-son pun appears in poems of *The Temple*, and a shooting star, on an errand from his lord's house, falls into the lap of the narrator of "Artillerie" and speaks to him. "I, who had heard of musick in the spheres,/But not of speech in starres, began to muse," reports the surprised narrator, letting the reader into the privileged space of his chamber (*Works*, 139, ll. 9–10). The following chapters chart the Herbert family's constellations, locating the lyrics of *The Temple* at the cynosure of a series of kin influences. These stars do not simply hum the theological music of the spheres, but also tell a compelling human story of a family, in verses shot from a master poet's house into our modern laps. Such stars are hard to ignore.

2 Joining Contrary Realms

࿐

The "Generous Ambiguity" of Magdalen Herbert

> . . . so much good there is
>   Delivered of her, that some Fathers be
> Loth to believe one woman could do this;
>   But, think these Magdalens were two or three.
> Increase their number, Lady, and their fame:
>   To their devotion, add your innocence,
> Take so much of th' example, as of the name;
>   The latter half; and in some recompense
> That they did harbour Christ himself, a guest,
>   Harbour these hymns, to his dear name addressed. J. D.
>   (John Donne,
>   "To Mrs. Magdalen Herbert," ll. 5–14)

Magdalen Herbert, the mother of George Herbert, has intrigued biographers and critics since the seventeenth century. John Aubrey gossiped of her marriage in 1609 to Sir John Danvers, who was some 20 years her junior, as of a family scandal: "She was old enough to have been his Mother. He maried her for love of her Witt. The Earl of Danby was greatly displeased with him for this disagreable match" (*Aubrey's Brief Lives*, 80–81). Similarly, in his funeral sermon for Lady Danvers in 1627, John Donne took great pains to inoculate her reputation against "any *halfe calumnies*" and "*whisperings*" concerning her second marriage, her love of witty conversation, and her occasional bouts of melancholy. The verbal acrobatics that Donne did to justify the marriage of the 20-year-old Danvers to the 40-something matron were quite incredible, even for a metaphysical poet. Simply by the force of metaphor, Donne attempts to deny the obvious age difference between Magdalen and John Danvers:

> For, as the well tuning of an *Instrument*, makes *higher* and *lower* strings, of one sound, so the inequality of their *yeeres*, was thus reduc't to an evennesse, that shee had a *cheerfulnesse*, agreeable to his *youth*, and he a *sober staidnesse*, conformable to her *more yeeres*. So that, I would not consider her, at so much more then *forty*, nor him, at so much lesse then *thirty*, at that time, but as their *persons* were made *one*, and their *fortunes* made one, by *mariage*, so I would put their *yeeres* into *one number*, and finding a *sixty* betweene them, thinke them *thirty* a peece; for, as twins of one houre, they liv'd. (*Sermons*, 8: 88)

One suspects that such creative computations did not impress John Danvers's unhappy brother, Henry, the Earl of Danby, but they did indicate something crucial about Lady Danvers's role in her family. As a social intermediary of considerable ingenuity, Magdalen Herbert brought contraries together (see figure 3). These contraries comprised not only the young and the old, but also the sacred and the profane, the common and the noble, the Reformed and the Roman, and the feminine and the masculine. As a courtly patroness and the mother of a large aristocratic family, "her *rule*," emphasized Donne, "was *mediocrity*" (*Sermons*, 8: 89). In contemporary language, she was a practiced mediator of family and social disputes who cultivated ambiguity.

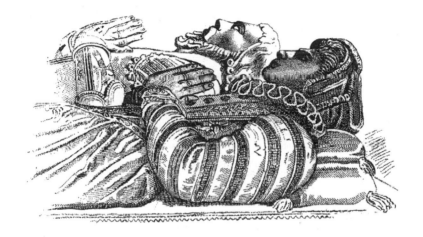

Richard and Lady Magdalene Herbert.

Father and Mother of George Herbert.

From the Monument in Montgomery Church.

Engraved by W. J. Alais from a Photograph by Owen Newton.

Figure 3

Magdalen and Richard Herbert. W. S. Alias's engraving for Grosart's edition of Herbert's *Complete Works*, 1874. By permission of the George Herbert Collection in the Special Collections Division, Walter Clinton Jackson Library, University of North Carolina at Greensboro.

Mario M. Rossi, the biographer of Edward, Lord Herbert of Cherbury, described this characteristic of Magdalen Herbert as "an earthly religiosity, a kind of roving moralism, which did not suppress the desire to enter and shine in a wider, more open world" (*La Vita*, 1: 39).[1] In fact, that "roving moralism" undoubtedly assisted Magdalen as a mediator and a social luminary. As incisively as any of the commentators, George Herbert summarized his mother's strenuous attempts to bring together opposite parties and realms of experience. In the thirteenth poem of *Memoriae Matris Sacrum*, an epitaph for his mother, he commemorated her efforts at mediation:

> Hic sit foeminei laus & victoria sexus:
>   Virgo pudens, vxor fida, seuera parens:
> Magnatúmque inopúmque aequum certamen & ardor:
>   Nobilitate illos, hos pietate rapit.
> Sic excelsa humilísque simul loca dissita iunxit,
>   Quicquid habet tellus, quicquid & astra, fruens.
>
>   (*Works*, 429, ll. 1–6)

> Here lies the honor and triumph of womankind:
>   Modest maiden, loyal wife, strong mother:
> The even and fiery contest of both great and poor:
>   She bears these away with dignity, and those with duty;
> So high and so humble, she has joined contrary realms together,
>   Possessing at once all that heaven and earth offer.
>
>   (My translation)

The climactic phrase "*loca dissita iunxit*" was translated "she unites opposing things" by Alexander B. Grosart, and "she unlinked/Regions linked" by Mark McCloskey and Paul R. Murphy (*The Complete Works*, 2: 77; *The Latin Poetry*, 149). The *loca* are not simply inert things, but opposing positions in society, ranks, or stations (OLD., locus, 17), as in the difference between the great and the poor in line three. However the lines are translated, it is clear that George considered his mother's "mediocrity" not as a passive form of compromise, but as an active assertiveness that resulted in social conquests. Indeed, her embrace of both *astra* and *tellus*, of heaven and earth, of graceful nobility and sacred poverty, exercised a profound influence on his religion and poetics.

The observation that George Herbert's mother deeply influenced his devotional poetry, made as early as 1670 in Izaak Walton's *Life of Herbert*, has been reiterated many times in the twentieth century. Walton cited George Herbert's letters and sonnets from Cambridge to Magdalen as evidence of his youthful piety and dedication to his mother. According to Walton, even as a grown man at Cambridge George Herbert "would by no means . . . prove an undutiful Son to so affectionate a Mother; but did always submit to her wisdom" (*The Lives*, 275). Much later in the biography, when Walton mentioned George Herbert's marriage and entrance into the priesthood, he added: "These had long been the desires of his Mother" (285). While David Novarr has documented many inaccuracies in Walton's *Lives*, biographer Amy M. Charles has also remarked on Magdalen's close direction of George Herbert's education and religious formation: "We shall not go far astray if we suppose that the woman to whom Donne addressed his *La Corona* sonnets took a deep interest also in the religious development of her children" (*The Making of Walton's Lives*, 1958, 301–41; *A Life*, 46). Primarily through a study of a kitchen account book of 1601, Charles demonstrated that Magdalen took particular care of her children's education in penmanship, Latin, music, and religion: teaching them to write, buying their primers, paper, and points, and appointing and sometimes boarding their tutors.

Not surprisingly, psychoanalytic critics have found in Walton's account of Magdalen ample material for speculation about George Herbert's psychic life. In his seminal article, "George Herbert's God," E. Pearlman suggested that the Latin verses of *Memoriae Matris Sacrum* show that Herbert wrote poetry as "his mother's surrogate," that "Herbert's sense of the sacred cannot be divorced from his relationship with his mother," and that his poems display "a confusion of gender, perhaps arising out of the incomplete differentiation of his own identity from that of his mother" ("George Herbert's God," 95, 97). Building upon the work of Pearlman, Michael C. Schoenfeldt has detected "gender lability" in George Herbert's portrayals of Christ, and Robert N. Watson has described the poet's "maternally imbued faith" (*Prayer and Power*, 237; *The Rest is Silence*, 257). Watson asserted that "Herbert fits the pattern of a man whose primary attachment to his mother—involving identification and a deeply conflicted eroticism—impairs some of the functions of conventional masculinity" (259). Similarly, Deborah Rubin has interpreted *Memoriae Matris Sacrum* as a therapeutic work that evinces the poet's unresolved mourning for his mother. In these poems, according to Rubin, "George Herbert extirpates the historical Magdalen and positions himself at the center of all gazes . . . Magdalen Herbert has become a secret sharer, an almost unspeakable double" ("The Mourner," 23).[2] In contrast with Pearlman and others, William Kerrigan found little evidence of "gender confusion" in Herbert's representations of his mother, but he did find in the crucifixion images of *The Temple* the representation "on the cross [of] a maternal nurturer" ("Ritual Man," 74).

Rather than speculating further about Magdalen's role in George Herbert's psychological conflicts, however, this chapter focuses on her historical role as a family and social intermediary. These roles were not exclusive. Magdalen's performance of her social role must have served her son as a preeminent example of mediation, which was to be a crucial political, theological, and aesthetic category in *The Temple*.

The recent work of women historians such as Barbara J. Harris, Caroline Bowden, and Vivienne Larminie has illustrated that women in the aristocracy and gentry participated vitally in the patronage and family networks of Tudor and

Stuart England. Harris, writing about early Tudor England, says that "overwhelming evidence exists that they [women] participated with . . . success in all the activities connected to forming, maintaining, and exploiting patronage networks" ("Women and Politics," 260).[3] These activities included petitioning patrons at court, giving gifts, boarding and visiting kin and clients, and arranging marriages—functions that often blurred the distinctions between the private and the public life, and between personal and political affairs. Similarly, Caroline Bowden has argued that in the seventeenth century upperclass women continued to play vital roles as intermediaries in social networks: "Women, participating in the informal arrangements by which patronage was distributed, understood the means by which influence could be obtained" ("Women as intermediaries," 223). In her study of the Newdigate family of the seventeenth century, Vivienne Larminie also concluded that "through hospitality and correspondence women were remarkably prominent in oiling the wheels" of kin, client, and patron interactions (*Wealth, Kinship, and Culture*, 5–6).

The evidence of Magdalen Herbert's letters and *Kitchin Booke*, as well as of George Herbert's poems, suggests that she was likewise adept at "oiling the wheels" of kinship and patronage. Four historical documents survive that attest to this role: Magdalen's account of her arbitration with her eldest son Sir Edward in 1603, preserved in the Guildford Muniment Room of the Surrey Record Office; her letter to Sir George More in 1608, also at Guildford; her letter to her eldest son Edward in 1615, now in the Public Record Office; and her kitchen account book of 1601, now in the possession of John Herbert, the Earl of Powis. All four documents concern matters of family fortunes and relations and speak eloquently of Magdalen's efforts at mediation. In the account of her arbitration with Edward, Magdalen summed up "the case betwene my sonne and me," noting that she had purchased Edward's

wardship, arranged his marriage to Mary Herbert, the heir of
Sir William Herbert of St. Julian's, and paid some of the debts
that encumbered the estate of the late Sir William (Loseley
Manuscripts 2014/103).[4] Magdalen asked that Edward pay, in
recompense for his inheritance, dowries for the marriages of his
sisters and modest annuities to his brothers. In the absence of
her late husband Richard Herbert, the widow Magdalen thus
mediated successfully between her eldest son's desire for an
estate and title and her other children's desires for a portion of
the patrimony. The arbitration involved not only the interests
of the Herbert children and tenants of the Herbert estates, but
those of Magdalen's own family, the Newports, and of Edward's
former guardian, Sir George More.

One result of Magdalen's management of family affairs was
to tie the Herberts closely to Sir George More of Loseley Park,
whom Edward addressed in his letters as "Noble Knighte" and
"Woorthy Father" (Kempe, *The Loseley Manuscripts*, 354–55).
One of Magdalen's two surviving letters was also written to
Sir George More. The letter written "In hast[e] late this 14th of
March 1607 [Old Style, i.e., 1608]" offers personal evidence of
Magdalen's efforts at mediation:

> S[r]
>
> where you cannot offend, you need make *no* excuse and though
> I desire nothinge more, then to heare of your health, yet when
> you are hindred from acquaynting me with it, eyther by your
> will, or occassions, so you be in health, I am contented with it.
> my Sonn Charlls hath so long been troublesom vnto you, as
> that I may *iu*stly feare, you are nearer being weary of him, then
> ridd of him, yet so farr am I from desyre of doeing you further
> trouble as that I shall beseech you not to suffer your Self to
> receive any wrong from him, whosoever [i.e., whatsoever] he
> and I doe Loose by it. since Wednesday Ned Herbert is rod hom
> towards his wife he hath put me in no less, but another feare,
> since the ending of that you know of, which makes me know
> the miseries of this lyfe, and to place my contentment in that,

I hope, and looke for, and in nothing I have or inioy. Forgive me for holding you so long in a discourse of my Self, and let me intreat your good oppinnion, to her that will not deserve the contrary

Magd: Herbert (Loseley Manuscript Correspondence 4/23)

The shell of the letter, its courtly salutation and close, shows Magdalen's confident mastery of the language of patronage— her ability to address a social superior and to maintain his "good oppinnion." The kernel of the letter appears to be a plea for assistance from Sir George in two family matters—one concerning young Charles Herbert, then about 16 years old, and the other concerning Sir Edward's relationship with his wife Mary. Like several of the Herbert children who lived for periods with schoolmasters apart from home, Charles, though a student at Westminster school, apparently received some additional training at Loseley Park. While expressing her deep concerns for Sir George's interests, Magdalen also reminded him how much both she and Charles would lose if their arrangement were broken.

The second matter, concerning Edward, is darker. The sentence "since Wednesday Ned Herbert is rod hom towards his wife he hath put me in no less, but another feare" suggests that Magdalen was likely involved in her son's marital conflicts. It was early in 1608, according to Edward's autobiography, that Mary Herbert disapproved of his plans for transferring properties to their son Richard, saying "that she would not draw the cradle upon her [own] head" (*Autobiography*, 47). After Mary had refused his proposal a second time, he resolved to go abroad with Aurelian Townsend to "attain the knowledge of foreign countries," even though Mary was then pregnant with another child. It was little wonder that Magdalen Herbert was distressed by the situation and sought George More's emotional support and advice, if nothing else, in the matter.

Magdalen's other surviving letter was written to Edward

Herbert on 12 May 1615, when he was traveling in France and Italy. Beginning with an assurance that "my thoughts are seldom remoued from you which must assuredly set me aworkinge of any thinge [that] may doe you good," she attempted to mediate between Edward and three other family parties—his stepfather John Danvers, his brothers, and his wife Mary and children (Herbert Family Correspondence, PRO 30/53/10). There appears to have been a strain between Magdalen's eldest son and her young husband, who were very near contemporaries. Magdalen reminded Edward "of Sʳ John Da[n]uers Loue which I dare sweare is to no man more" and of Danvers's financial assistance to his eldest step-son: "He is and hath beene so carefull to keep you from lake of money now you are abroad." The point is sufficiently important that she repeats: "Beleeue me there was neuer a tenderer hart or a louinger minde in any man then is in him [i.e. Danvers] towards you who haue power to Com[m]aund him and all that is his." Given Edward's own economic straits, he must have found the prospect of Sir John's assistance quite appealing.

While Magdalen sought to sweeten Sir Edward Herbert's disposition toward his stepfather, she also reminded him of his responsibilities toward his six brothers, to whom he owed several quarterly annuity payments, and towards his wife and children, from whom he was long absent. Rather tactfully, she blamed the lapse in annuity payments on Edward's financial officers, rather than on Edward himself.

> Now for your Baylifs I must tell you they haue not yet payd your Brothers all there Anuities due at Midsom[m]er past, and but half due at Christmas last and no news of the rest. this yf aduauntadge were taken might be preiuditiall to you and it is ill for your Brothers, and very ill you haue such officers.

Sir Edward Herbert could not have missed his mother's deep concern for the younger brothers, nor her rather stern warning of a possible legal suit: "this yf aduantadge were taken . . ."

Even more warmly, she appealed to him to return home to his wife and children: "Your wife and sweet Children are well, and herein I send you little Florence letter to see what comfort you may haue of your deare Children. Let them my Deare Sonn draw you home." Praying for Edward's "safe retorne to Your euer Louinge mother," Magdalen closed her letter skillfully, having mediated with her son in three vexing family matters.

Yet perhaps the best and most overlooked evidence of Magdalen Herbert's role as an intermediary is the last of these documents—her *Kitchin Booke* of 1601, which was noted by only one of George Herbert's nineteenth century biographers, J. J. Daniel (*The Life of George Herbert*, 27). It has been studied by only two critics in the twentieth century, Mario M. Rossi and Amy M. Charles. Rossi was interested in the kitchen book primarily as evidence that corroborated Edward Herbert's account of his early marriage and of his households in Oxford, London, and Montgomery (*La Vita*, 3: 379–81). In his autobiography, Edward wrote that in his eighteenth or nineteenth year he and his wife Mary moved with Magdalen from Oxford to a Charing Cross residence in London and that they "kept a greater family than became either my mother's widow's estate, or such young beginners as we were" (*Autobiography*, 43). Amy M. Charles's more detailed study of the *Kitchin Booke* demonstrated that the Herberts must have kept a very large house indeed in order to accommodate so many children, servants, and guests, that the house was probably near the Swan and the George inns, and that Magdalen provided generously for the Latin education, musical training, and religious instruction of her young children (*A Life*, 36–47; "Mrs. Herbert's *Kitchin Booke*," 164–73). One more point about the *Kitchin Booke*, however, which Charles only glanced at, needs to be made explicitly: the daily accounts illustrate that Magdalen brought together and literally nourished a network of kin. This family network included relatives of her late husband

Richard Herbert, of her daughter-in-law Mary Herbert, and of her own Newport family, as well as local gentry from Shropshire and Montgomeryshire.

If one counts names and titles of all Magdalen Herbert's guests at dinner and supper from 11 April to 4 September 1601, the total comes to well more than 150 individuals.[5] The number is all the more impressive because most of the Herbert household dispersed after dinner on 6 July, when Magdalen left London to spend the summer in the country—probably in Eyton, Shropshire, or in Montgomery. There were six "gentlewomen," eight "gentlemen," four "Nurses & Chambermayds," and ten "Seruingmen," or 28 individuals in the immediate Herbert household itself.[6] This means that Magdalen Herbert presumably invited, or at least allowed, well over 100 other distant family members, clients, special guests, and their servants to partake of her hospitality in the 12 weeks from 11 April to 6 July of 1601. Some of these family guests—Mr. Harley, Thomas Lawley, Edward Cooke, the servant William from Montgomery, and others—ate dozens of meals in the Herbert household. When Edward complained of the "greater family" his mother obliged, he was undoubtedly referring not to his brothers, sisters, and long-time family servants, but to the extended network of kin that ate at the Herberts' table. Charles wrote that "Some of those who came [to the house at Charing Cross] most often were linked to the Herberts by ties of blood or of origin" (*A Life*, 41). Indeed, Magdalen Herbert boarded a great many distant kin in order to buttress the Herbert family network.

Magdalen's support of a network of kin began with her own Newport family and neighbors. She kept her brother Francis's son Richard Newport as a regular member of the household, and she frequently boarded her sister Elizabeth's son (or second husband of the same name) Thomas Lawley, his servant, and his relative George Lawley; her sister Mary's husband Robert Harley; and the Lady Bromley, who was a cousin on her mother's side, and the Lady's servant. Charles also surmised that the Cooke family that ate so many meals at the Herbert house—Mr. Edward Cooke, his "boy" and sister, Mr. John Cooke, Mrs. Frances Cooke, and another Mr. Cooke, who ate suppers on 27 June and 28 June—were related to either the Newports or the Herberts, and that the Elizabeth Detton who was listed as a member of the Herbert household was "probably the daughter of friends or relatives in Shropshire or Montgomery" (*A Life*, 39; "Mrs. Herbert's *Kitchin Booke*," 170).

Other Newport relatives that Magdalen hosted, not mentioned by Charles, included Magdalen's youngest sister Margaret's husband, John Barker of Haumond, and his servant; and a Mr. Smallman, very possibly Stephen Smallman of Wildertop, who would marry Jane Lawley of Spoonhill and serve as a justice of the peace in 1623 (*Kitchin Booke*, fol. 11r, 19r).[7] It is clear that the Barkers lived near Shrewsbury and wished to please their Herbert kin, as Mr. Barker's servant presented Magdalen with "Shrosburie Oakes from his master" and Mr. Barker himself gave "one great pigion" to the steward (fols. 26v, 27r). Magdalen also hosted one of the leading gentry of Shropshire, when Sir Robert Needham of Shenton dined at her home on 7 May 1601. Sir Robert's father Thomas Needham had been sheriff of the county three times, a military commander in Ireland, and vice-president of the council in the Marches of Wales. Sir Robert was to become sheriff of the county in 1606, and advanced to the peerage of Ireland in 1625, when Charles I created him Viscount Kilmory (Brydges, *A Biographical Peerage*, 4: 194–95; Foster, *Alumni Oxonienses*, 2: 1055). Such a powerful neighbor would be a welcome ally at court and in county affairs.

If Magdalen provided hospitality for many Shropshire kin and gentry, she by no means neglected the Herbert kin of her late husband Richard and those of her daughter-in-law Mary Herbert of St. Julians. Many of the Welsh names that appear in the *Kitchin Booke* were likely their kin and neighbors. The Lloyds who often dined and supped at Charing Cross— Mr. Jenkin Lloyd, Mr. Charles Lloyd, Mrs. Lloyd, and Mr. Lewis

Lloyd—were relatives of Magdalen's husband Richard. Richard's third sister Ann had married Charles Lloyd, Esq., and his fourth sister Joyce had married Jenkin Lloyd, Esq., of Montgomery, who had attended Balliol College, Oxford, and was about 40 years of age in 1601 (Meyrick, *Heraldic Visitations*, 1: 312; Foster, *Alumni Oxonienses*, 2: 925). The Pryces and Powells who appear in the *Kitchin Booke*—Mr. Powell and Mr. Reece Powell; Mr. Richard Pryce, and two of Mr. Pryce's men—may also have been kin of the late Richard Herbert. His eldest sister Catherine married Edward Pryce, Esq., and his sixth sister Margaret married David Powell (Meyrick, *Heraldic Visitations*, 1: 312). Certainly, news came to London from the family's Montgomery estate—a messenger arrived from Montgomery for dinner on 20 May and stayed through dinner on 15 June. The steward John Gorse referred to the messenger as "Willm ffootman from home" in the *Kitchin Booke* entry for dinner on 2 June (fol. 37r). News came also from Mary Herbert's home, the Herbert estate of St. Julians in Monmouthshire. Two bailiffs from Monmouthshire arrived on 26 June, probably with pressing financial matters in hand, and stayed for only one meal. The Mr. Myles Herbert and Mr. Walter Herbert who stayed at Charing Cross from 13 to 16 June were probably kin of Edward Herbert's wife Mary, as she had an uncle named Myles and other relatives named Walter (Herbert Family Pedigrees, N.L.W. Ms. 1739B; Walter, *Herbert in England*). One unspecified Herbert kinsman, "Mr. Herbert of [Blank]," appeared for dinner on 1 June 1601 (fol. 36v). Apparently even the family steward had difficulty in keeping track of the distant Herbert kin.

What emerges from this survey of names in the *Kitchin Booke* is that during George Herbert's childhood, he would have known his mother as the manager of an immense, bustling household, and as the cynosure of a very large constellation of kin. Her roles as family intermediary and household manager must have consumed a great deal of her time, and left lasting impressions on her children. Barbara J. Harris says of the elite households of Tudor England: "Life in such households made heavy social and managerial demands on the time and energy of aristocratic women," often separating them from their children ("Property," 611). Such was Magdalen Herbert's role at the house in Charing Cross, arranging lodgings and schoolmasters for her children, visiting and welcoming the visits of kin and family allies, managing a large cadre of servants, and supervising household accounts. "The wife," said George Herbert's *Outlandish Proverb*, "is the key of the house" (*Works*, 351, no. 904).

Although Magdalen's responsibilities might have diminished some after her marriage to Sir John Danvers, George Herbert still commemorated his mother's management of Danvers's Chelsea house in *Memoriae Matris Sacrum*:

> Ratione certâ vita constat & domus,
> Prudenter inito quot-diebus calculo.
> Totâ renidet aede decus & suauitas
> Animo renidentes priùs. Sin rarior
> Magnatis appulsu extulit se occasio,
> Surrexit vnà & illa, seseque extulit:
> Occasione certat, imò & obtinet.
> Proh! quantus imber, quanta labri comitas,
> Lepos seuerus, Pallas mixta Gratijs.

> Her life and house run on a fixed schedule,
> Beginning wisely with a daily account.
> Grace and sweetness shimmer through the house,
> Shining first in her spirit. But if a special event
> Brought the entrance of a noble person,
> She arose and elevated herself to it,
> Striving and indeed winning the contest.
> Oh! What a shower, what a bath of courtesy,
> Stern grace, wisdom mixed with charm.
>
> (*Works*, 423, ll. 22–30, my translation)

In this portrait, as in Donne's funeral sermon for her, Magdalen Herbert appears as a singular combination of discipline and pleasure, of self-assertion and graciousness. Her sociability never fails to enchant, and her wit never fails to impress her guests. She is a perfect hostess and a powerful intermediary. This quality of mind, which George Herbert styled "lepos seuerus" and which Rossi called her "roving moralism," is also aptly summarized in Louis L. Martz's phrase "generous ambiguity."

In his brilliant essay "The Generous Ambiguity of Herbert's *Temple*," Martz described how the poet's lyrics often elude theological categorization as Calvinist or Arminian and how *The Temple* represents "the tense and delicate equilibrium that prevailed in the Church of England for most of Herbert's lifetime" (*From Renaissance*, 70). While some of the poems sound "Calvinist in tone," they fail to express the strict Calvinism of the Lambeth Articles, and many other poems exhibit traditional eucharistic and sacerdotal imagery. "In such ambiguity," says Martz, "lies the source of Herbert's popularity and acceptance by Christians of all creeds" (72). To put Martz's point another way, George Herbert's lyrics are much less interested in pure theological argument than in religious experiences that mediate the various doctrinal positions. In "Divinitie," he upbraided the theological disputants who "jagg'd" Christ's "seamlesse coat . . ./With curious questions and divisions," and he urged them to follow the gospel's simple instructions: "*Love God, and love your neighbour. Watch and pray./Do as ye would be done unto*" (*Works*, 134–35, ll. 11–12, 17–18). Such gospel instructions also illustrate "lepos seuerus," or stern grace—a social stance that is forceful in its religious devotion, aristocratic in its manner, and yet generously inclusive of all Christians.

In "The Invitation" and "The Banquet," George Herbert urges all Christians to join in the noble banquet of the Eucharist and to experience Christ's mediation. In "The Invitation," the speaker calls evocatively to his Lord and to all Christians—

to the "All," who is Christ the host, and to the "All," who make up Christ's body, the Church.

> Lord I have invited all,
> > And I shall
> Still invite, still call to thee:
> For it seems but just and right
> > In my sight,
> Where is All, there All should be.
>
> > (*Works*, 180, ll. 31–36)

The invitation is striking not only because it expresses a latitudinarian impulse, but also because it represents Christ's mediation in sensuous domestic imagery.

"The Banquet" is one of the most exquisite of the many exquisite lyrics in *The Temple*. It begins with the poet's characteristically intimate and loving address.

> Welcome sweet and sacred cheer,
> > Welcome deare;
> With me, in me, live and dwell:
> For thy neatnesse passeth sight,
> > Thy delight
> Passeth tongue to taste or tell.
>
> > (*Works*, 181, ll. 1–6)

The feast opens with an enchanting lute-song, the sacred equivalent of Marlowe's "Come live with me and be my love." The "neatnesse" that "passeth sight" suggests the personal refinement of an aristocrat, and the sheer sensuality of the verse, enticing the reader's tongue with its promise of pleasure, is intoxicating. The verse proceeds with such a concrete and luxurious description of wine bowls, perfumes, and pomanders that George Herbert might have taken the list of delicacies from his mother's own *Kitchin Booke*:

> O what sweetnesse from the bowl
> > Fills my soul,
> Such as is, and makes divine!

Is some starre (fled from the sphere)
　　　　Melted there,
As we sugar melt in wine?

Or hath sweetnesse in the bread
　　　　Made a head
To subdue the smell of sinne;
Flowers, and gummes, and powders giving
　　　　All their living,
Lest the Enemy should winne?

Doubtlesse, neither starre nor flower
　　　　Hath the power
Such a sweetnesse to impart:
Onely God, who gives perfumes,
　　　　Flesh assumes,
And with it perfumes my heart.

But as Pomanders and wood
　　　　Still are good,
Yet being bruis'd are better sented:
God, to show how farre his love
　　　　Could improve,
Here, as broken, is presented.

　　　　　　　　　　(*Works*, 181, ll. 7–30)

Throughout the poem, Herbert maintains a remarkable balance between the sensuous appreciation of the feast, with its sugary wine, aromatic bread, and bruised pomanders, and the sacred meaning of the Eucharist—in which Christ's sacrifice of his body and blood is presented to the faithful. Perhaps it was no coincidence that John Donne used very similar imagery to describe Lady Danvers's house: "The love of . . . *ministring to the sicke*, was the *hony*, that was spread over all her bread; the *Aire*, the *Perfume*, that breath'd over all her house" (*Sermons*, 8: 89). This is the sensibility of a vital, worldly religion, none less devout for being associated with the worldly matters of social invitations and table manners.

Just as Magdalen Herbert had united contraries at her table, serving knights and ladies along with vagrant street musicians ("a Blinde harper and his boy") at her house in Charing Cross, so George Herbert imagines the eucharistic banquet as a form of community that permits social elevation. Christ's redemption of fallen man is like a patron's acceptance of a humble petitioner at court. In "The Banquet," the communion wine becomes the "wing" by which the poor suitor is carried heavenward to his Lord:

> Having rais'd me to look up,
> In a cup
> Sweetly he doth meet my taste.
> But I still being low and short,
> Farre from court,
> Wine becomes a wing at last.
>
> For with it alone I flie
> To the skie:
> Where I wipe mine eyes, and see
> What I seek, for what I sue;
> Him I view,
> Who hath done so much for me.
>
> (182, ll. 37–48)

In lines 37–38, Christ's salvation of the fallen ("Having raised me to look up") is equated with a host generously asking his humble guest to rise to drink a toast ("In a cup/sweetly he doth meet my taste"). The meeting of speaker's eyes with his Lord's dramatizes the mediation of a social superior. As in "Easter-wings," the poet combines the doctrine of *felix culpa* with the idea of social ascent through submission: "Then shall the fall further the flight in me" ("Easter-wings," 43, l. 10). Before communion, Herbert's country parson prays, "Lord . . . thou art not only the feast, but the way to it," acknowledging Christ's role as the divine mediator of the feast.

Eating was for George Herbert, as Schoenfeldt points out, a

profound fixation: "Food offered Herbert a kind of radium iso-
tope which could trace, when consumed, the lineaments of
the Christian devotional self" ("George Herbert's Consuming Subject," 127). Schoenfeldt demonstrates amply the poet's
intense concern with eating, drinking, feasts, and the ceremonies of noble tables. Table matters figure prominently in many
of the lyrics of "The Church," including some memorable and
some curious lines: "Prayer the Churches banquet" ("Prayer
I"); "But can he want the grape, who hath the wine?" ("The
Bunch of Grapes"); "Welcome deare feast of Lent" ("Lent");
"If thou hast wherewithall to spice a draught,/When griefs
prevail;/. . . is't not fair?" ("The Size"); "Thy board is full, yet
humble guests/Finde nests" ("Longing"); "Thy creatures leap
not, but expresse a feast,/Where all the guests sit close, and
nothing wants" ("Providence"); "Distinguished, our habitation;/Below, our drink; above, our meat" ("Man"); ". . . at a
board, while many drunk bare wine" ("Love unknown"); and
"What cordials make this curious broth,/This broth of smells,
that feeds and fats my minde" ("The Odour").

Of course, the consummate example of table matters, and
of table manners, occurs in "Love III," where the unworthy
guest and the gracious host engage in a courtesy contest
before the guest is finally obliged to eat his Lord's meat.
Together, these poems form what one critic has called *The
Temple's* Eucharistic structure, and they illustrate that table
matters, which so often involve the issues of social precedence
and desert (Who is to sit at the head of the table? Who carves?
Who invites? Who is invited? Who offers thanks?) require
mediation (Patrides, "A Crown of Praise," 18).

As Magdalen Herbert provided many lessons in mediation
to her children at the family's large table, it is not surprising
that George Herbert's Christ is characterized by her "lepos
seuerus"—by intimate addresses, stern sacrifice, domestic
familiarity, and generous succor. The adjectives "sweet" and
"dear," words of familiar and courteous address, typify the

poet's language, especially as he speaks to his Lord: "Ah my deare God! . . . I am clean forgot" in "Affliction I" (l. 65), "Sweetest Saviour, if my soul/Were but worth the having" in "Dialogue" (ll. 1–2), and "My love, my sweetnesse, heare!" in "Longing," (l. 79). In his anagram poem "Jesu," Herbert's broken-hearted speaker discovers that his Lord's name also spells "I ease you" (I-ES-U), a remarkably intimate, almost maternal consolation. In fact, in "Longing," Herbert ascribes to his savior the source of all maternal love:

> From thee all pitie flows.
> Mothers are kinde, because thou art,
> And dost dispose
> To them a part:
> Their infants, them; and they suck thee
> More free.
>
> (*Works*, 148, ll. 13–17)

Likewise, in the remarkable Latin poem "In Johannem," he equates Christ with a nurturing mother, from whose breast he wishes to suck: "But he poured out blood for me as well/ And the right to his breast following from this,/I ask for the milk flowing down with his blood" (*Works*, 421, ll. 4–6, my translation). The passage is striking, in large part, because it combines visceral and infantile appetites with the legal language of mediation—the speaker claims a child's juristic right to share the maternal breast. This Christ, like a nurturing mother, must mediate the claims of all Christian children to eat at (and from) his breast. Even if one puts aside the considerable psychological dimensions of this imagery, one still finds throughout George Herbert's poetry the presence of a courteous, maternal mediator, performing gracious service at a noble table.

In his funeral sermon for Lady Danvers, Donne emphasized her "mediocrity" not only in her marriage, but also in her religion. Recently, in *Conforming to the Word*, Daniel W.

Doerksen has asserted that she provided "an important pattern of [religious] conformity" to both Donne and George Herbert (42). What George called his Mother's "lepos seuerus" Donne called her "holy cheerfulnesse": "From this I testifie her *holy cheerfulnesse*, and *Religious alacrity*" (*Sermons*, 8: 86). As an example of this attitude, which reconciled wit with spiritual devotion, he cited Magdalen's "cheerful provocation" of her family to hurry to Sunday worship: "*For God's sake let's go, For God's sake let's bee there at the Confession*" (8: 86). Apparently, there was something amusing and a little absurd about the noisy scurrying of so large a family together toward penitence. After this anecdote, Donne went on to characterize Lady Danvers as the epitome of the Church of England's middle way between Roman and independent churches:

> Shee never diverted towards the *Papist*, in undervaluing the *Scripture*; nor towards the *Separatist*, in undervaluing the *Church*. But in the *doctrine*, and *discipline* of that *Church*, in which, *God* seal'd her, to himselfe, in *Baptisme*, shee brought up her children, shee assisted her family . . .; And, in that forme of *Common Prayer*, which is ordain'd by that *Church*, and to which she had accustom'd her selfe, with her family, twice every day, she joyn'd with that company, which was about her *death-bed*, in answering to every part thereof. (8: 90–91)

In managing her family's religious practices, Magdalen, like the Church of England itself, mediated between the Protestant emphasis on scripture and the Roman emphasis on liturgical prayer. Thus, she manifested the same kind of "generous ambiguity" that Martz finds throughout *The Temple*.

Following Donne's sermon for Lady Danvers closely, Heather Asals has suggested that Magdalen's person and demeanor served as a "Topos for the Anglican Church" in *The Temple*: she "presents to the literary critic a key to the ontology of Herbert's poetry itself" ("Magdalene Herbert," 1). For example, Donne commented that Magdalen's clothing was "never sumptuous, never sordid," and George described "The British Church" as moderately attired and placed in a middle state. Perhaps the poet's address of the Church as "deare Mother" is more than an accident of ecclesiastical phrasing:

> I joy, deare Mother, when I view
> Thy perfect lineaments and hue
> > Both sweet and bright.
>
> > *   *   *   *
>
> A fine aspect in fit aray,
> Neither too mean, nor yet too gay,
> > Shows who is best.
>
> > *   *   *   *
>
> But, dearest Mother, what those misse,
> The mean, thy praise and glorie is,
> > And long may be.
> > > (*Works*, 109–10, ll. 1–3, 7–9, 25–27)

Like his mother, Herbert's British Church strikes the perfect balance between lavish and bare decoration, achieving a glorious "mean" that is not "too mean." The apparently self-effacing mediator is still able to show "who is best," asserting herself circumspectly.

The golden mean of Herbert's church and mother is by no means a purely external matter of ornament. Professor Asals has located Magdalen's influence on George primarily in her confidence in the mediative ability of language: "Her method in language presents to Herbert an idea of the middle way of the condition of language itself, its paradoxical reconciliation of extremes" ("Magdalene Herbert," 1). Such language began in a family and patronage network through which efforts at mediation in religious, political, and personal matters were constantly ongoing.

Of course, this argument—that Magdalen's family and social role as an intermediary decisively influenced George Herbert's poetics—does not discount the significance of gospel stories and Reformation theology in *The Temple*. In fact, Magdalen Herbert's role as the host of a generous family table fit well the gospel parables of heavenly banquets, where beggars and castoffs are seated alongside the rich. In his *Table Talk*, Luther described Christ's service of his disciples at table as a symbol of God's ministry to humankind:

> The communion or fellowship of our blessed Saviour Christ, was doubtless most loving and familiar; for he who thought it no dishonour, being equal with God, to be made man like unto us, yet without sin, served and waited upon his disciples as they sat at table. . . . In such wise did Christ fulfil his office; as is written: "He is come to minister, and not to be ministered unto." Ah, 'tis a high example . . . (101).

While maintaining her own noble social status, Magdalen followed Christ's "high example" after the Herbert fashion: "So high and so humble, she has joined contrary realms together." In other words, inasmuch as the wine and bread of *The Temple* is certainly Eucharistic, representing Christ's mediation for humankind, the gracious banquet is also very much perfumed by Magdalen Herbert's presence as a family intermediary.

In summary, I wish to endorse the old Waltonian conclusion that Magdalen Herbert had a formative influence on George Herbert's religion and aesthetics, but for a new reason: her role as an intermediary in a very large network of kin, patrons, and clients. If the poet learned the language of mediation from his mother, as he seems to have done, it was because his family's economic and social welfare depended on such mediation. The "generous ambiguity" of Magdalen Herbert was not a social affectation, but a strategy of forceful accommodation of social and personal conflicts. Undoubtedly, in a network of kin with diverse religious and political views, such a strategy was beneficial. One hears the enchanting music of mediation in many lovely verses of *The Temple*: in the proverb of "Repentance," "Fractures well cur'd make us more strong" (l. 36); in the humble admission of "The Flower," "We say amisse,/This or that is:/Thy word is all, if we could spell" (ll. 19–21); and in the winsome appeal of "Affliction I," "Ah my deare God! though I am clean forgot,/Let me not love thee, if I love thee not" (ll. 65–66). Such winning ambiguity was a cultural asset that George Herbert learned, generously, at his mother's table.

3 "The Church-porch" and George Herbert's Family Advice

Were a man to write so now, the boys would throw stones at him.

(Dr. Samuel Johnson
on Francis Osborne's *Advice to a Son*)

To offer aduyse vnrequested: what is it els but to vaunt youre selfe wiser then he is, whom you do counsell: nay rather, it is a pleyne checke to him, for his Ignoraunce and folly.

(Giovanni Della Casa,
Galateo)

George Herbert's "Church-porch" has been an embarrass-
ment to modern readers. Critics usually have been content
to neglect the longest poem in *The Temple*, passing over it
quickly with muffled distaste on their way to readings of
"Love III," "The Pearl," or virtually any other lyric in "The
Church." Most readers find the 462-line poem intolerably pro-
saic, preachy, and boring. C. A. Patrides called it "excellent
advice . . . but questionable poetry" and Arnold Stein damned
the poem with faint praise: "There are some things to be
learned in the poem . . ., but they are almost all things that
can be learned from more attractive poems" ("A Crown of
Praise," 9; *George Herbert's Lyrics*, 14). Helen Vendler suggested that George Herbert "abandoned, after *The Church-
porch*, the long homily" since "a purely homiletic purpose by
itself never engenders a successful poem" ("The Poetry of
George Herbert," 163). Richard Strier, in a thorough critique
of the poem's theology, characterized it as "the crudest and
nastiest of the texts" influenced by Saint Francois de Sales'
devout humanism, the one which most typified the "straight-
forward spiritual commercialism" that the poet rejected in
his mature lyrics ("Sanctifying the Aristocracy," 38, 50).
Debora K. Shuger said similarly, "Most of the poem is not
about being morally good at all" (*Habits of Thought*, 96). And
in perhaps the most revealing criticism of the poem, James
Boyd White frankly vented his impatience with it: "I find this
an impossible poem to read through without a rebellion of
my own at this didactic voice, telling the reader what to do. . . .
It is all too true, and boring; or in another sense not true, after
all, for it is false to one's experience of moral life" ("*This Book
of Starres*", 69).

The modern critical disfavor toward "The Church-porch"
is all the more striking when one considers its remarkable
popularity in the seventeenth century. Robert H. Ray's survey
of seventeenth century allusions to George Herbert's poetry
reveals that "The Church-porch" was by far the most cited

poem of *The Temple*. Ray lists 70 contemporary allusions to the poem, including 19 references to the couplet: "A verse may finde him, who a sermon flies,/And turn delight into a sacrifice" ("Herbert's Seventeenth-Century Reputation," 4–5). The poem's combination of self-advancement and sanctification inspired a great many imitations and adaptations, including Christopher Harvey's own "Church-porch" in *The Synagogue* (1640), Henry Vaughan's "Rules and Lessons" in *Silex Scintillans* (1650), Francis Cockin's *Divine Blossomes: A Prospect or Looking-Glass for Youth* (1657), G.B.'s *The Way to Be Rich* (1662), Nathaniel Wanley's "Alphabet" (1667), John Bryan's fifth sermon in *Dwelling with God* (1670), William Dillingham's Latin translation of "The Church-porch" in *Poemata Varii Argumenti* (1678), Thomas Willis's "Counsel to Young Men" in *The Key of Knowledge* (1682), Dame Sarah Cowper's "Precepts out of Herberts Poem" (circa 1700), and Thomas White's "Youth's Alphabet: Or, Herbert's Morals" (ante 1702).[1]

And if seventeenth century writers found the poem worthy of imitation, they also found it deserving of praise. Thus, the editor of *The Works* of Joseph Mede (1664) compared Mede's charitable demeanour to the Christian cheerfulness of "The Church-porch": "Upon this score does that Prince of Divine Poets, Mr. *G. Herbert*, not impertinently in his *Church-porch* (a piece enrich'd with most Divine Morality) persuade to a chearfull and frank Beneficence" (qtd. in Pritchard, "Additional Seventeenth-Century Allusions," 41). Apparently, seventeenth century readers did not feel the poem's prudential advice was stuffy, overbearing, venal, or "false to one's experience of the moral life." What, then, are critics to make of this verse that seventeenth century readers relished but that modern readers dislike?

Here, Dr. Johnson's remark to Boswell about Francis Osborne's *Advice to a Son* also seems apropos of "The Church-porch": "Were a man to write so now, the boys would throw

stones at him" (Boswell, *The Life*, 424). The Johnsonian barb
fits an advice poem whose ethical assumptions are strange
and inimical to contemporary readers. The poem's didactic
injunctions leave modern readers in an unenviable position—
a position that authors of early modern courtesy books sensed
keenly—of listening unwillingly to advice unrequested. The
"Verser" or speaker of the poem seems to "vaunte" himself
over the reader, offering a "pleyne checke" to one's intelligence, or at least an affront to one's sensibility. As Sir William
Cornwallis put it in his essay "Of Advise," "Eyther wee will
not endure Aduise or not beleeue it" (*Essayes*, 11). Should
critics, then, do what Cornwallis recommended to his readers: "Infranchize Aduise and perswade our eares to become
good common-wealth's men"? Or should they, instead, as
Richard Strier and James Boyd White have done so deftly,
launch verbal stones at "The Church-porch" and dispute its
ethical cogency?

In fact, critics should do both in turn: explore appreciatively
the proverbial wit and rhetorical gestures of "The Church-
porch" and critique the social order that underlies the poem.
Like other advice and conduct literature of the period, the poem
presents a systematic view of social expectations at the time,
situating the speaker and listener in the Stuart world of courtly
and mercantile ambition, class expectations, domestic struggles, formal manners, and suffusive piety. What Konrad Eisenbichler and Kenneth R. Bartlett say of courtesy literature in
general is true in particular of "The Church-porch": "Courtesy
books have a special relationship to the age which produces
them. By attempting to codify the manners, styles, ideals and
values of society, the author reveals the principles and pre-
suppositions that shape and animate his world. . . . They
provide an *entre* into the complex social and intellectual structures of the past" ("Introduction," *Galateo*, xvi). This particular "entre" into the world of George Herbert's poetry sums up
the exacting rules and energetic attitude that young men

needed to find a place in Stuart society. The atmosphere of this world is one of gentlemanly piety and ardent vocationalism, the bracing atmosphere of Lord Burghley's salty and religious *Precepts*.

Some of the more appreciative critics of "The Church-porch" have simply accepted the poem's didactic onus and its place in the literature of courtesy, proverbs, and family advice. Joseph Summers conceives of the poem as a necessary "preparation" of a young nobleman, one which puts "the traditional, classical (and Jonsonian) mixture of pleasure and profit to the uses of Christian didactic verse" (*The Heirs*, 89). Chana Bloch contends that "portable wisdom" occurs throughout *The Temple* and that "The Church-porch" is "a lineal descendant of [the Book of] Proverbs" (*Spelling the Word*, 177, 180) Likewise, Robert Hinman states: "[George] Herbert's 'Church' encompasses his 'Church-porch' and his 'Church-porch' pervades his 'Church.'" In the same vein, Michael C. Schoenfeldt asserts that "the relation between the shrewd maxims of 'The Church-porch' and the devotional utterances of 'The Church' is contingent rather than transcendent" (Roberts, ed., *New Perspectives*, 88). If these various critical approaches to "The Church-porch" seem at all at odds with George Herbert's saintly reputation, they reflect admirably the simultaneous piety and pragmatism of early modern advice books.

George Herbert was himself an inveterate reader and writer of advice literature, in a family keen on advice, in a period that saw a literary explosion of the advice genre. As a family advice poem, "The Church-porch" is thoroughly sententious, but it is by no means a crude, cynical, or arrogant poem. In fact, George Herbert's *Country Parson* frequently echoes the advice of "The Church-porch." The poem was seminal in its day, containing the germ of "the Protestant ethic," and it now admits a fascinating comparison with other advice works in the Herbert family, especially with Edward Herbert's Latin precepts to his heirs and Sir Henry Herbert's "Instructions to his Son upon Going to Oxford." While all three Herbert brothers emphasized cautious self-regard and piety, it was the two younger brothers, George and Henry, whose social positions forced them into service, who stressed a young man's need for vibrant industry. "The Church-porch" adapts the commonplaces of the family advice book to the poet's position as an ambitious younger son, born into vocational struggle. As a transitional work, midway between courtesy books like Castiglione's *Il Cortegiano* and bourgeois conduct books like Franklin's *Advice to a Young Tradesman*, "The Church-porch" is a singular example of gentlemanly piety and the vocational urgency required of a place-seeker in Jacobean society. Indeed, it was the poem's strenuous vocationalism, its blasting of "idlenesse" and all the vices that smacked of it, that made it so popular later in the seventeenth century. Advice that has sounded vulgar or officious to modern critics of "The Church-porch" was the Stuart period's clarion call to "brave employments."

Advice on conduct was a ready commodity in the early modern period. Humanists such as Machiavelli, More, Erasmus, Vives, Ascham, and Elyot instructed princes on education and government, and courtesy books like Castiglione's *Il Cortegiano*, Della Casa's *Galateo*, and Stefano Guazzo's *Civile Conversation* found an eager audience, spawning translations by Thomas Hoby, Robert Peterson, and George Pettie, respectively. In the Elizabethan and Stuart periods, courtly conduct books proliferated at an ever-increasing rate: John Lyly's *Euphues* and *Euphues his England*, Robert Greene's *Euphues his Censure to Philautus*, Barnabe Barnes's *Four Books of Offices*, Henry Peacham's *Compleat Gentleman*, and *Truth of our Times Revealed*, and Richard Braithwaite's *The English Gentleman* and *The English Gentlewoman*, among others. Some of the most powerful and notorious figures in Elizabethan and Jacobean England (Sir Walter Ralegh, Lord Burghley, and Lord Henry Percy, Earl of Northumberland) wrote advices to their sons, which were subsequently printed. Perhaps the most famous of these books, James I's *Basilikon Doron*, generated flattering imitations, like James Cleland's *Institution of a Nobleman* and Patrick Scot's *Omnibus & Singulis*.

The market for advice manuals in the seventeenth century also enabled a series of women authors to voice their opinions on domestic issues: Dorothy Leigh in *The Mother's Blessing*, Elizabeth Jocelin in *The Mothers Legacie to Her Vnborn Child*, Countess Elizabeth Clinton in *The Countess of Lincoln's Nurserie*, M.R. in *The Mother's Counsell*, and Elizabeth Grymeston's *Miscelanea. Meditations. Memoratiues*. Specialized advice books on travel in Europe, husbandry (e.g., hops-growing), pastimes (e.g., fishing), avoidance of vice (e.g., swearing, drinking, and tobacco-smoking), and sundry other pursuits appeared as well. Finally, many popular genres, such as the essay, the familiar letter, the character, the proverb, the epigram, and the emblem, were also replete with domestic advice.[2]

This literary outpouring of advice was as socially diverse as it was prolific. John E. Mason wrote of the emergence of conduct literature among all social and political groups: "Such works, indeed, became a standard form of personal literature, written both in prose and verse, by men and women, the illustrious and the obscure, the Puritan and the Royalist, the aristocrat and the man of humble origin" (*Gentlefolk*, 86). The causes of this literary emergence were many and complex, including the dwindling of church and feudal authority in the Reformation, the decline of medieval hospitality, the gradual redefinition of public and private spheres, the growing population of European cities, and the rise of the Protestant mercantile ethic. Siegmund A. E. Betz speculated that the "moral and religious confusion" created by the Reformation led people to "revert to an adherence to that simple prototype of all tradition, the precept handed down from generation to generation, from father to son" ("Francis Osborn's," 53–54). The traditional elements in family advices made them conservative in nature but seldom reactionary, as they aggressively promoted Protestant and humanistic ideals of marriage, education, labor, and domestic life.

And the participation of women in advice literature suggested something further. Kristen Poole writes of Jacobean "Mothers' Manuals": "Such manuals are indicative of a larger process of cultural self-definition occurring in the early seventeenth century, in which the very concepts of 'private' and 'public' were being worked out" ("The fittest closet," 70). Historians of the family have determined that the early modern period was crucial in the decline of feudal hospitality and the rise of modern individualism. Philippe Ariés writes: "The sixteenth and seventeenth centuries saw the triumph of individualism in daily life . . . The social 'space' liberated by the rise of the state and the decline of communal forms of sociability was occupied by the individual" (*A History of Private Life*, 3: 7). During this period, the medieval hall was transformed into the manor house, as large open spaces gave way to smaller rooms, "closets," vestibules, and passageways. So, "it became possible to create a closed private preserve, or at any rate a private realm totally divorced from the public service and completely autonomous. This liberated zone would be filled by the family" (10). Similarly, in England, as Lena Orlin says, "With the Reformation was inaugurated a glorification of the individual household," leading to changes in domestic relations (*Private Matters*, 1–2). As the household sphere was reified and isolated from other social institutions, a literature was needed to redefine the concrete particulars of social roles and to speak with the authority of religious discourse. Advice literature served just such a need.

But perhaps the greatest function advice literature served was to trumpet the Protestant call to work: to enjoin Christians to sanctified industry, cost and time accounting, and the rigorous pursuit of a vocation. Almost all of the advice books warned of drunkenness and idleness, and more and more of them, even of the highest ranks, urged a zealous dedication to one's calling. Weber, citing examples from Baxter's sermons and Franklin's advice, called this religious involvement in economic affairs "worldly asceticism," "the spirit of capitalism," and, most famously, "the Protestant ethic." It was Luther's concept of the *Beruf,* translated into English as "the calling": "Euery person of euery degree, state, sexe, or condition without exception, must haue some personall and particular calling to walke in. . . . Adam so soone as he was created, euen in his integrity had a personall calling assigned him by God." (Perkins, *A Treatise of the Vocations,* 755). While "the Protestant ethic" did not deprive English in the seventeenth century of all recreation nor even demand the accumulation of savings, it insisted upon a rigorous dedication to one's worldly profession. This Protestant notion of the calling, which rejected the traditional hierarchy of clerical and secular vocations, was the "one thing" that "was unquestionably new" in Reformation attitudes toward work, and which "gave everyday worldly activity a religious significance" (Weber, *The Protestant Ethic,* 80).[3] In the seventeenth and eighteenth centuries, this "unquestionably new" ethic inspired a robust tradition of vocational advice, from Perkins to Baxter to Franklin.

In this age of advice, the Herbert family was eminent. In his second Latin elegy for his mother, George Herbert punningly praised Magdalen's genius for advice and skill in conversation. He presents her as "slipping through" tangled discourse with the shrewdness of Cato in her own maxims (*Works,* 423, ll. 32–34). Magdalen's few surviving letters in the Public Record Office and Guildford Muniment Room contain some incisive advice, suggesting the praise was well merited. Her eldest son Edward, Lord Herbert of Cherbury, also shared this penchant for advice. In addition to writing three versions of his Latin "Precepts and Counsels," Edward included other advice for young gentlemen in his unfinished *Autobiography.* His advice on training young men in riding "the great horse," in fact, closely resembled George's in *The Country Parson* (The *Autobiography*, 39; *Works*, 277). According to his autobiography, Edward projected yet another treatise on the subject:

> I could say much more concerning all these points of education . . ., but this work would grow too big; and that many precepts conducing thereunto may be had in *Guazzo de la Civile Conversation, and Galateus de Moribus.*
>
> It would also deserve a particular lecture or *recherche*, how one ought to behave himself with children, servants, tenants, and neighbours; and I am confident, that precepts in this point will be found more useful to young gentlemen, than all the subtleties of schools. I confess I have collected many things to this purpose, which I forbear to set down here; because, if God grant me life and health, I intend to make a little treatise concerning these points. (42–43)

Sir Sidney Lee thought this "little treatise" may have been the philosophical discourse *A Dialogue Between a Tutor and His Pupil*, but, as John Lievsay pointed out, "it does not fulfill [Edward] Herbert's promise" as a work of advice literature (*Stefano Guazzo*, 52, 309). At any rate, Edward clearly shared with his mother and brothers the confidence that "precepts . . . will be found more useful to young gentlemen, than all the subtleties of schools."

As a successful courtier, Master of the Revels, and "man of letters," George's brother Sir Henry was adroit with proverbs. His surviving news-at-court letters to Viscount John Scudamore bristle with vivid, witty similes, as do his letters in Rebecca Warner's *Epistolary Curiosities*:

> A man may be lowzy at more certainty than cleanly.
>
> *   *   *   *
>
> Men of one mynde, like saylers in a storme; one and all; all laboringe at their taclings. (Warner, ed., *Epistolary Curiosities*, 21, 23)

And Henry's dedicatory poem to his cousin Sir Thomas Herbert's *A Relation of Some Yeares Travaile* (1634) brims with proverbs:

> The Worlds a Lott'ry; He that drawes may win:
> Who nothing ventur's, looks for nothing; Sin
> Multiplies and shall thy honour barren be;
> Lanch out and prosper, let not thy modestie,
> Be counted a crime. . . .
>
> ("No sooner Welcome home," A4v, ll. 7–11)

In their epigrammatic compression and conjunction of piety and worldly advice, Henry's lines sound a good deal like the couplets of "The Church-porch."

Quite possibly, Henry Herbert was inspired to write and collect apothegms by his brother George: "The delight in proverbs that he and George shared . . . continued well into their adult years." Amy M. Charles speculated that George Herbert wrote "The Church-porch" for Henry's instruction, when his younger brother traveled abroad to France, perhaps in 1615. Charles also noted George's use of proverbs in his letters to Henry, and Henry's manuscript listing of 72 proverbs in the National Library of Wales (Charles, ed., *The Williams Manuscript*, xxiii.). This manuscript list in Sir Henry's hand, NLW Ms. 5301E, is identical, with only two exceptions, to the first 72 proverbs printed in George Herbert's *Outlandish Proverbs*. On the basis of this evidence, Herbert G. Wright, F. F. Hutchinson, and Charles concluded that Henry Herbert transcribed some of George's proverbs before they were first printed in 1640.[4] More recently, Susan Anne Dawson has argued that Sir Henry Herbert did not simply transcribe George's proverbs, but rather that he contributed his own proverbs to *Outlandish Proverbs* (1640) and helped to shape the collection (*Sir Henry Herbert*, 186–93).[5]

Whatever Henry's part in the *Outlandish Proverbs*, he certainly authored at least one other advice work. When young

Henry Herbert prepared to matriculate at Trinity College, Oxford in January of 1670, Sir Henry wrote two pages of instructions and advice to his son. Young Henry subscribed to the instructions with his signature, and the family servant Walter Vaughan also signed as a witness, as if it were a legal contract (Herbert Family Correspondence, PRO 30/53/7). The instructions, accented by proverbs and Latin phrases, bear comparison with both Edward's and George's advice poems, especially with "The Church-porch." Sir Henry may also be the author of 26 pages of Latin verses on the virtues of sobriety, continence, industry, thrift, fortitude, and constancy, preserved on vellum sheets in the National Library of Wales (NLW Ms. 5300B). Charles declared that the nine Latin verses "may well be related to George Herbert's admonitions in *The Church Porch*," but she did not acknowledge the uncertain ascription of the manuscript ("Sir Henry Herbert," 11). The NLW handlist of manuscripts says the Latin verses are *"probably* by Sir Henry Herbert, Master of the Revels, circa 1650" (my emphasis). Although the verses descended to the NLW with other Herbert family papers, they are not, however, in Sir Henry's characteristically slanted hand. Nor does the author's name or signature appear anywhere on the manuscript.[6]

In a family of advisors and proverb collectors, George Herbert was the resident master of aphoristic writing, both in English and in Latin. The catalog of works in which proverbs and pithy advice occur is very nearly George Herbert's complete bibliography: his Latin and English letters; his Latin poems, especially, *Lucus*; the poems of *The Temple*; *The Country Parson*; his translation of Luigi Cornaro's *Treatise of Temperance and Sobrietie*; and, of course, *Outlandish Proverbs*. In his *Country Parson*, he urged parsons to use proverbs didactically in their sermons: "Sometimes he tells them stories, and sayings of others . . . for them also men heed, and remember better than exhortations" (*Works*, 233). Having been a lecturer in rhetoric at Cambridge, he undoubtedly agreed with his contemporaries about the persuasive and mnemonic power of proverbs. In Guazzo's *Civile Conversation*, a courtesy book from which George Herbert extracted proverbs, Annibal advises Guazzo similarly to employ "Sentences, pleasant Jestes, Fables, Allegories, Similitudes, Proverbes, Comptes, and other delightfull speache . . ., which hath no small force to content the hearers" (136–37).[7]

Despite the mixed reception of "The Church-porch," critics agree almost unanimously on George Herbert's pervasive use of proverbial advice. James Thorpe noticed "how much [George] Herbert is given to the use of proverbs all through his . . . writings" ("Reflections and Self-Reflections," 37); Diana Benet suggested that the poet "coined proverbs of his own" (in *Like Season'd Timber*, 140); Heather A. R. Asals wrote, "Proverbs, both 'outlandish' and Biblical, play an important part in the development and meaning of *The Temple*" (*Equivocal Predication*, 76 ff.); and Bloch summed up: "In its impulse to aphorism, the didactic intent of Herbert's poetry openly proclaims itself" (*Spelling the Word*, 177).

As a poem of advice, "The Church-porch" is seriously sententious. As witty discourse, it fails to impress. In a clever critique of the poem's stylistic defects, Michael Piret indicts its failed wit and apparent lack of purpose: "In his more mature poems, the proverbial impulse is controlled and contributes to some palpable end; only in 'The Church-porch' do we find its particular brand of moral scattershot" ("Herbert and Proverbs," 239). The poem is neither as gracefully witty as Chesterfield's letters nor as delightfully cynical as Wilde's aphorisms. Nor does it not mean to be. Indeed, other critics, notably Summers, Strier, and Bloch, have argued effectively that the poem has a "palpable end": warning against the Seven Deadly Sins, espousing devout humanism, promoting the Biblical wisdom of the Book of Proverbs, and so on. In addition to these purposes, "The Church-porch" has another very palpable

end: to infuse in the "sweet youth" a desire to follow a vocation, a willingness to observe the rules that make a vocation
possible, and an imperative to shun the vices that interfere
with it. The "bait of pleasure" that the Verser uses to catch
the youth is not Epicureanism (as the subjunctive verb in line
60 indicates: "*Were* I an *Epicure* . . ."), but a heroic vocationalism: "Fool not: for all may have,/If they dare try, a glorious
life, or grave" (*Works*, 10, ll. 89–90).

Citing proverbs such as "A penny spar'd is twice got" and
"Bee not idle and you shall not bee longing," Timothy Hall
Breen remarked that "the similarity between Herbert's *Outlandish Proverbs* and Benjamin Franklin's *Poor Richard* al-
manacs . . . is as startling as it is obvious." Breen's overarching
point was that Protestants throughout the Church of England,
not simply dissident Puritan groups, participated in "the very
spirit of disciplined work that Herbert praised" ("The Non-
Existent Controversy," 273 ff.). Similarly, Christopher Hill has
suggested that George Herbert "derived directly from Luther
when he wrote [in "The Elixir"] that labour was dignified or
degrading according to the spirit in which it was done," and
Cristina Malcolmson says, "*The Country Parson* preaches
the 'gospel of work' and the Protestant ethic" (*Essays in the
Economic*, 30; "George Herbert's *Country Parson*," 265).
Malcolmson's forthcoming study will show that "the Protestant ethic" pervades *The Temple* and that the poet attempted
throughout his life to link devotion and business.[8] From this
point of view, Baxter's well-known comment, "*Heart-work*
and *Heaven-work* make up his books," says as much about
George Herbert's vocational ethic as it does about the interiority of his poetry. The subtitle of Baxter's collection of poetical
fragments, *Heart-Imployment With God and It Self*, expresses
the same concern with sanctified industry (*Poetical Fragments*, A5v).

Two crucial ideas in "The Church-porch," the necessity of
a vocation and the sin of idleness, were consistent themes in

George Herbert's writings. His *Country Parson* advises young gallants "that *ingenuous and fit* imployment is never wanting to those that seek it." He assumes that all young men "are either to have a Calling, or prepare for it" (*Works*, 275). The parson condemns "Idlenesse" as "the great and nationall sin of this Land," and he "represents to every body the necessity of a vocation" (274). Both as a layman and as a pastor, George Herbert preached the gospel of work, taking pointers from Luther and William Perkins. In his *Treatise of the Vocations*, Perkins, the reforming Cambridge theologian, likewise required that "euery person . . . must haue some personall and particular calling," and condemned "the idle body, and the idle braine" as "the shop of the diuell." For Perkins, as for George Herbert and the next generation of English Protestants, the *sine qua non* of holiness was the individual's combination of the general calling to Christianity with the personal calling to an employment: "A Magistrate must not onely in generall be a Christian, as euery man is, but he must be a Christian Magistrate" (*A Treatise of the Vocations*, 752, 755, 756).

In "The Elixir," George Herbert illustrates this doctrine of the personal calling in terms remarkably like those of Perkins. The speaker prays for the sanctification of his labor:

> Teach me, my God and King,
>   In all things thee to see,
> And what I do in any thing,
>   To do it as for thee:
>
> Not rudely, as a beast,
>   To runne into an action;
> But still to make thee prepossest,
>   And give it his perfection.
>
>   *   *   *
>
> A servant with this clause
>   Makes drudgerie divine:
> Who sweeps a room, as for thy laws,
>   Makes that and th' action fine.

> This is the famous stone
> That turneth all to gold:
> For that which God doth touch and own
> Cannot for lesse be told.
>
> (*Works*, 184–85, ll. 1–8, 16–24)

Perkins wrote likewise that a labor done apart from God's grace "is worse then the labour of the beast," and that "the true end of our liues is, to do seruice to God, in seruing of man" (*A Treatise of the Vocations*, 766, 757). Perkins also concluded that the "base" occupation of household servants, when done for God's sake, "is not base in his sight" and "reward at Gods hand, shall not be wanting." "And thus," he continued, "may we reape marueilous contentation in any kind of calling, though it be but to sweepe the house" (757). Finally, while Perkins reproved the idleness of the "Alchymist" and the seekers of "the Philosophers stone" (764), George Herbert cleverly urged them to seek instead the truly supernatural transformation of dross into gold in the doctrine of the Christian's personal calling.

At the heart of "The Church-porch" is the same earnest call to industry and the same excoriation of idleness. While the cardinal sin of pride scarcely appears in the poem, the sin of idleness takes a preeminent place, menacing the youth's "early hopes" for "treasure." The poet scourges idleness and enjoins the youth to pursue a life of ardent industry, seeking "brave employments" and "a glorious life, or grave." He is to "embrace" the "activenesse" of foreign industry and to scorn its "vanities" (*Works*, 21, l. 363). He is to let his mind "be bent, still plotting where,/And when, and how the businesse may be done" (20, ll. 337–38). Inasmuch as he is diligent, the youth will be a "sure traveller" that "still goeth on," like a merchant's mill, without rest. "Active and stirring spirits," the Verser says, "live alone" in their excellence, while one may write "Here lies such a one" (that is, Rest in Peace) on the slackers (20, ll. 341–42). The slothful are already dead, or at least tottering on the grave. "Slacknesse," says the speaker, "breeds worms," the Herbertian equivalent of Franklin's "Sloth, by bringing on Diseases, absolutely shortens Life. Sloth, like Rust, consumes faster than Labour wears" (*The Complete*, 2: 367). The most passionate advice of "The Church-porch" is fueled by the burning urge to "be up and doing," to employ every moment of life for material and spiritual gain.

In the poem's most sustained treatment of the vocational ethic, the speaker exhorts the young man to escape "idlenesse," the sin that has made England's gentry effeminate, and to "chase" real vocations. The speaker's emphasis on bravery, glory, and martial employments implied the youth's nobility, but the accent on energetic industry also appealed to the socially mobile merchants of the period:

> Flie idlenesse, which yet thou canst not flie
> By dressing, mistressing, and complement.
> If those take up thy day, the sunne will crie
> Against thee: for his light was onely lent.
>   God gave thy soul brave wings; put not those feathers
>   Into a bed, to sleep out all ill weathers.
>
> Art thou a Magistrate? then be severe:
> If studious, copie fair, what time hath blurr'd;
> Redeem truth from his jawes: if souldier,
> Chase brave employments with a naked sword
>   Throughout the world. Fool not: for all may have,
>   If they dare try, a glorious life, or grave.
>
> O England! full of sinne, but most of sloth;
> Spit out thy flegme, and fill thy brest with glorie:
> Thy Gentrie bleats, as if thy native cloth
> Transfus'd a sheepishnesse into thy storie:
>   Not that they all are so; but that the most
>   Are gone to grasse, and in the pasture lost.
>   (*Works*, 9–10, ll. 79–96)

In such passages, the poem reflects values that George Herbert held tenaciously throughout his career, reiterating them almost verbatim in *The Country Parson* at the end of his life.

As the Verser warns the youth against "dressing, mistressing, and complement," the country parson also cautions young men about "the unlawfulness of spending the day in dressing, Complementing, visiting, and sporting" (*Works*, 277). As the Verser laments, "O England! full of sinne, but most of sloth," so the parson declaims, "The great and nationall sin of this Land he esteems to be Idlenesse" (274). As the Verser mocks the "sheepishnesse" of the bleating "Gentrie" that are "gone to grasse," the parson deplores the condition of "all Gentlemen, that are now weakned, and disarmed with sedentary lives" (277). Such constant echoing proves that the country parson in no way rejected the vocational ethic of the earlier "Church-porch," but, indeed, advocated it as a spiritual principle.

Although the words "calling" and "vocation" themselves do not appear anywhere in "The Church-porch," synonyms are used frequently. Words like "businesse" and "employments" appear at significant junctures of the poem, preparing for the vocational poems titled "Business" and "Employment I" and "Employment II" in "The Church." Readers of the time certainly had no difficulty making this connection. George Ryley, the poet's eighteenth century annotator, applied the "Magistrate" stanza of "The Church-porch" to "diligence to the several callings in which the providence of God has placed us" (*Mr. Herbert's Temple*, 6). "We may be *employed* and about good work," Ryley went on, "yet, if it be not our proper sphere, it will not entitle us to the character of diligent" (6, my emphasis). Like a number of Ryley's glosses, this one seems perceptive, but not entirely correct. The speaker is urging effort in one's calling, but the emphasis is on energetic dedication to the work ("If studious, copie faire, . . . If souldier,/ Chase . . ."), rather than on the meditative choice of a calling. While the danger of idleness is just as clear in "The Church-porch" as in *The Country Parson*, the method of choosing a vocation is not so fully treated in the earlier work.

Perhaps this difference occurs because the mature country parson could give vocational counseling more authoritatively than the Verser? Or was the Verser simply appealing to secular desires, what Perkins called the "bare will and pleasure of man himself," in choosing a profession? The latter alternative fits Strier's analysis of the poem as a debased form of devout humanism, but it does not explain why George Herbert repeated so many passages of the poem in writing his pastoral manual, *The Country Parson*. Dozens of phrases, especially ones concerning vocational advice, echo between the two works. Also, why would the poet have chosen, in the years that intervened between the Williams and Bodleian manuscripts, to retain an "early poem" of dubious morality within his devotional collection? If Herbert had thought of "The Church-porch" as a profane poem from his wayward youth, he could have done with it what he did with his "Aethiopissa ambit Cestum" ("The Ethiopian Woman Embraces Cestus") and "To the Right Hon. The L. Chancellor." That is, he could have excluded it from *The Temple* and left it to be forgotten. Instead, he chose to revise and polish the poem, as the many differences between The *Williams Manuscript* and the *Bodleian Manuscript* illustrate. He also chose to use titles ("The Church-porch" and "The Church") and an architectural analogy that would incorporate the poem within the very structure of *The Temple*. In a word, "The Church-porch" is of a piece with *The Temple*, introducing the vocational ethic and struggles that so dominate the collection.

Allied to the call to work, the insistence upon discipline and rule is a central motif of "The Church-porch." The imperative voice of the poem reminds the reader, again and again, to observe rules: "Man is a shop of rules, a well truss'd pack,/ Whose every parcell under-writes a law" (*Works*, 12, ll. 141–42). The Verser's deep impulse to give rules corresponds to the youth's inherent unruliness, his need for authority to validate his identity as a social being: "Who breaks his own bond,

forfeiteth himself:/What nature made a ship, he makes a shelf"
(11, ll. 119–20). Without rules, the youth is an accident waiting to happen, a walking shipwreck of the self. "Who lives by
rule then, keeps good companie," but "Who keeps no guard
upon himself, is slack,/And rots to nothing at the next great
thaw" (12, ll. 138–40). Without rules, the youth "rots to nothing," becoming a social no-account. Thus, Schoenfeldt writes:
"Only by strict adherence to rules and regulations does the
consuming subject [of Herbert's poems] avoid dissipating into
its appetites" ("George Herbert's Consuming Subject," 111).
Unlike Romantic notions of the self as oppressed by social
conformity, the self of "The Church-porch" requires constant
and social regulation of its appetites. In seeking employment,
the youth needs intense self-discipline, what Weber called
"worldly asceticism."

According to Weber's analysis, two impelling motives urged
the "worldly asceticism" of labor for God: first, it was an "approved ascetic technique," a means of serving and commun-
ing with God; and, second, it was "the specific defence against
all those temptations which Puritanism united under the name
of the unclean life" (*The Protestant Ethic*, 158). The youth of
"The Church-porch" is to "look not on pleasures as they come,
but go," to live by the rules and virtues of "worldly asceticism." Herbert's country parson required three virtues in a
"compleate servant": "Truth, and Diligence, and Neatnesse,
or Cleanlinesse" (240), which his Verser also required of the
"sweet youth." These values of honesty, constancy, and clean-
ness were the cardinal virtues of "worldly asceticism," just as
idleness, drunkenness, and whoring were the signal vices. As
well as marking social distinctions between merchants and
the idle poor, these Protestant values guaranteed productive
mercantile activity, while the vices disrupted that activity. It
was in horror at the vice of inconstancy that George Herbert
wrote in "Giddinesse": "Surely if each one saw anothers heart,/
There would be no commerce,/No sale or bargain passe" (127,

ll. 21–23). Much more cynically, Benjamin Franklin recognized the material effects that the display of virtue or vice had on one's business: "The most trifling actions that affect a man's credit are to be regarded. The sound of your hammer at five in the morning, or eight at night, heard by a creditor, makes him easy six months longer; but if he sees you at a billiard-table, or hears your voice at a tavern, when you should be at work, he sends for his money the next day" (qtd. in *The Protestant Ethic*, 49).

"Constancie," according to Perkins, was the "perseuerance in good duties" in one's calling (*A Treatise of the Vocations*, 773). It was the internal glue that kept a laborer dedicated to a calling, rather than to sensual pleasures. The Verser lauds it highly to the young man: "Constancie knits the bones, and makes us stowre,/When wanton pleasures bcckcn us to thrall" (*Works*, 11, ll. 117–18). "Stowre" means "strong, sturdy, stalwart" (OED, stour, 5a): it is the internal strength of "season'd timber" in "Vertue," the unbudging will to "never give" in to the enticements of sensuality. In "Constancie," the poet proposes the "character" of the ideal laborer:

> Who is the honest man?
> He that doth still and strongly good pursue,
> To God, his neighbour, and himself most true:
> Whom neither force nor fawning can
> Unpinne, or wrench from giving all their due.
>
> (*Works*, 72, ll. 1–5)

Here, as in the constancy couplet of "The Church-porch," the body of the laborer is "wrenched" by force in various directions, but, thanks to the constitutional strength of "constancie," he withstands the vocational bone-breaking. This ideal of constant, honest labor seems to critics like James Boyd White "terrifying" and "inhuman," but all critics should admit that the ideal is profoundly Protestant ("*This Book of Starres*", 180).

Cleanliness was a crucial mark of social standing and moral purity in the Reformation. In "Cleanliness and godliness in early modern England," Keith Thomas writes that "this theme was taken up with enthusiasm by some of the Puritan wing of the Church of England" (Hamilton and Strier, eds., *Religion, Literature and Politics*, 62). The character of the slothful man, as Bishop Hall depicted him, was a "standing pool," excelling in "uncleanness" (*Characters of Virtues and Vices*, 115–16). Godly laborers were, on the contrary, scrupulously "neat," as George Herbert said, or "clean." Well before John Wesley coined the phrase, "Cleanliness is next to Godliness," the Jacobean preacher Richard Bernard declared: "God required of his people cleanlinesse. Our Christian profession is pure and holy, which outward cleannes well befitteth" (qtd. in Thomas, "Cleanliness and godliness," 63). Herbert's country parson likewise reinforced the metonymy between interior and exterior cleanliness: "His apparrell plaine, but reverend, and clean, without spots, or dust, or smell; the purity of his mind breaking out, and dilating it selfe even to his body, cloaths, and habitation" (*Works*, 228). Employing the same analogy and some of the same phrases, the Verser advises the youth:

> Affect in things about thee cleanlinesse,
> That all may gladly board thee, as a flowre.
> Slovens take up their stock of noisomnesse
> Beforehand, and anticipate their last houre.
> Let thy mindes sweetnesse have his operation
> Upon thy body, clothes, and habitation.
>
> (*Works*, 21, ll. 367–72)

Here, "board" means to approach or come near, expressing the social approval of "cleanlinesse." No one fears to approach the godly cleanliness of the flower or of the "sweet youth," whereas they fear the rank putrescence of the "slovens" as much as death itself. The "mindes sweetnesse" of the cleanly laborer has its "operation" (from the Latin "operor," *work*) on the external parts of the youth. His clean body, brushed clothes, and well-tended room all show his diligence and trustworthiness as a laborer.

In the minds of seventeenth century writers, constancy and cleanliness were directly linked to sobriety. Cornwallis praised the sober youth: "What a precious sight it is to see a temperate young man. How he shines. Glorie and admiration attends all this [sic] actions" (*Essayes*, 13). In advice books of the period, no sin is more constantly and monotonously reprehended than drunkenness. Henry Peacham repeats the conventional warning in his *Complete Gentleman*: "Above all, learn betimes to avoid excessive drinking . . .; remembering that hereby you become not fit for anything, having your reason degraded, your body distempered, your soul hazarded, your esteem and reputation abased, while you sit taking your unwholesome healths" (152). In comparison with these conventional sentiments, the Verser's warning against drunkenness is vivid, brutal, and shocking.

> Drink not the third glasse, which thou canst not tame,
> When once it is within thee; but before
> Mayst rule it, as thou list . . .
>
> He that is drunken, may his mother kill
> Bigge with his sister: he hath lost the reins,
> Is outlawd by himself: all kinde of ill
> Did with his liquour slide into his veins.
>   The drunkard forfets Man, and doth devest
>   All worldly right, save what he hath by beast.
>   (*Works*, 7, ll. 25–27, 31–36)

This is a "beastly" passage about alcoholic "beastliness." This story of the murder of a pregnant woman by her son leads James Boyd White to comment: "If a patient on a couch spoke of the evils of drunkenness in such terms, the analyst would have something to say about the desires he was unconsciously manifesting, and they are not attractive" ("*This Book of Starres,"* 70). And yet, if the passage divulges a psychic disturbance, it was not George Herbert's alone, but that of his culture at large.

George Ryley explained helpfully that the story behind the passage was not original, but was a commonly told legend of a man who was tempted by the devil to kill his family and who initially refused, but, when intoxicated, murdered his mother (pregnant with his sister) in a fit of anger (*Mr. Herbert's Temple*, 4). What is striking about the Verser's adaptation of the story is that the devil's part has been internalized within the drunkard himself. This drunkard cannot say, "The devil deceived me," since his own vicious loss of self-rule is damnable in itself. Hell is not waiting with gaping and fuming jaws for the man—he is already there. Much more subtly than other theologians of his day, Herbert combined the Protestant abhorrence of drunkeness with a psychological understanding of hell as a state of self-hatred and self-inflicted violence. If anything, the analyst sitting beside Herbert on the couch should be impressed by his insights.

Although "Life is a businesse, not good cheer" for the author of "The Church-porch," his vocational ethic was not identical to Franklin's or even to Baxter's. "His attitude toward work is no less complex" than his attitude toward play, says Anna K. Nardo (*The Ludic Self*, 80). One need only think of the poet's many playful forms (shaped poems, anagrams, emblem poems, beast fable) and his parody of secular verses to realize that George Herbert combined Godly industry with noble amusements. Throughout "The Church-porch," the speaker's injunctions to work are spiced with the piquant rhetoric of nobility: "God gave thy soul brave wings" (*Works*, 9, 1. 83); "Chase brave employments" (10, 1. 88); "Fool not: for all may have/. . . a glorious life or grave" (10, ll. 89–90); "Then march on gallant: get substantiall worth" (15, 1. 209); "A grain of glorie mixt with humblenesse/Cures . . . lethargicknesse" (19, ll. 335–36); and "In brief, acquit thee bravely; play the man" (24, l. 457). Such aggrandizing gestures complicate the idea of a calling, mingling service of God with the pursuit of social eminence.

Like Perkins, the poet praises "drudgerie" done for God in "The Elixir," but, quite unlike Perkins, the poet also devises a witty alchemical allusion to prove his wit ascends higher than "household stuff." When he urges godly gravity, he does so with the aristocratic flourish of military conquest: "A sad wise valour is the brave complexion,/That leads the van, and swallows up the cities" (16, ll. 247–48). This paradox of gentlemanly toil or "drudgerie divine" makes "The Church-porch" a transitional work, halfway between courtly conduct books and bourgeois advice. The paradox also gives the poem its awkwardly in-between quality—too gritty to appeal to readers of Chesterfield, too grandiose to appeal to readers of Franklin.

If the poet's vocational ethic differs from that of later advice writers, so does his precise advice about courtesy and religion. As the young man relies on patronage to win places, his courtesy is of a more accommodating and venturesome kind than the civility of Puritan conduct books. Like King James in *Basilikon Doron*, but unlike the more severe Puritans, George Herbert reluctantly allows the youth to play at cards. He does not, however, allow the youth to gamble: "Play not for gain, but sport" (*Works*, 14, l. 193). Also like King James, he allows for witty talk, but insists, with a metaphor from husbandry, that the youth "Pick out of mirth, like stones out of thy ground,/Profanenesse, filthinesse, [and] abusivenesse" (16, ll. 235–36). His four-part advice on successful conversation is a nicely modulated synthesis of bourgeois work ethic and refined leisure:

> In thy discourse, if thou desire to please,
> All such is courteous, usefull, new, or wittie.
> Usefulnesse comes by labour, wit by ease;
> Courtesie grows in court; news in the citie.

> Get a good stock of these, then draw the card
> That suites him best, of whom thy speech is heard.
>
> 　　　　　　　　　　　　　　　　(*Works*, 18, ll. 289–94)

In order to succeed in Stuart society, the youth must coalesce these opposite realms of court and city, of ease and labour, of courtesy and news. The clever final couplet of the stanza also combines these opposites in the double metaphors of mercantile stock and cavalier card-playing. The advice to "draw the card/That suites him best" puns on the suits of the deck of cards and the suits of petitioners for employment, seeking their places in society. Diligence and recreation both have a part in this gentlemanly work ethic.

As nearly all writers of advice did, George Herbert urged the young man to be thrifty, yet he despised the parsimony of the Franklinesque merchant: "Never was scraper brave man. Get to live;/Then live, and use it: els, it is not true/That thou hast gotten" (*Works*, 12, ll. 153–55). "Surely use alone," the speaker says, "Makes money not a contemptible stone" (12, ll. 155–56). That is, only the coin's exchange in commerce—not the intrinsic worth of gold—makes the coin truly valuable.[9] Similarly, the Verser scorns parsimonious saving as a form of avarice, which is both spiritually and materially harmful:

> What skills it, if a bag of stones or gold
> About thy neck do drown thee? raise thy head;
> Take starres for money; starres not to be told
> By any art, yet to be purchased.
> 　None is so wastefull as the scraping dame.
> 　She loseth three for one; her soul, rest, fame.
>
> 　　　　　　　　　　　　　　　　(*Works*, 13, ll. 169–74)

In the competing economies of mercantile wealth and noble grace, the youth accounts both values at once. Even when he cannot count the stars, he is busy purchasing them. He will not deign to lose his earthly fame, his rest, and his heavenly soul for the meager value of money. Noting the poet's ambivalent attitude toward money, Strier says of these passages: "This is a moment in which Herbert seems to want to distinguish aristocratic from bourgeois behavior, but early capitalism would certainly have shared Herbert's emphasis on the *use* of money" ("Sanctifying the Aristocracy," 52).

Concerning charity toward the poor, the Verser's advice is also ambivalent, reflecting both the medieval ideal of sanctified poverty and the Reformation discrimination between the infirm poor and the idle poor. As an aristocratic family, the Herberts stressed the *noblesse oblige* of alms-giving. In his funeral sermon for Magdalen Herbert, Lady Danvers, John Donne called the Danvers house "an *Almeshouse*, in feeding the *poore*" and "an *Hospitall*, in ministring releete to the *sicke*" (*Sermons*, 8: 89). Likewise, in *The Country Parson*, Herbert urged pastors to use alms for the poor and hospitality toward parishioners to encourage religious piety. Felicity Heal says of this advice: "There was nothing in [it] . . . that was not suitable to an incumbent of any persuasion, even though his detailed preoccupation with social duty is indicative of an Anglican sensitivity to Second Table obligations" (*Hospitality in Early Modern England*, 292). While promoting almsgiving with the ideal of holy poverty, the poet still discriminated, albeit generously, between the "good poore man" and others:

> Give to all something; to a good poore man,
> Till thou change names, and be where he began.
>
> Man is Gods image; but a poore man is
> Christs stamp to boot: both images regard.
> God reckons for him, counts the favour his.
>
> (*Works*, 21, ll. 377–81)

This complex passage, with its multiple puns on "counts" and "favour" bespeaks the complexity of George Herbert's attitude toward charity. By an act of grace, God "counts" (i.e., imputes) the "favour" (or face) of the poor man to be Christ's suffering face, and he "counts" (i.e., adds) Christ's "favour" (or merit) to the benefit of the almsgiver. Poverty is not holy for its own sake, as in the medieval vow of poverty, but it becomes so by God's grace and Christ's reverse reckoning.

As Herbert's country parson is "a Lover of old Customes" in the church, so the speaker of "The Church-porch" also prefers formal piety. In "The Church," the poet's affinity to formalism comes out in the "perfect lineaments" of "The British Church," the golden mean between the "painted" falsehood of the Roman church and the "naked" barrenness of other Reformation churches. In "Lent," the "good use" or custom of fasting during Lent is approved as a form of *imitatio Christi* recommended by "Temperance" and the "Authoritie" of the church: "Who goeth in the way which Christ hath gone,/Is much more sure to meet with him, then one/That travelleth by-wayes" (*Works*, 87, ll. 38–39). So, the Verser warns the youth to be reverent in church, since "God is more there, then thou: for thou art there/Onely by his permission" (22, ll. 404–05). He is instructed to attend Sunday service scrupulously in order to "Restore to God his due in tithe and time" (22, l. 385). The Verser also elevates daily public prayer in Church above private prayer, expecting all to arrive on time for services ("Stay not for th' other pin," 23, l. 411) and to kneel to pray: "Kneeling ne're spoil'd silk stocking," 22, l. 407. However noble the youth, he is to defer to the priest as his spiritual authority: "Judge not the preacher; for he is thy Judge" (23, 427). However poor the priest, the youth is to honor him in his ordained office: "His condition,/Though it be ill, makes him no ill Physician" (24, ll. 443–44). As well as combining industry with courtly play, George Herbert also united formality and religious intensity in his gentlemanly asceticism.

While little read in this century, Edward Herbert's "Haeredibus ac Nepotibus suis Praecepta & Consilia"—"Instructions and Advice to His Grandsons and Heirs"—offers a fascinating comparison with George Herbert's "Church-porch." The comparison is significant, not simply because two Herbert brothers wrote poems in the family advice genre, but because their advice is so different, and the differences say a great deal about the brothers' careers and places in the the family. In his introduction to Edward, Lord Herbert's poems, G. C. Moore Smith says that the precepts "bring us still nearer to [Edward] Herbert as he lived" than his other Latin poems (*Poems*, xxii), and "The Church-porch" likewise says much about George Herbert as a social being. Readers in the seventeenth century may well have compared the Herberts' advice poems and noted the differences. At least one learned reader, the Reverend William Dillingham, the Master of Emmanuel College and Vice Chancellor of Cambridge, appears to have done so.[10] Such readers would have noticed striking differences between the Herberts' morality.

Although Lord Herbert's advice poem has been criticized in some of the same terms as "The Church-porch" (as dry, tedious, etc.), the poems differ markedly in their theology and advice. While George's "Church-porch" is an optimistic challenge to younger brothers to realize their social and religious ambitions, Edward's "Praecepta & Consilia" is a disappointed counsel to heirs, born of disillusionment with the social institutions of the time. With wit and bravado, "The Church-porch" leads the "sweet youth" toward successful vocations both in the world and in the church; "Praecepta & Consilia" leads Lord Herbert's heirs toward a stoical and privileged retirement, still cherishing humanistic ideals and aristocratic manners, but with little dependence on the church. In fact, while George Herbert's poem leads the young gentleman step-by-step into the church, Edward Herbert's advice leads them away, and instead, into the cultured retreat of a gentleman's library.

"The Church-porch" is probably among George Herbert's earlier works, but Edward, Lord Herbert certainly wrote "Praecepta & Consilia" late in his career. Between 1642 and 1643, Edward drafted at least three versions of his Latin poem, expanding the poem considerably in the last draft. The first version of the poem, discovered in manuscript by Mario M. Rossi, was dated in 1642 and contains 110 lines. The second version, also dated in 1642, contains 116 lines and was printed in the 1646 edition of *De Causis Errorum*. The third version of "Praecepta & Consilia," dated in 1643, was expanded to 372 lines and was printed in the 1645 edition of *De Causis Errorum* (Rossi, *La Vita*, 3: 391–92). George Herbert also made some significant changes in his "Church-porch" between the Williams and Bodleian manuscripts of the poem. He excised a remark about "ffrench sluttery" in stanza 62, removed a full six lines between stanzas 15 and 16, and revised many other passages considerably. Both advice poems are written in six-line stanzas and use aphoristic expressions, although Lord Herbert's elegiac couplets are intended for a more bookish audience than his brother's English poem. He wrote the advice, at least nominally, to his grandsons Edward (the third Lord Herbert of Cherbury) and Henry (the fourth Lord Herbert of Cherbury), although he also shared the advice with the readers of his philosophy.

Mario M. Rossi, Lord Herbert's Italian biographer and one of the few critics of the twentieth century to have read "Praecepta & Consilia," disparaged the poem in some of the same terms that critics have used for "The Church-porch." Rossi considers it one of Edward's least provocative works, marked by conformity, philistinism, and tediousness: "The counsels continue with tedious flatness." The tenor of the work, according to Rossi, is dull, ending "on a note of weariness, like an incomplete work and one that could be prolonged indefinitely." While Rossi viewed the advice of "Praecepta & Consilia" as sensible, he thought it contradicted Lord Herbert's theological radicalism and his libertine lifestyle as a Jacobean courtier. Rossi adduced this contradiction with good humor:

> Thus the revolutionary, the paradoxist, the old, unbridled knight approaches in old age to being a bit of a philistine when

he dealt with giving counsel to his grandson. A normal phe-
nomenon: there is no one who is as much the moralist with
his own family than the libertine. Not because he is disgusted
with and repentant of his past life or his past extravagant ideas.
But precisely because from youth he did and thought in that
mode in order to be different from others, he cannot counsel
the same kind of life for youths in his family. . . . He wishes to
render his grandson or heir happy: and thus the grandsons and
heirs inherit a belated reasonableness, a sacrifice of the feck-
less past. (*La Vita*, vol. 3: 161–62)

Rossi's criticism of "Praecepta & Consilia" is much less caus-
tic than the criticism of "The Church-porch," but, in the end,
it has much the same effect. It disconnects the writer's advice
poem from his major achievements and the central themes of
his work.

While Lord Herbert moderated his more radical ideas in
the poem, his "Praecepta & Consilia" still concisely presents
the major tenets of his deistic worldview. These tenets are his
five "notitiae communes" or common notions, the five truths
of natural theology, which he held to apply to all religions:
the existence of God, the need to worship God, the true worship of God in virtue and in piety, God's forgiveness of sins
through repentance, and God's just reward of good and punishment of sin in an afterlife (*Poems*, 106–07, ll. 7–30). Also,
although Edward Herbert softened his mocking of priests as
self-seeking charlatans, he still warned his grandsons against
untrustworthy and dogmatic priests:

> If any man wishes to compell faith, let him proclaim publicly
>   What he teaches, so that you may believe it is necessary.
> For if he reveals new doctrines from dubious texts and confines
>   God within these narrow corners, in order to be known
> To a few, or expedient to a few, then a straitened faith
>   Or even a slight one should be extended to this man.
>   (*Poems*, 108, ll. 73–78)

Rather than repeating "Judge not the preacher" as "The Church-porch" does for three stanzas, Edward encouraged his grandsons to judge their priests according to the dictates of reason and the "common notions." Concerning deficient priests, George pleaded: "If thou mislike him, thou conceiv'st him not," and "God sent him, whatsoe're he be: O tarry,/And love him for his Master" (*Works*, 23–24, ll. 428, 442–43); and Edward opined: "*Illi/Arcta quidem levis aut est adhibenda fides*" (*Poems*, 108, ll. 77–78). That is, if the priest is a sham, treat him as a sham. Clearly, George Herbert, as a younger brother, found a measure of social authority through the priesthood and exalted the office, but Edward, as an eldest brother, insisted on the prerogatives of his own conscience and held priests indifferently at best.

In place of George Herbert's many injunctions to the youth concerning tithes, timely attendance of services, public prayer, and kneeling, Edward Herbert advised his grandsons to remain aloof from the doctrinal and liturgical arguments that were tearing apart the Church of England. His ties to the church were weakened by his skepticism of revealed religion, and so he gave his grandsons this ambivalent advice: "Moreover, while accepting those things that the holy Church hands down,/Reverently deny a doctrine that you cannot fully believe" (109, ll. 91–92). Faith, as Edward Herbert defined it, was a matter of the individual conscience, not of church creeds. He advised his grandsons to care for their conduct and conscience first, and let God resolve the vexed matters of doctrine.

> Lest the disputes that are pitched around religion
>   Rack your mind, let your life only be upright,
> And your faith firm, which, aware of its destiny,
>   Will give you joy when evil is all around.
> Unless heaven's gate swings open, setting aside disputes,
>   There is no safe or certain way to on-high.
>
> (*Poems*, 109, ll. 97–103)

George Herbert had written that "churches are either our heav'n or hell," and they appear to have been the latter to his eldest brother—a place where doctrinal disagreements torture the spirit: "*Ne crucient animum . . . Lites*" ("Lest the disputes . . ./Rack your mind," ll. 97–98). Whereas George sprinkles the youth with his sanctifying precepts and leads him confidently toward "the churches mysticall repast," Edward sprinkles caution on his heirs, leading them away from implicit trust in the church. His philosophical faith is a kind of stoical tranquility. He views the mind as a lone fruit tree, most productive when undisturbed by the flocking birds of emotional conflict (110, ll. 121–26). "There is not safe or certain way to on-high" meant, among other things, that Edward Herbert could not lend his ultimate allegiance to either faction in the Civil Wars. Given his attitude of philosophical detachment, it is little wonder that when his library and properties were threatened in September 1644, he surrendered Montgomery Castle to Sir Thomas Middleton, the leader of the parliamentary forces in North Wales. While royalists dubbed him "the treacherous Lord Herbert," Edward Herbert was remaining true to the individualistic principles of *De Veritate*.[11]

In contrast to the employment stanzas of "The Church-porch," Edward Herbert's "Praecepta & Consilia" says little about the pursuit of a vocation, but much about gentlemanly avocations and refinements. He encourages his grandsons to be trained in riding, fencing, and dancing, to study languages, to read in the sciences, philosophy, and history, to travel in Europe, to visit military camps and learn the "ars Belli," to know the court, to marry to advantage, and to manage the family estates with thrift and prudence. Since the precepts are addressed to "Haeredibus," there is little question of the youths' vocations: they are to inherit the family properties, enrich them through marriage and courtship, and pass their riches on to their heirs, the paternal estates descending undiminished to the eldest son (*Poems*, 114, ll. 229–34). In keeping with their rank, they are to have fitting clothes, handsome tapestries and furniture, and superior horses: "As long as your mount exceeds the common hack,/You will receive motion, power, and grace from him" (111, ll. 143–44). The sense of entitlement in "Praecepta and Consilia" diverges markedly from the vocational ethic of "The Church-porch." Of course, as a younger son who lived most of his life on a modest annuity, George Herbert had no such expectation of the inheritance of estate, title, and the accoutrements of leisure.

As much as "The Church-porch" differs from Lord Herbert's "Praecepta & Consilia," it resembles Sir Henry Herbert's advice to his son Henry, who matriculated at Trinity College, Oxford, in January of 1670. As younger brothers, both George and Sir Henry Herbert struggled to find places in the Stuart court, and both cultivated a strenuous work ethic. Sir Henry directed his son "To pursue your education in the wayes of Piety, vertue, Learning and industry: *Quoniam non progredi est regredi*" ("Instructions to His Son," PRO 30/53/7). The Latin tag, translated freely, reads as a careerist slogan: "Get ahead, or be left behind." Sir Henry's instructions also reminded his son "to be constantly up and ready" early in the morning, and "to pray on your Knees before you leave your Chamber for gods blessing on y^t dayes worke." Young Henry was to be abstemious and thrifty in his meals, remembering that "*Natura paucis contenta est*" (Nature is satisfied with a little), and was "to be a good husband in your Clothes and expences & to appeare alwayes cleanly, and well habited." He was "not to be seen in Taverne or Alehouse." The Latin verses in the National Library of Wales that have been attributed to Sir Henry likewise praise the virtues of "Constantia," "Fortitudo," "Vigilantia industria," and "Labor," and preach relentlessly against drunkenness, vanity, and idleness. In fact, if Sir Henry wrote the Latin verse entitled "Contra Ebrietatem," his son was not to have undiluted drink at all:

Undiluted drink is no improver of your judgment:
I warn too that it will suffuse all the veins,
Weigh down the body, agitate the blood,
Parch the intestines, tamper with the head,
Clog the brain, besetting it with vapors.
It will venture everywhere, through the whole man,
From sole to crown, it will take possession of all,
It will snatch away the key of reason itself.
(*Latin Verses on the Virtues*, ll. 11–18)

Although Sir Henry was an adroit and successful Caroline courtier, his ethics, like George's, often sound rather stoical, and at times almost puritanical.

Also like George's advice, Henry's instructions to his son concerning religion favored traditional worship, especially public ceremonies in church and sanctified almsgiving. He instructed his son to pray in his chamber on his knees, and to be "timely" in attending morning chapel and evening prayers daily ("Instructions to His Son," PRO 30/53/7). Like the Verser in "The Church-porch," he preferred public prayer to private, although he encouraged both. In exercising Christian charity, young Henry was "to be Civill to all the persons in the Colledge upon occasion, and to speake kindly to the meanest person y^t comes in your way." He was to give alms "when the occasion is offered," since "ye best way of spending is giving." In the spirit of *vanitas vanitatum*, he is to remember "that life is but a vapor, a winde, a shadow, a bubble, grasse, smoke, and compared to every fadeing thing that consumeth in a moment." Thus, while working diligently, he is to seek ascetically "to be rich towards god, & to provide only necessaries here for your journey to heaven." The *memento mori* tone of Henry Herbert's instructions to his son, as Amy Charles has explained, was no doubt influenced by his age and his bitter experiences during the Civil Wars. These were "stern instructions not to place too high a value on this world's goods, nor to see this world as other than a delusion of no lasting worth"

("Sir Henry Herbert," 3). In its stern frankness, Sir Henry's monition to his son "y^t all ye land that you shall enjoy after death is but a graue: all ye pallace but a C[offin]," recalled his brother's trenchant lines in "Mortification": "When man grows staid and wise,/Getting a house and home . . ./That dumbe inclosure maketh love/Unto the coffin, that attends his death" (*Works*, 98, ll. 19–20, 23–24). There was no mistaking the pungency of the Herbert brothers' advice.

In summary, "The Church-porch" was a work of advice literature by a skillful advice writer from a family of such advisors. The same didactic and aphoristic impulses appear in all of George Herbert's writings: his *Outlandish Proverbs, Country Parson*, and many of his sacred lyrics. Critics like Strier, who have distinguished "The Church-porch" from the rest of *The Temple* as an early and aberrational poem, have neglected how persistently Herbert's country parson gave the same advice. Clearly, the poet considered this advice about industry, constancy, diligence, and reverence to be sound from the beginning of his career to the end, or he would not have so thoroughly polished his early advice poem and included it in the architectural metaphor of *The Temple*. The ethical core of the advice, however, is not Salesian but thoroughly Protestant, the "worldly asceticism" of Perkins and Baxter with some gentlemanly embellishment.

As a work of advice literature, midway between courtesy manuals and bourgeois conduct books, "The Church-porch" is of a piece with George Herbert's other works because of the vocational struggle it invokes. The same yearning for profitable employment, as in "Employment I" or "Businesse," and the same attempt to find one's ultimate meaning through work, as in "The Elixir" and "The Pearl," resonate throughout *The Temple*, making the collection an extended drama of vocational search. Nicholas Ferrar, in his preface to the first edition of *The Temple*, witnessed to the vocational theme of the work: "He betook himself to the Sanctuarie and Temple of God, choosing rather to serve at Gods Altar, then to seek the honour of State-employments. As for those inward enforcements to this course (for outward there was none) which many of these ensuing verses bear witnesse of, they detract not from the freedome, but adde to the honour of this resolution in him" (*Works*, 3). Advice literature, after all, was about such inward and outward "enforcements," about the internal injunctions and rules that constituted the self and gave it a place in Stuart society. While identifying the vocational ethic in "The Church-porch" does not suddenly transform the preachy poem into a lyric masterpiece, it does demonstrate how well the poem fits into George Herbert's overall achievement.

4 "Lovely enchanting language"

ا&ع

Sir Henry Herbert and the Language of Courtship

Lovely enchanting language, sugar-cane,
Hony of roses, whither wilt thou flie?
>> ("The Forerunners," ll. 19–20)

I know the wayes of Honour, what maintains
The quick returns of courtesie and wit:
In vies of favours whether partie gains,
When glorie swells the heart, and moldeth It
To all expressions both of hand and eye.
>> ("The Pearl," ll. 11–15)

The New Historicist criticism of *The Temple* has made one point abundantly clear: George Herbert mastered the language of courtship as an orator and favor-seeker at Cambridge, and even as a writer of devotional verse, he deployed that courtly language persistently. Translating courtly flatteries and obeisances into prayers, he telescoped the realms of worldly and divine favor-seeking into one edifice of supplication. "There is not just a humble Christian but also a worldly courtier within *The Temple*," wrote Marion White Singleton (*God's Courtier*, 49), and Michael C. Schoenfeldt ventured more boldly: "Herbert does not just run away from the social and political world but also turns the language of this world into the medium for his lyric worship of God" (*Prayer and Power*, 17). This central argument of Schoenfeldt's *Prayer and Power*, especially, has been so influential that it need not be recapitulated here. Despite the New Historicist exploration of *The Temple*, however, little attention has been focused on the courtier George Herbert knew most intimately, his brother Sir Henry Herbert, the Master of the Revels. Of all the Herbert brothers, Sir Henry was the most "dexterous in the ways of the court, as having gotten much by it," and the closest to George in age and demeanor (Edward, Lord Herbert, *Autobiography*, 12). It comes as something of a surprise, then, that Sir Henry's early career as courtier and his most significant group of courtly writings have not been studied alongside George's verses. This chapter will correct that omission and present a needed biographical supplement to New Historicist criticism of *The Temple*.[1]

Of course, many facets of Sir Henry Herbert's career have been well known by George Herbert's biographers and by scholars of Caroline drama. The entries in Sir Henry's "office book," first published by Joseph Quincy Adams and most recently by N. W. Bawcutt, have long been regarded as significant records of the political control and censorship exercised on the Stuart stage. In *The Dictionary of National Biography*, Sir Sidney

Lee noted King Charles I's love of Sir Henry for his "'excellent parts' as a scholar, soldier, and courtier" (9: 642). Amy M. Charles styled him a "man of letters" ("Sir Henry Herbert," 12), and Bawcutt depicted him as "worldly-wise," a man who "could make friends and keep them, and knew how to manage his own interests" (*Control and Censorship*, 1). Noting Henry's ties to his Pembroke cousins, Richard Dutton has argued that William Herbert, the Third Earl of Pembroke, "engineered" Henry's replacement of Sir John Astley as Master of the Revels in 1623, and Michael Brennan has suggested that Henry, as Master of the Revels, "could pull strings" for his cousin Philip Herbert, the Earl of Montgomery (*Mastering the Revels*, 228). In March 1622, he was sworn a Gentleman of the Privy Chamber to King James, and in August 1623, he was knighted at Wilton, home of the Earl of Pembroke, and King James received him as Master of the Revels. It is clear that Sir Henry profited handsomely from his post of Master of the Revels, taking perhaps as much as £500 annually from fees, gifts, and related investments, gaining estates in Worcestershire, Essex, and Buckinghamshire, and obtaining a house in London. His brother Edward's comment that Henry had "gotten much" by his knowledge of court is, as Bawcutt says, "an entirely appropriate account" (*Control and Censorship*, 41).

Indeed, Sir Henry long thrived at court, enjoying a kind of success that his brothers George and Edward sought at times but never attained. This prosperity appears to have depended on two factors: his ambitious use of his office to obtain new benefits and his skillful cultivation of allies from all factions of the court. While the fundamental responsibilities of the Master of the Revels were to choose plays for royal performances, make politic "reformations" in the play scripts, and license new and revised plays for performance, Henry Herbert took on other functions, for which he was also remunerated. These functions included licensing the printing of plays and some works of nondramatic poetry and prose, and licensing other entertainments, such as animal exhibitions, puppet shows, fencers, dancers, circus performers, monstrosities, and mountebanks. In 1627, for example, he licensed an entertainer at Norwich to exhibit "A rare portraycture or Sight"; he allowed Humfry Bromley and three associates to "show a childe with 3 heads for a y^r"; and he permitted Bartholemew Cloyse and his four assistants to "shew an Organ," probably but not necessarily one of the musical kind (Bawcutt, ed., *Control and Censorship*, 165–66). And if the Master of the Revels' licensing of spectacles seems bizzare or tawdry to our modern sensibilities, it nonetheless testified to his shrewdness.

Ever ambitious, Sir Henry Herbert expressed his earnest desire to "win" at court in his commendatory verses ("No sooner welcome home . . .") for his cousin Thomas Herbert's *A Relation of Some Yeares Travaile*. Henry urged his cousin to venture boldly in publishing his book:

> The Worlds a Lott'ry; He that drawes may win:
> Who nothing ventur's, looks for nothing; Sin
> Multiplies and shall thy honour barren be;
> Lanch out and prosper. . . .
>
> (A4v, ll. 7–10)

This gamesman's ambition undoubtedly served Henry well in serving as a diplomatic emissary to King James in Europe and in securing his first places at court. The "No sooner welcome home" verse very much resembles the bold call to employment that George issued in his "Church-porch" (10, ll. 89–90). While George sometimes disclaimed worldly preoccupation with gain in poems like "Dotage" and "Home," Henry apparently suffered few such inhibitions as a young courtier. Fame and profit were his spurs, and they drove him fiercely.

Just as important to Sir Henry's success was his thorough

command of courtly politics. Not for mere amusement did he copy passages from Machiavelli, Tacitus, and Sallust in his commonplace books, translate and publish Jean de Silhon's *Minister of State* in two books in 1658 and 1663, and write his own political treatises and a Restoration drama of courtly intrigue, entitled *The Emperor Otho*. He studied and practiced the courtier's arts deftly for over 50 years, under three kings. In his life of George Herbert, Walton commented that Henry's place as Master of the Revels "requires a diligent wisdom, with which God hath blest him" (*The Lives*, 262). This blessing was manifest in his ability to maintain friendships with many courtiers of contrary factions. Thus, while he was family ally of the Earls of Pembroke and Montgomery, who expressed distaste for Buckingham and who favored militant protestantism, he was also the close friend of John, Viscount Scudamore (1601–1671), who was an ardent supporter of Buckingham and of Archbishop Laud. His numerous friends at court included Richard Weston, the Earl of Portland; Henry Danvers, the Earl of Danby; Catherine Stuart, the Duchess of Lennox; Oliver St. John, the Earl of Bolingbroke; Henry Montagu, the Earl of Manchester; his Puritan cousin Sir Thomas Herbert; the diarist John Evelyn; and the Puritan divine Richard Baxter.

In this regard, it seems particularly telling that Sir Henry admired the Lord Treasurer Weston, who was the soul of politic pragmatism and encouraged Charles I's policy of peaceful personal rule. On 1 July 1631, he wrote to Scudamore after having attended the King's review of his navy: "The King hath byn Lately at Chatham to see his royall Navy, wher he founde his ships In very good order, & was as well pleased to see them, which ads to my Lord Threasurors [i.e., Weston's] greatness" (Public Record Office, PRO C115/N3/8547). Likewise, it is not at all surprising that, even though his Pembroke cousins disliked Weston, Sir Henry censored Philip Massinger's play *Believe as You List* in 1631 for its caricature of Weston and its criticism of Charles's peaceful foreign policy (Gardiner, "The

Political Element," 499–501).[2] Henry Herbert's political mind was, above all, shrewd and flexible, placing service to his friends and patrons above ideological conflicts.

Although little known until recently, Sir Henry's letters to Scudamore are the best evidence of his knowledge of the ways of court and an important resource for future studies of George Herbert. From the beginning of his career at court almost to its end, Henry wrote letters filled with news and gossip to his friend and confidant Scudamore. There are 42 surviving letters, dating from 1624 to 1671: of these, 39 are in the Duchess of Norfolk's exhibit of deeds in the Public Record Office (C115/N3/8536–74), and three are among the Scudamore Papers in the British Library (MS Add. 11043, ff. 80, 93–94, 95–96). The letters are extraordinary, not only for their canvassing of political topics, but also for the candor with which they address the affairs of court and for their connections to George Herbert's life and letters. While the letters have been studied recently by Stuart historians such as Kevin Sharpe and Thomas Cogswell and by scholars of the Caroline stage such as N. W. Bawcutt and Susan Anne Dawson, none of George Herbert's biographers, including Hutchinson and Charles, have made use of them. These letters, like the poems of *The Temple*, speak the "Lovely enchanting language, sugar-cane,/Hony of roses" of a courtier, while also making shrewd and heartfelt criticisms of the court (*Works*, ll. 13–14).

Scudamore, who was created Viscount Scudamore in 1628, served beside George Herbert in Parliament in 1624, received reports of the stormy Parliament of 1626 from Sir Henry, and shared many of the Herberts' ambitions and allegiances. Like Henry and Edward Herbert, he strongly supported Buckingham's expedition to the Isle of Rhé in 1627, and like all of the Herbert brothers, he was intensely interested in military and political affairs on the continent. The greatest part of Henry's news to Scudamore during the 1620s and early 1630s concerns events in the Thirty Years' War and the employments of Charles I's court. Scudamore was eager for both kinds of news, as he periodically sought offices that involved state affairs. He was named England's ambassador in Paris in 1635, the position formerly held by Henry's brother Edward. The letters imply that Sir Henry was offering privileged news of court to Scudamore, who was in retirement at his estate in Herefordshire, in exchange for his political allegiance and benevolences. In a letter dated 23 May 1626, Henry inquired about the gift of a horse that Scudamore was to have sent him, and in a letter which followed on 8 June, he thanked Scudamore for his gifts of "a fine horse" and five pounds: "Commande mee as surely, as you bestowe on mee & then I am sure to haue some employment, which will much agree wth the desires of your servant" (PRO C115/N3/8537 and 8538).

One of the most fascinating letters in the collection and one that relates most directly to George Herbert's biography was written by Sir Henry from his lodging at Lombard Street in London on 2 March 1631/32. The letter largely concerns the King's spring entertainment at Newmarket and his upcoming visit to Cambridge on 22 March.

My Lord

The same hande that receiud your favour this afternoone, conveyes the thanks & giues waye only In the time, that your L. [Lordship] may take notise of my diligense which is wound vp to make y⁰ Lesser wheeles goe the faster. It maye supplye some of my defects by yʳ Lordships toleration; but neuer mende them. Yett I have heard of diligense Commended In a servant & I know you loue it.

The season & Company conspiringe together make Newmarket yᵉ Theater of our world wheron all maner of pleasures are acted & In as delicious a mannr as Bruts [?] favord which was deliciously every day. By yᵉ Computation of our Jockeys, learned in yᵉ arte of Cousening ther owne Masters, ther are not so few as 300 runninge horses, wherof tis to bee presumed that some runn as now for their Ease whilst others beate yᵉ Carpett wayes wth their feete. Many a man may boaste himselfe to bee worse helde then ye worste of those horses. . . .

This day I heare that my Lord of Holland hath receiud such a Curtsy from his Horse as layd him for deade for a great while, & leaves him dangerously, which is ye best success of this Jokyng [i.e. Jockeying] mysterye.

On monday next I sett forward God willinge towards Cambridge, wher I hope to see my master & mistris on wensday followinge to receiue ye best Enterteynmts of ye Vniversity, which consists of Too [i.e., two] speeches only; The one In latin thother [i.e., the other] in Englishe; the first being dedicated to ye honour of ye Vniversity, & understoode I hope only by themselves, thother to Ladys & Courtiers who understande alyke, for I Knowe y^r L. [i.e., Lordship] will conclude him a very ill Courtier, who cannot *Iurare In verba magistrae.*

I could wishe our thoughts did crosse ye watrs a little more that sorrows might bee mingled with merry things. However, ye Kinge of Suede goes on & prospers. . . .

The secretarys plase stands vndisposed of, and by Consent almost, tis caste vpon sir Isack Wake. My L. Thresuror [i.e., Weston] is gone for Newmarket on whom ye voyce runs, but I doe not thinke he will embrace so muche.

What your L. [i.e., Lordship] may finde of this to bee shorte of my meaninge, which is only to deliver truthe, may be bee attributed to ye absence of Courte and presence of ye Exchange, wher they minte more news then silver at the Tower. But as that Coine only is Currant which hath ye Kings stampe, or his allowance, so I hope y^r Lordship will make ye differense twixt true & adultrate metalls & thus I Kiss y^r Lordships hands desyringe the Continuance of y^r good opinion In the Constant protestations of

Your L. [i.e., Lordship's] faithfull frend & servant
H. Herbert (PRO C115/N3/8548)

Henry's letter is of the same kind, bristling with names and court gossip, that George Herbert wrote to his cousin-by-marriage Sir Robert Harley in 1618, and the elegant metaphysical conceits of clock hands and coining recall George's Latin letters as Cambridge University Orator (*Works*, 456–73). Henry's shrewd observation about the Newmarket jockeys' "Cousening ther owne masters" and his barb directed against the Earl of Holland (his political enemy and Weston's) bespeak his canniness. Furthermore, this letter of Henry's bears a definite relation to George Herbert's letter to Henry of late March 1632, which begins, "I was glad of your Cambridge newes. . . ." By comparing these letters, it becomes clear that Henry's "Cambridge newes" in March of 1632 was a report of the festivities attending the King's visit to Cambridge on 22 March.

A record of the royal visit in *The Annals of Cambridge* details that King Charles and Queen Henrietta Maria proceeded through jubilant crowds in Cambridge to Trinity College Court, where the University Orator Robert Creighton and the Master of the College delivered speeches. The King and Queen then dined, attended two college comedies, heard another speech by Creighton, and toured the choir of King's College Chapel, before retiring to their palace at Royston (Cooper, ed., 3: 249–50). Henry's report of the events would have no doubt reminded George of his office as University Orator at Cambridge, which he had ceded to Creighton, of his own attendance upon King James's procession in March 1622, and the ceremonial speeches he delivered at Trinity College. In a word, Henry's "Cambridge newes" would have reminded George of his own aborted career as a courtier, and George's hasty dismissal of the news speaks eloquently about the course of his life: "I was glad of your Cambridge newes, but you joyed me exceedingly with your relation of my Lady Duchess's forwardnes in our church building" (*Works*, 377). So George expressed tepid interest ("I was glad") in the kind of royal festivities at which he once presided but passionate interest ("you joyed me exceedingly") in turning courtly arts toward godly ends. In abandoning the court for his rural parish church, he continued to apply his courtly arts and those of his well-placed family to projects like the reconstruction of the Leighton Church (Walton, *Lives*, 278–80; Charles, *A Life*, 151–52).

It is also curious that Henry's letter to Scudamore mentions the kind of orations that his brother George once delivered: the witty, flattering speeches, usually in Latin, and sometimes also in English, that ordinarily won the King's simpering acceptance, but that also caused unease among members of the court. Certainly, his brother George's Latin orations a decade earlier on the explosive subject of the Spanish Match might have made courtiers nervous.[3] Perhaps this is the reason that Henry wishes that the University's Latin oration is "understoode . . . only by themselves," although he protests that most in the court know Latin. Even this protestation says something important about the *savoir faire* expected of a courtier: "I Knowe y^r L. [i.e., Lordship] will conclude him a very ill Courtier, who cannot *Iurare In verba magistrae*." The Latin phrase means "to converse in the language of the master," referring primarily to the schoolmaster's language of Latin, but punning on another sense of master. The courtier is one who, by definition, must speak his master's language, the language of servitude and supplication, and Henry's letters to Scudamore offer plentiful examples of this language.

Two related charactertistics of courtly discourse that are evinced in Henry's letters are evoked powerfully in George Herbert's poetry: a courtier's appeal for patronage and political alliance, and a courtier's penchant for indirection in addressing dangerous subjects. The language of servant and master pervades Henry's letters from the opening, "My Lord" to the closing "Your L. [i.e., Lordship's] faithfull frend & servant H. Herbert." Constantly, as was the custom, he proffered his services to Scudamore, and just as constantly he excused his services as insufficient to his patron Scudamore's gifts. While one might easily exaggerate the importance of commonplace phrases, one cannot escape the fact that Henry Herbert and

John Scudamore were bosom political allies, who often served one another's material interests. In a letter dated 25 November 1626, for example, Henry's assured Scudamore that he would assist one of Scudamore's kinsmen in securing employment: "I shall bee most ready to serue you in him upon this occasion" (PRO C115/N3/8540). And on 1 August 1628, Sir Henry consoled Scudamore himself, who had unsuccessfully sought the position of Chancellor of the Exchequor: "The Lord Barrets plase [Chancellor of the Exchequor] *I did & do wishe your Lordship hereafter* which may easilier happen in apparance; for no man seemd vnlikelier for itt then himselfe. Nor was he so much as named when I came from london" (my emphasis; PRO C115/N3/8543; Foster, ed., *Alumni Oxonienses*, 1: 77). When such occasions came, Sir Henry pledged his support to his friend seeking a high office at court. In the parlance of the day, Sir Henry was a "faithfull frend"—not merely an affectionate well-wisher, but a loyal ally, whose faith was tested in the crucible of the court. In his poem "Unkindnesse," as explained in the first chapter, George Herbert describes just this political form of friendship: "In friendship, first I think, if that agree,/Which I intend,/Unto my friends intent and end" (*Works*, 93, ll. 2–4).

   In part because friends at court served one another's interests, they also traded in controversial and confidential information. Henry Herbert wrote candidly to Scudamore about such dangerous matters as the attempted impeachment of Buckingham in 1626, the Forced Loan of 1626–1627, and the Isle of Rhé expedition of 1627. While the surface of Henry's letters was often glistening and artificial, ornamented by witty tropes, the heart of the letters was punctuated by harsh truths, sometimes told roundly, sometimes thinly disguised. In several cases, Sir Henry, troubled by the conscience of a censor, actually urged Scudamore to burn his letters or to await a personal interview. One of these cases came in the Forced Loan crisis, when it became clear in early 1627 that recalcitrant officials and citizens, especially in Essex, were refusing to participate in the loan. Sir Henry detailed the plight of the refusers with sympathy, but then on 2 February 1626/1627 asked for his own letter to be burned:

> Ho. Sir
> If mine of the 26. of January kiss your hands, this may receaue the like favour and give you notis of the committment of diuers gentlemen who . . . are sent to one prison; Many of them being of Northamptonshire; some of Bedfordshire; some of Warwicke; some of Huntington & Sir John Strangny is one of the number and much pitied for his behauiour and good partes. . . . Tis feared that your sheir [Herefordshire] & Shropsheir will bee refractory but I hope the worst newes is come already & and that wee shall heare better. The Collections goe on scurvely in Essex & hereabouts. Thus I write as if wee were alone, & beleeue that you will free [me] from the danger of accusers or wittnesses by com[m]ittinge itt to the fyer. . . . (PRO C115/N3/8541)[4]

Sir Henry was willing to confess his dissatisfaction with the King's policy to his confidant Scudamore, but not to acknowledge it publicly. The phrase "Thus I write as if wee were alone" implies a privileged confidentiality within the more formal relations of the court. Undoubtedly, Renaissance courtship required distinguishing between public and private communications and between distant and privileged auditors: alliances were cemented by secrecy, and secrets were proofs of courtly service.

Likewise, in "'Secret' Arts," her study of Elizabethan miniatures and Sir Philip Sidney's sonnets, Patricia Fumerton has identified a "sense of secrecy" that informs a range of courtly arts. This "sense" of privileged intimacy in the midst of lavish ornament and ceremony was shared by sonnets, miniatures, and even Elizabethan architecture and furniture. Through labyrinthine chambers and anterooms of a palace, one came to the inner room of a lord's or a lady's bedchamber, where tiny writing cabinets concealed sonnets and where the enamelled golden cases were removed from Hilliard's miniature portraits. In reading Henry's letters or Sir Philip Sidney's sonnets, one frequently encounters the illusion of entering such a private, privileged space. Here, the writer's declaration of secrecy "creates for the reader the sense of a door opening onto the poet's most inner self" ("'Secret' Arts," 74). This sense of confidentiality is created by venting not only dangerous political viewpoints, but also the scandalous affairs of the heart. So Sidney wrote as to a confidant in *Astrophil and Stella*: "And [I] now employ the remnant of my wit,/To make my selfe beleeve, that all is well,/While with a feeling skill I paint my hell" (Sidney, *The Poems*, 166, ll. 12–14).

While Sidney's poems were famous for the amorous speculation they aroused, Sir Henry's writings also trafficked in a few intimate tales of court. In his *Proverbs and Extracts* manuscript, his sincere Christianity did not prevent him repeating bawdy anecdotes such as: "Another Lady standing by her husband in good Company who bragd of his braue acts in Leachery . . . Twas neuer to mee, says shee, naturally" (NLW 5301E). Similarly, in a letter to Scudamore on June 8, 1626, he told of his cousin Lady Catherine Vaughan, daughter of Sir William Herbert, Lord Powis, who was seduced by the court painter Sir James Palmer, while sitting for a portrait:

> James Palmer Like an excellen[t] painter hath taken the face of my Lady Vaughan the dainty widowe so longe, that now he hath taken her heart & is maryed to her: wherin she hath deceived all her frends & many sutors; As Mr. William Craven. & who was much in Loue in her. He hath gott his pension of 500 £^{i}, per annum to bee setled vpon her and hath setled himself in her too. (PRO C115/N3/8538)

The gossipy account, with its ribald suggestions about the seductive painter and the two-timing lady, means to entertain a privileged listener. Here, as in so many Elizabethan sonnets, "painting" is synonymous with deception, and the writer caustically scans the deception of the portraiture. The amorous and political meanings of "court" were very much entangled, and the court imagined as a realm of artifice, whose facades were peered through only by the *cognoscenti*, those wise in the ways of love, wealth, and power.

Providing the literary model for the exposure of courtly art was Sidney's *Astrophil and Stella*, and especially the famous first sonnet. In it, the speaker appears to reject artificial wit and "painting" for the direct effusions of his heart:

> Loving in truth, and faine in verse my love to show,
> That the dear She might take some pleasure of my paine:
> Pleasure might cause her reade, reading might make her know,
> Knowledge might pitie winne, and pitie grace obtaine,
>   I sought fit words to paint the blackest face of woe,
> Studying inventions fine, her wits to entertaine:
> Oft turning others' leaves, to see if thence would flow
> Some fresh and fruitfull showers upon my sunne-burn'd braine.
>   But words came halting forth, wanting Invention's stay,
> Invention, Nature's child, fled step-dame Studie's blowes,
> And others' feete still seem'd but strangers in my way.
> Thus great with child to speake, and helplesse in my throwes,
>   Biting my trewand pen, beating my self for spite,
>   "Foole," said my Muse to me, "looke in thy heart and write."
>   (*The Poems*, 165, ll. 1–14)

In other words, the epitome of courtly art was to appear to shun courtly art, to act with spontaneous grace or *sprezzatura*, and to create a factitious sense of natural interiority in contrast with artifice. Paradoxically, no one could be as dismissive of the ways of court as courtiers themselves, and in this sense, Shakespeare's Hamlet is the truer representation of a courtier than Osrick, Hamlet's dupe and foil. This principle of courtly behavior was summarized neatly by Castiglione in *The Book of the Courtier* as "true art is what does not seem to be art" (67), and Fumerton says of Sidney's speaker: "Only through con-vention can he find in-vention" ("'Secret' Arts," 85).

George Herbert, as John N. Wall illustrated in *Transforma-tions of the Word*, was decisively influenced by his cousin Sidney's secular poetry (224–37). Herbert's "Jordan" poems, in particular, enact sacred parodies of Sidney's poems, con-trasting the godly plainness of the shepherd with the "wind-ing stair" and "painted chair" of courtly verse. His "Jordan II" clearly recalls Sidney's sonnet "Loving in truth":

> When first my lines of heav'nly joyes made mention,
> Such was their lustre, they did so excell,
> That I sought out quaint words, and trim invention;
> My thoughts began to burnish, sprout, and swell,
> Curling with metaphors a plain intention,
> Decking the sense, as if it were to sell.
>
>   *   *   *   *
>
> As flames do work and winde, when they ascend,
> So did I weave my self into the sense.
> But while I bustled, I might heare a friend
> Whisper, *How wide is all this long pretence!*
> *There is in love a sweetnesse readie penn'd:*
> *Copie out onely that, and save expense.*
>
>   (*Works*, 102–03, ll. 1–6, 13–18).

In both poems, art is created by the contrast of artificial rhetoric and abrupt idiomatic speech, and while the art pretends to naturalness, it remains essentially courtly. The truth-telling "friend" in Herbert's poem, like the muse in Sidney's, plays the role of the courtly confidant, whispering insistent advice to a stunned listener. The prudential nature of the advice is stressed by the phrases "readie penn'd" and "save expense," and the whispered exchange gives a sense of privileged interi-ority to the verse. Thus, George Herbert's devotional verses imitated the rhetoric of courtly secrecy and truth-telling, which he might have known from his brother Henry's letters as well as from his cousin Philip's poetry.

A second way in which George and Henry Herbert employed

the courtly language of secrecy came in their turn to riddling, allegorical language as they addressed scandalous or dangerous subjects. This kind of secret language was common to Hilliard's miniatures, with their Latin and French mottoes and elaborate visual puns, to Shakespeare and Sidney's sonnets, with their quibbling upon names like Will and Rich, and to many courtly letters, satires, and dramas that concerned political subjects (Fumerton, "'Secret' Arts," 74–75). As Master of the Revels, Sir Henry Herbert approved performances of one such political work in 1624, Thomas Middleton's anti-Spanish *A Game at Chess*, only to see the play suppressed by the Privy Council. The political allegory of the play, including its caricature of the Spanish ambassador Gondomar, was so well disguised that Herbert probably did not anticipate a controversy. In this regard, T. H. Howard Hill wrote in "The Origins of Middleton's *A Game at Chess*": "Had [the acting company] refrained from exaggerating the political features of the play by impersonation and striking subtextual action, the play might have escaped official attention" (11). Certainly, Henry Herbert himself knew the value of riddling and disguised political commentary. In his letter to Scudamore dated 23 June 1632, he referred to his friend as "ye best Interpreter of my meaninge," it being rather obvious that his meanings sometimes required considerable political knowledge to construe (PRO C115/N3/8549).

In writing to Scudamore on 1 July 1631 about affairs on the continent, for example, Sir Henry also made a glancing allusion to affairs in Charles's court: "At home wee have our wars too, but they are ciuill ones as yett, but of an vnciuill nature, as you shall heare more at large hereafter for what is not safe to Enquire after is less safe to write" (PRO C115/N3/8547). What was the nature of the war at court? Was Henry alluding to the rumors then current that James Hamilton was plotting against Charles I?[5] In this case, Henry seems to have been whetting his friend's appetite for news to be delivered in a private interview, but without revealing any details. In other cases, Sir Henry resorted to more elaborate allegory in order to deliver political commentary.

On 4 November 1641, he wrote to Scudamore about his premonitions of an actual civil war:

> My Lord,
> To heare of your health Is the best news this tyme affords which is so full fraughte of the variety of Ill tydinges that like waues at sea In a storme, One begets another and without beginninge or endinge.
> The winde did blowe colde out of the Northe & does so still, but a westerne wynde Is rysen that denotes a storme, & a great One too; A Lande storme which Is the worst of stormes. . . .
> Haste was made Into Scotland to disturbe the three Kingdomes; no auoyding of destinye; what Is apoynted must come to pass & our Day of punnishment Is at hande. (PRO C115/N3/8556)

The wind from the North clearly referred to the Scottish opposition to Charles I's church and government, which was supported by Puritan members of the House of Commons; the western wind presumably referred to the Catholic rebellions in Ireland, which called for the perilous measure of raising another army. Like waves crashing ever further, the disaster of Scotland was breaking into the disaster of Ireland, and then, Henry rightly feared, the disaster of England. The "Lande storme" of war was soon to involve all three kingdoms, and in November of 1641 there seemed "no auoyding" of it. Sir Henry was using allegory that was deeply portentous of political disorder.

Just as clearly, George Herbert also used political allegory in the poetry of *The Temple*. One striking example in "Church-rents and schismes" parallels closely his brother Henry's description of political storms. In the poem, George allegorized the divisions within the English church as the tearing apart of a "Brave rose" by jealous worms and winds. The division of the Church of England is complete in the third stanza, when the rose is trampled in the dust:

> Then did your sev'rall parts unloose and start:
> Which when your neighbours saw, like a north-winde
> They rushed in, and cast them in the dirt
> Where Pagans tread.
>
> (*Works*, 140, ll. 21–24)

Even though George Herbert wrote this verse many years before the English Civil War, he, like Henry, expressed fears about the "north-winde" and the "neighbours" of Scotland and Ireland, which eagerly sought to cast off the Church of England. Like his brother Henry, George used an allegorical language of secrecy to make political commentary of a particularly ominous kind. As an experienced courtier himself, George Herbert knew the special protections and rhetorical power afforded by this kind of veiled language.

Although "Church-rents and schismes" offers the most blatant example of covert political allegory, a handful of poems in *The Temple* make similar allusions. "The British Church" famously allegorizes the differences between the British, Catholic, and Reformed churches, presenting the Church of England as a golden mean of liturgical correctness, "double-moat[ed]" by God's grace. Herbert's "The Familie," on the other hand, represents noisy divisions within the Church of England as the domestic "wrangling" of dissenting servants. According to Claude J. Summers and Ted-Larry Pebworth, the allegory of the poem presents the Church's threat to expel dissenting ministers and laity. In "The Politics of *The Temple*," Summers and Pebworth say of the poem's speaker: "He calls on God to thrust out these intruders, praying that they be replaced by . . . genuine members of God's household" (6).

Still other poems in *The Temple* extend Herbert's political critique beyond the church gate. Sidney Gottlieb, for one, has read Herbert's "Peace" as a criticism of the hollow rhetoric of

peace during Charles I's personal rule. In the course of "Peace,"
an ardent peace-seeker ventures into an elegant garden, where
he discovers a worm at the root of "A gallant flower,/The
Crown Imperiall" (*Works*, 125, ll. 14–15). Thus, says Gottlieb:
"Herbert seems to have written 'Peace' as a sobering, allegorical but demystifying anti-masque" (Summers and Pebworth,
eds., "*The Muses Common-Weale*", 110). Similarly, Cristina
Malcomson has found in Herbert's garden poem "Paradise" a
justification for the colonialism of the Virginia Company: "The
'end' of this religious and social order, which in 'Paradise' and
the 'Church Militant' is understood as individual and universal salvation, included as well the acquisition of foreign
territory and the development of a world-wide trade nexus"
(*Heartwork: George Herbert and the Protestant Ethic*). Finally,
the beast-fable of Herbert's "Humilitie," which very much resembles the political allegory of Spenser's "Mother Hubbard's
Tale," makes a sustained critique of corruption throughout
the Stuart court and bench. The riot of the beasts in the poems,
who battle for a peacock's plume, represent "a powerful and
precise description of what many contemporary observers felt
was a crumbling social hierarchy and a court made impotent
and volatile by bribery." ("Herbert's Anti-Court Sequence,"
482).[6] While readers may dispute some or all of these particular interpretations, that George Herbert used the secretive language of political allegory seems beyond question. Like his
brother Henry, a skillful courtier, he remained shrewdly critical of the court, while still in a manner attached to it.

The manner in which George Herbert, as a somewhat disaffected country parson in distant Bemerton, remained attached
to the court was necessarily complicated. His employment at
Bemerton meant he had foregone many of his ambitions for a
place at court, but he did not, and probably could not, forsake
all of his family's courtly ties. Through his brothers Henry
and Edward, his stepfather John Danvers, and his Pembroke
cousins, he maintained connections to court, which he used

for the rebuilding of the Leighton-Bromswold church. Writing to his brother Henry "at Court," George said, "I am glad I used you in it [i.e., in procuring patronage], and you have no cause to be sorry, since it is God's business" (*Works*, 377). God, he felt, blessed courtiers too, though sometimes reluctantly. John Aubrey also asserted that George Herbert served as a chaplain to his cousin Philip Herbert, the Fourth Earl of Pembroke, and "his Lordship gave him a Benefice at Bemmarton" (*Aubrey's Brief Lives*, 137). In fact, one of Herbert's surviving letters from Bemerton was written to Lady Anne, the Countess of Pembroke, and is itself a courtly letter, although it disclaims the "Court-stile" (*Works*, 376–77). His "Church-porch" was written for the instruction of young gallants who fled sermons, and he repeated some of the same advice in *The Country Parson*.

Yet the final and deepest tie of George Herbert to court was in the language of supplication shared by both church and court. It was more than coincidence that many of Sir Henry's letters to Scudamore began with the same salutation, "My Lord," as George's devotional poems. The same addresses were used to denote absolute forms of power, whether terrestrial or divine, and similar attitudes of humility accompanied them. Rather than denying or neglecting the common forms of prayer to God and King, George Herbert played upon them ingeniously. There is in his poety, as Schoenfeldt says, a "parallel between the courts of heaven and earth" that "culminates in a deployment of the language of secular supplication appropriate to terrestrial courts in the act of petitioning God" (Roberts, ed., *New Perspectives*, 91). In "Jordan I," for example, the speaker rejects the "fictions," "false hair," and "winding stair" of courtly love verse, but supplants them with a courtly religious verse: "Shepherds are honest people; let them sing: . . ./ Nor let them punish me with losse of rime,/Who plainly say, *My God, My King*" (*Works*, 57, ll. 11, 14–15). Just as Herbert's "honest shepherds" refers both to country parsons and to the pastoral speakers of courtly eclogues, so his prayer to God and

King has a double application. Like Sidney's, his plain speech artfully disdains—and employs—artifice.

In other poems, George Herbert's love of courtly language is stated explicitly. In the sonnets he wrote during his first year at Cambridge and sent to his mother for the New Year of 1610, he expressed his ambition of transforming secular love poetry into divine poetry: "Doth Poetry/Wear *Venus* Livery? only serve her turn?/Why are not *Sonnets* made of thee?" (*Works*, 206, ll. 3–5). Clearly, he wished poetry would wear God's "livery," devoting itself to a heavenly love and master. And such was the success of his courtly religious lyrics that he lamented the effects that aging might have upon his witty and elegant language. In "The Forerunners," he wrote:

> Farewell sweet phrases, lovely metaphors.
> But will ye leave me thus? when ye before
> Of stews and brothels onely knew the doores,
> Then did I wash you with my tears, and more,
>   Brought you to Church well drest and clad:
> My God must have my best, ev'n all I had.
>
> Lovely enchanting language, sugar-cane,
> Hony of roses, whither wilt thou flie?
> Hath some fond lover tic'd thee to thy bane?
> And wilt thou leave the Church, and love a stie?
>   Fie, thou wilt soil thy broider'd coat,
> And hurt thy self, and him that sings the note.
>
>   (*Works*, 176, ll. 13–24)

The speaker's obvious pride in his reclamation of courtly, amorous language for the church puts him in the position of Christ to a Mary Magdalene: he has made a holy lady of formerly lewd poetry, and he is reluctant to forfeit his association with her. Later in the poem, he asserts again that "[Divine] Beautie and beauteous words should go together" (177, l. 30), words befitting a religious poet from a courtly family.

Amy M. Charles was certainly right in asserting that "Sir Henry's reputation as a man of letters ... will not compete with those of his elder brothers [George and Edward]." His courtly letters, however, unknown to Charles and other biographers, bear study alongside his brothers' poetry and enhance New Historicist interpretations of *The Temple*. The Scudamore letters suggest that Sir Henry was indeed "dexterous in the ways of the court," that accounts of his intense piety may have been somewhat exaggerated (see appendix B), and that he wrote to his brother George of affairs at court that reflected back upon George's career as Cambridge University Orator. Henry's letters also illustrate a courtly language of confidential speech, which was able to shun artifice and political corruption without forsaking the court. George used this "enchanting language" in *The Temple* to create a distinctive religious idiom and a sense of interiority, but he directed it to a much more powerful confidant than Viscount Scudamore—to his "friend" and Lord, Jesus Christ.

5 Comparing Fruits

ॐ

Edward Herbert, Sonship, Sacrifice, and Time

Our Orenge-trees grow ripe with time.
> (Edward Herbert of Cherbury,
> "I am the first that ever lov'd," l. 20)

Oh that I were an Orenge-tree,
> That busie plant!
>> (George Herbert,
>> "Employment II," ll. 21–22)

George Herbert and Edward, Lord Herbert of Cherbury both wrote of oranges, but on first reading it seems improbable that one brother's orange poem influenced the other's. In Edward Herbert's witty seduction song "I am the first that ever loved," he compared a slow-maturing and secret love to the growth of oranges "in our Northern clime" (*Poems*, 28, l. 25). Once the speaker's love has finally grown for the lady, he begs her, with more than a little sexual innuendo, to pluck the unexpected fruit: "Then gather in that which doth grow/And ripen to that fairest hand;/'Tis not enough that trees do stand,/If their fruit fall and perish too" (29, ll. 33–36). In George Herbert's poem, however, the speaker yearns for a vocation that would bear fruit: "Then should I ever laden be,/And never want/Some fruit for him that dressed me" (*Works*, 79, ll. 23–25). Despite the palpable differences in these orange poems, however, they are the fruit of the same family tree.

In fact, Cristina Malcolmson has argued that George and Edward Herbert exchanged lyrics within their Herbert-Pembroke family coterie in order to win esteem at court. In "George Herbert and Coterie Verse," she wrote: "It is clear that George Herbert's famous and compelling representations of spiritual intimacy owe more to his family circle than has previously been noticed" (174). George's offering of "fruit for him that dressed me," then, may refer not only to God, but also to Herbert family patrons such as the Earls of Pembroke. The speaker of the poem is, after all, seeking "employment"— i.e., a place, whether in church or court, which could be obtained only through a patron. Although the brothers took different positions in the literary debate over sacred and profane love, both Herberts imitated their courtly cousin Sir Philip Sidney and their family friend John Donne. "For the Herbert coterie," says Malcolmson, "poetry was a social ritual evoked by and participating in an upper-class world that included evenings of entertainment and the exchange of verse, as well as the forging of political alliances and client-patron relations"

(176–77). Among the brothers' coterie verses are their Sidneian echo poems ("Echo in a Church" and "Heaven"), their Donnean progress poems ("The State progress of Ill" and "The Church Militant"), their metaphysical elegies for Prince Henry, their Marinist poems on black beauty ("La Gialletta Gallante" and "Aethiopissa ambit Cestum"), and their distinctively Herbertian poems of repentance ("A Sinner's Lament" and "Sinnes round").

By their own account, George and Edward Herbert shared not only literary rivals and patrons, but also a family likeness in their temperaments. "My brother George," Edward recalled in his autobiography, was "not exempt from passion and choler, being infirmities to which all our race are subject" (11). And in a letter to his younger brother Henry, George commented, "My brother [Edward] is somewhat of the same temper, and perhaps a little more mild, but you will hardly perceive it" (*Works*, 366).[1] It was precisely this "infirmity" of his race that George represented in "The Collar," with its well-known pun on "choler" and its intemperate speaker, who angrily wishes to fly abroad. Perhaps Edward Herbert's own footloose example and amorous verse beckoned to his brother: "Leave then thy Country Soil, and Mothers home,/Wander a Planet this way . . ." (*Poems*, 70, ll. 25–26).

The brilliant American essayist Margaret Fuller, 150 years ago, wrote a provocative sketch about "The Two Herberts." While little known today, it is a creative piece, rich with implications about their poetry and theology. In the piece, Fuller sought to "mark some prominent features in the minds of the two Herberts, under a form less elaborate and more reverent than that of criticism," and so wrote a fictive dialogue, depicting the brothers discussing their religious views and reciting their poetry along the green lane of George's Bemerton parish in the shadow of Salisbury Cathedral ("The Two Herberts," 15–34). By enacting the dialogue of the Herberts' poems, Fuller demonstrates how the works speak to one another about religious and family differences, the differences between a religion of "the Master" and a religion of philosophical world-liness. The sketch contains some purple prose, but, as Eugene D. Hill points out, it foregrounds well the intriguing relation of the Herbert brothers (*Edward, Lord Herbert of Cherbury*, 118–20).

Other critics since Fuller have sometimes commented on similarities between George and Edward's poems. In "Rhyme-craft in Edward and George Herbert," Mary Ellen Rickey first noted the kinship between George's "Heaven" and Edward's "Echo in a Church" (506–07).[2] George Held has also remarked on the domestic tensions between George Herbert and Edward, and the opposition of George's orthodox poems and Lord Herbert's deistic and anticlerical philosophy ("Brother Poets," 19–35). And as mentioned, Malcolmson has recently suggested that the Herbert brothers took part in a coterie exchange of verses of the Sidney-Herbert clan. Other critics of the period have sometimes generalized broadly about the contrasts between Lord Herbert's abstract Neoplatonic poetry and his brother George's sensuous devotional verse. Yet no critic since Fuller has investigated the intriguing family dialogue of their poems—how the verses speak to one another about important matters of fatherhood and sonship, free and constrained love, merit and sacrifice, domestic affliction, beatific visions, and secular and sacred time.

In this dialogue, two distinctive voices emerge, indicating the brothers' different positions in the family. The first is that of the elder brother, ostensibly independent, placing his trust in his own will and reason, assuming the prerogatives of the heir, and conducting an autonomous, minute-by-minute accounting of his life. The second is that of younger brother, ostensibly dependent, unable to do the will of a Father, but relying on the generous mediation of the Son, and ordering his life by the sacramental calendar of the church. While the brothers' dialogue is animated by these differences, it is also harmonized by their common assumptions about inheritance, marriage, and conduct in a patriarchal social order.

Both Herberts took for granted the traditional economic system of aristocratic and gentry families, which was one of primogenitural inheritance and arranged marriage. "The prime factor affecting all families which owned property, was . . . the principle of primogeniture," says Lawrence Stone (*The Family, Sex and Marriage*, 87), and Miriam Slater adds, "The virtually untrammeled authority of the family patriarch rested on the primacy of primogeniture" (*Family Life in the Seventeenth Century*, 30).[3] By virtue of primogeniture, when the father died, "the eldest son took the lion's share of the estate, while the younger sons were provided either with a small property in land, which reverted to the elder brother at death, or an annuity which also terminated at death" (Thirsk, "Younger Sons," 362). Marriage for the heir was arranged by the father or guardian, principally to enhance the family's estate and political position; portions or dowries were provided for the arranged marriages of daughters according to the family's means; and marriage for younger sons, if it became possible, was usually delayed until they found profitable employment.

In his "Praecepta & Consilia," an advice poem written for his grandsons, Edward Herbert of Cherbury (see figure 4) obliges them to accept primogenitural inheritance and arranged marriage.

Quos latè fundos Proavorum cura relinquit,
    Sit Primogenito tradere cura tuo.
Nam quaecunque aliis tradas haeredia Natis,
    Ex emptis prorsus suppeditabis agris.
Providus at cures, ut Dos satis ampla paretur,
    Filia connubio si qua locanda foret.

Figure 4

Edward, Lord Herbert of Cherbury. Portrait by an unknown artist.
By permission of the National Portrait Gallery, London.

Whatever lands your ancestors' care bequeathed you,
   Take care to pass them down to your first-born son.
And for those inheritances you pass on to other sons,
   You will supply them entirely from other properties.
But take diligent care to provide a sufficient dowry,
   If you have a daughter to contract in marriage.
(Poems, 114, ll. 229–34, my translation)[4]

Edward Herbert of Cherbury's advice provides a neat summary of the implicit *dos* and *don'ts* of primogeniture: *do* transfer all the paternal inheritance intact to the eldest son; *don't* divide or diminish the estate; *do* provide lesser inheritances for younger sons from "exemptis agris," lands acquired through marriage or good fortune; *don't* take from the eldest son to pay the younger son; *do* arrange marriages and pay portions for daughters; and *don't* deprive the sons of their inheritance because of the cost of the daughters' dowries. Henry, Lord Delamer advised similarly later in the seventeenth century: "To provide convenient matches for your daughters if you can, is without doubt your Duty, as also to give them good portions, but not such as will make your eldest sonne uneasy . . ." (qtd. in Beatrice Gottlieb, *The Family in the Western World*, 221). The force of Edward Herbert's advice, in the end, is not so much to insist on the respective bequests to the children, as to encourage the financial prudence that would make such bequests possible.

Likewise, in *The Country Parson*, George Herbert instinctively divides young men into two groups: "Now, for single men, they are either Heirs, or younger Brothers" (*Works*, 276). For the first group, he assumes that they should "mark their Fathers discretion in ordering his House and Affairs," as they will one day inherit the property; they should study law and attend the sessions of the local Justice of the Peace, as they may become justices themselves in time; and they should attend Parliament, as they may also become Members of Parliament (276–77). As for younger brothers, Herbert recommends the studies of law, commerce, fortification, and navigation so that they might be "ingaged into some Profession by their Parents" (277–78). Even for children of the humble country parson, Herbert assumes the distinction between the eldest son, who is given "the prerogative of his Fathers profession" and educated at a university, and the younger sons who cannot be thus educated: "Happily for his other children he is not able to do" the same. Thus, the younger sons are apprenticed in trades that befit "the reverence of their Fathers calling" (239–40).

George and Edward Herbert of Cherbury's support of the primogenitural system was by no means surprising, given how the lives of all ten of Richard and Magdalen Herbert's children had been shaped by it. According to his *Autobiography*, as the eldest son and heir, Edward Herbert received a privileged gentleman's education. He was taught Latin at age seven, Welsh at age nine (so that as a landowner he might negotiate with his Welsh tenants), and Greek literature and logic at age ten (19–21). In 1596, Edward Herbert matriculated at University College, Oxford, and Izaak Walton says that Magdalen Herbert, "being desirous to give *Edward* her eldest son, such advantages of Learning, and other education as might suit his birth and fortune," later moved to Oxford to superintend his education (*The Lives*, 263).[5] When Magdalen wrote to Edward on 12 May 1615, she addressed her letter: "To my best beloued Sonn." (PRO 30/53/10). In 1598, at about the age of 16, Edward married his cousin Mary Herbert of St. Julian's, who was then aged 21. It was a contractual marriage, arranged by his mother and uncle in order to enlarge the Herberts' lands.[6] The marriage was in George Held's words "an unfortunate attempt at hypergamy," and Michael D. Bristol characterized it as one of "chilly feelings" and "convenience" ("Herbert and His Brothers," 22; "Sacred Literature," 21).

As heir to the family estates, Edward agreed to pay an annuity of 30 pounds to each of his six brothers (Richard, William,

Charles, George, Henry, and Thomas), and portions of a thousand pounds for his sisters (Elizabeth, Margaret, and Frances) (Charles, *A Life*, 49). All three sisters were married early, in matches presumably arranged by their mother Magdalen. While the Herberts were remarkably well-educated for such a large family (William and Charles also attended Oxford, and George, Cambridge), the younger brothers were heavily dependent on their elder brother, their stepfather John Danvers, and on Herbert relatives. Only two of the younger brothers, Henry and George, were able to marry, and George waited until he was almost 36.

Again, according to "the principle of hypergamy," Henry married a wealthy widow, and, after a long wait, George made a semi-arranged marriage to his stepfather's cousin, Jane Danvers. Walton says that Charles Danvers of Wiltshire commended Jane to George and "so much commended Mr. *Herbert* to her that *Jane* became so much a Platonick, as to fall in love with Mr. *Herbert* unseen" (*The Life*, 286). Richard, William, and Thomas adopted the common and unfortunate profession of younger brothers, military service, in which the former two died. Henry Herbert served as a secretary and emissary of Edward Herbert, before and during Edward's tenure as French Ambassador, but eventually received preferment at court through the offices of his cousin, the Earl of Pembroke. George Herbert also hoped for preferment, but, according to Walton, after the death of his patrons the Duke of Richmond and the Marquis of Hamilton, he finally dedicated himself to the priesthood, another common profession of younger brothers (*The Lives*, 276).

All of the younger Herbert brothers must have felt some resentment toward Edward, for his mother Magdalen admonished him in a letter dated 12 May 1615 about his failure to pay their annuities (see chapter 2). In his letters from Cambridge, George begged for money for books from his stepfather and lamented: "I am scarce able with much ado to make one half years allowance, shake hands with the other" (*Works*, 365). Thus, Held speculates that George Herbert resented both "the relative pittance received annually through Edward" and "the cavalier manner in which his eldest brother absented himself abroad" ("Herbert and His Brothers," 29). "His Lordship deales like an Elder brother, & the Lord forgive him" was Sir Henry Herbert's comment in a letter of 12 June 1634 about one of his occasional disputes with Edward (PRO 30/ 53/7). Even in 1670, in his instructions to his son Henry, old Sir Henry bitterly recalled his status as a younger son: "Your grandfather did not give to your father a foot of Land in England or Wales, but an annuity for life of 30$^£$ a year wch was neaver well payed, & is now in Arreare, nor any goods w^{t}soever" (PRO 30/53/7).

The conflicts that primogeniture created among the Herberts were quite typical of families of their class. Detailing the difficulties of the inheritance system, Stone said that "primogeniture inevitably created a gulf between the eldest son and heir and his younger brothers who, by accident of birth order, were destined to be thrown out into the world and would probably become downwardly mobile" (*The Family, Sex and Marriage*, 114). It was the primary reason that, as the *Outlandish Proverb* put it, "In great pedigrees there are Governours and Chandlers" (*Works*, 328, no. 222). As for the elder brothers, according to Stone, they were "sapped" of their "entrepreneurial drive" while awaiting the deaths of their fathers (88).[7] Such an arrangement effectively consolidated family properties and patriarchal power, but at the cost of aggravating sibling rivalries between brothers and Oedipal tensions between the patriarch and sons. Joan Thirsk says that in this period "to describe anyone as '*a younger son*' was a short-hand way of summing up a host of grievances" ("Younger Sons," 360). The strife between the heir Oliver and his younger brother Orlando in *As You Like It* is only the best known dramatic example of this conflict. In pamphlets published in the

Jacobean and Caroline periods, there developed a "more serious debate on the disadvantages of primogeniture for society as a whole and on the practical measures that might remedy the situation" (Thirsk, "Younger Sons," 361). As writers of the time, George and Edward Herbert expressed little extraordinary criticism of the aristocratic family pattern. On the whole, they merely assumed it.

There were, of course, countervailing advantages of the system of preferences given to heirs. Younger brothers, as Linda Pollock points out in "Younger Sons in Tudor and Stuart England," often served their elders as key political allies within family patronage networks, and the entire family benefited from the arrangement. "Rather than viewing the heir and younger brother tie as one predicated on rivalry and in which the younger sibling had no valuable role to perform," says Pollock, "it should be placed in the overall context of patron-client relations of the early modern period" (29). Elder brothers often sought and secured employments for younger brothers. Edward Herbert's various travels in Europe, for example, led not only to his career as French Ambassador, but to his brother Henry Herbert's education in France and service on foreign diplomatic missions. For his part, Henry assisted his brother in setting up his office as ambassador and in "writing numberous letters for him and otherwise acting as his confidential secretary" (Charles, "Sir Henry Herbert," 2, 5). And when conflicts between brothers arose, as they inevitably did, it was in the family's interest to resolve them peaceably. In their courtly and religious writings, George and Edward Herbert sublimated their personal conflicts into literary art that gave honor to the entire family coterie.

The family differences between George and Edward Herbert are manifested frequently in their religious disagreements. In contrast to Edward Herbert's radical anticlerical philosophy, George Herbert's sacred verse combined, as had the Elizabethan Settlement, a Calvinist soteriology with an episcopal church government, traditional liturgical rites, and the ancient calendar of sacred feasts. Patrick Collinson has described George Herbert well as "a formalist" who was not "as remote from the prevalent Calvinist churchmanship of his age as Izaak Walton and others who subscribed to his posthumous hagiography" (*The Religion of Protestants*, 109); and Christopher Hodgkins says that "Herbert, even more than the Elizabethan Settlement, which formed his ecclesiastical ideal, was Calvinist in the essentials of theology" (*Authority, Church, and Society*, 2).[8] Edward, Lord Herbert of Cherbury, on the other hand, practiced a radical form of Arminianism, influenced strongly by Grotius, by Donne's early theology (as in "Satire 3"), and perhaps by Sebastian Castellio, urging the freedom and perfectibility of individual believers apart from the strictures of any church polity.[9]

The Herberts' opposing theologies imply not only political disagreements over the status of the "State-Ecclesiastical," but also domestic differences over the status of sons. In George Herbert's poetry, the tormented Son is exalted as hero, the crucifixion sacrifice is considered the center and meaning of history, the speaker's greatest desire is to ingest the Son's body and blood, reenact his sacrifice, sup with the Son in heaven, and become one with him by faith, as a suffering member of his body, the church. In contrast, in Edward Herbert's poetry and philosophy, the character of the Son is elided, and the imagery of sacrifice is eschewed. Lord Herbert's God is a providential Creator and Judge of free and reasonable agents, requiring them to observe universal laws and express private penitence for sins, and proffering to them the hope of eternal happiness as the reward for a moral life.

First among their theological disagreements was the Herberts' understanding of the roles of the human will, faith, and reason in salvation. For George Herbert, the human will was principally determined by God's election, and the soul was chosen to be saved or destroyed eternally according to God's inscrutable wisdom. The soul has, as Luther put it, "no free will, but is a captive, servant and bond slave" (Winter, ed., *Erasmus-Luther*, 113). Concerning this doctrine, George Herbert's stated in his commentary upon Juan de Valdés' *Considerations* that "a mans fre-wil is only in outward, not in spirituall things" (*Works*, 313). While he appears to have held firmly to the doctrine of double predestination, he also, characteristically, made a generous qualification: "This doctrine however true in substance, yet needeth discreet, and wary explaining" (*Works*, 314).

The related Reformation doctrine of salvation by God's grace alone is illustrated in his lyric "The Thanksgiving." When the speaker of "The Thanksgiving" imagines momentarily that he can repay Christ's sacrifice, he then realizes, as with a sudden jolt, his utter inadequacy: "Then for thy passion—I will do for that—/Alas, my God, I know not what" (*Works*, 36, ll. 49–50). The *anacoluthon* trope Herbert uses in this line, wrenching the sentence's structure and meaning, voices the speaker's exasperation and powerlessness. Again, in "Clasping of hands," the speaker admits his impotence apart from God: "If I without thee would be mine,/I neither should be mine nor thine" (*Works*, 157, ll. 9–10). The message is clearly *sola fide, sola gratia*: without faith and God's grace, he is a nonentity.

For his part, Edward, Lord Herbert of Cherbury rejected Calvin's doctrines of predestination and irresistible grace, defining free will as the *imago dei* in every soul, and extending salvation to all on the basis of merit rather than faith alone. Edward's cousin by marriage Sir Robert Harley reported that "he says he loves a puritan, but not a predestinator" (qtd. in Sharpe, *The Personal Rule of Charles I*, 300). Lord Herbert expressed the concepts of human freedom and individual merit most forcefully in *De Veritate*:

> . . . if, finally, you prefer faith to reason—do you not bring the entire edifice of the understanding to ruin by wretchedly abusing the gifts of God and wickedly destroying free will,

> without which you would be as constrained as a slave or a
> beast of burden. . . . For what is free is divine and infinite, nor
> can it grow old nor suffer constriction. Rejoice in your free-
> dom, for if your goodness were a matter of compulsion and
> produced against your will, it would belong to God; and you
> would have no part in it (204–05).

Lord Herbert wrote, further, that the idea of predestined damnation is "so dreadful and consorts so ill with the providence
and goodness, and even the justice of God" that he could not
abide it (299). As he expressed his opposition to the concepts
of the bound human will and predestination, Edward Herbert
summarized remarkably well the main points of his brother's
"Thanksgiving": that goodness is a matter of divine intervention, that it belongs to God, and that man has "no part in it,"
save through God's grace. George Herbert gladly accepts the
role of God's "bond servant," while Edward chafes against this
role as inhuman, refusing to be a "slave" or "beast of burden."

Consistent with their notions of free will and predestination were the Herberts' respective emphases on reason and
faith. For Lord Herbert, the faculty of reason has constructed
religion upon a foundation of intuitively understood and universally accepted truths. He amplifies this metaphor in *De
Veritate*: "So we must establish the fundamental principles of
religion by means of universal wisdom, so that whatever has
been added to it by the genuine dictates of Faith may rest on
that foundation as a roof is supported on a house" (290). That
is, reason built the house, and faith covered it. To begin with
faith, however, was absurd, like constructing a roof before the
foundation. It was to invite the disaster of religious enthusiasm: "Anything that springs from the productive, not to say
seductive seed of Faith will yield a plentiful crop. . . . Is there
any fantastic cult which may not be proclaimed under such
auspices?" (*De Veritate*, 289). While Lord Herbert's philosophy did not require a complete rationalization of religion, he
did "expect a rational justification of any belief to which . . .

assent was demanded by an external authority" (Hutcheson, ed., *De Religione Laici*, 31).[10] Edward Herbert promoted a humanistic ideal of the self-sufficient soul, an almost secular form of works righteousness, and an elitist contempt for fideism. He bristled against the *sola fide* message of the Reformation: "What pompous charlatan can fail to impress his ragged flock with such ideas?" (*De Veritate*, 289).

In stark opposition to these views was George Herbert's insistence on the priority of faith. When "Reason triumphs," he wrote in "Divinitie," "faith lies by," and "Faith needs no staffe of flesh, but stoutly can/To heav'n alone both go, and leade" (*Works*, 134–35, ll. 8, 27–28). Richard Strier has shown that a Lutheran "theological attack on reason pervades Herbert's poetry," marking the vanity of self-centered reasoning in verses like "Sinnes round" (*Love Known*, 31 ff.). For George Herbert, reason could not well explain, nor very well accommodate, the central mystery of Christianity—that of Christ's love. "Philosophers have measur'd mountains," he noted, but they could measure out God's love with human reason. In "Agonic," he meditated on this theme: "Love is that liquour sweet and most divine,/Which my God feels as bloud; but I, as wine" (37, ll. 17–18). The synesthetic paradox of Herbert's couplet, combining Christ's pain with the believer's palate, suggests how far the Christian mystery transcends reason.

In fact, reason implied a self-sufficiency, to which George Herbert could not pretend and which he shunned heartily. In "Faith," he proclaims the levelling effects of faith on the social order:

> If blisse had lien in art or strength,
> None but the wise or strong had gained it:
> Where now by Faith all arms are of a length;
> One size doth all conditions fit.
>
> A peasant may beleeve as much
> As a great Clerk, and reach the highest stature.

> Thus dost thou make proud knowledge bend & crouch,
>   While grace fills up uneven nature.
>
> (*Works*, 50, ll. 25–32)

Through faith, the speaker finds a paradoxical freedom through submission—so much freedom that he verges on spiritual egalitarianism and Antinomianism.[11] This "grace" that "fills up uneven nature" also levels the differences between elder brothers like Edward, with manorial estates and extensive libraries, and younger brothers like George, with £30 annuities, worn Bibles, and dearly purchased copies of Augustine.

Without at all vitiating the sincerity of George Herbert's Christian faith, it can be observed that his powerful identification with Christ the Son was encouraged by social factors such as his family position. Jesus Christ was, after all, the ideal elder brother, the heir who was still humble enough to serve, and who sacrificed himself to give "eternal treasure" to God's adopted sons, his brothers. As such, the crucified Son could serve as the locus of a younger brother's undifferentiated anger, guilt, and desire: "The bloudie crosse of my deare Lord/Is both my physick and my sword" ("Conscience," ll. 23–24). Alluding to the story of the brothers Jacob and Esau, Jean Calvin had made precisely this identification of Christ with the "first-born brother":

> ... noting that, as he did not of himself deserve the right of the first-born, concealed in his brother's clothing and wearing his brother's coat, which gave out an agreeable odor..., he [Jacob] ingratiated himself with his father, so that to his own benefit he received the blessing while impersonating another. And we in like manner hide under the precious purity of our first-born brother, Christ, so that we may be attested righteous in God's sight. (Olin, ed., *John Calvin*, 113)

The younger brother was characterized similarly by John Earle in *Microcosmography* as the Jacob ever "at his [Esau's] heels" (23). George Herbert took his personal motto from

Jacob's words in Genesis 32.10. It was this motto, "Lesse then the least of Gods mercies," that Arthur Woodnoth recalled in a letter to Nicholas Ferrar in August of 1633, persuading him to excise a dedication to Lord Herbert from the first edition of *The Temple* (Doerksen, "Ferrar, Woodnoth, and *The Temple*," 25–27). As Malcolmson notes in "Herbert and Coterie Verse," the passage in Genesis is followed by the appeal: "Deliver me, I pray thee, from the hand of my brother . . ." (175–76). Jacob was, thus, the proverbial upstart brother, as well as the Old Testament type representing God's blessing of his faithful sons, irrespective of their birth rank or social merit. It is no wonder, then, that when George spelled "Jesu," he "perceived/That to my broken heart he was *I ease you*" ("Jesu," 112, ll. 8–9).

And it is also no wonder that in Edward Herbert's writing, as Robert Ellrodt says, "Christ does not appear at all. Likewise, God is only very rarely invoked as the personal God of Donne and George Herbert, the God that one dreads or that one loves" (*Les Poètes Métaphysiques Anglais*, 2: 26).[12] Rather, the God of Edward Herbert's worship was "Mens Divina," the Eternal Spirit, the Good and the Beautiful. This Divine Mind is a reflection of the human mind, just as divine love is a reflection of human love. So the sky serves as reflection of perfect human love in "An Ode upon a Question moved": "As if so great and pure a love/No Glass but it [Heaven] could represent" (*Poems*, 62, ll. 35–36). This Divine Mind is so ethereal that it seems at times a narcissistic reflection of Lord Herbert's own privileges and desires: "And from hence, Lord, with how much comfort do I learne the high estate I received in my creation, as beinge formed in thy owne similitude and likenesse" (Warner, ed., *Epistolary Curiosities* 188).

For Lord Herbert, no sacrificial death is needed for human salvation. In *A Dialogue Between a Tutor and his Pupil*, priestly sacrifices are eschewed completely: "For had it both, in the beginning and end, been destitute of religious rites, a sacrifice would have appeared no better than a butchery" (255). Rather, as in "A Meditation upon his Wax-Candle burning out," the pure soul is seen as a spiritual flame, consuming the candle wax of the body and rising inevitably toward a heavenly destiny (*Poems*, 83–84, ll. 19–24). For such breaches of Christian orthodoxy, Lord Herbert's biographer Mario M. Rossi censured him as a Platonist: "He never understood the significance of the Resurrection, he never possessed the humility necessary to consider also this sick and fragile flesh as part of himself. It was the absurd vanity of Platonism" (*La Vita*, 3: 277). One wonders, however, whether Edward's failure to identify with Christ the Son might indicate, instead, that he understood the significance of the Resurrection only too well, and that he wanted nothing to do with its claims upon his status and person.

George and Edward Herbert's theologies were not *direct* functions of their family positions, certainly, but there was an influential relation, an "elective affinity" in Weber's phrase, between their positions of entitlement and service and their theologies of freedom and dependence. As Lawrence Stone, Jonathan Goldberg, and Lena Cowen Orlin have shown, seventeenth century texts often employed analogies between the powers of God the Father, the Stuart monarch, and the family patriarch.[13] References to a just Father or an obedient Son were never merely theological, but always potentially domestic and political statements. In this context, Susan Dwyer Amussen writes: "Everyone . . . agreed that the model for relations in the family and the state was the relationship between God and man. . . . The combination of supreme power (creation and the ability to condemn us to damnation) and unmerited mercy (the salvation of at least a few) was a powerful tool in the rhetoric of power relations" (*An Ordered Society*, 36–37).

Naturally, this rhetorical tool was used in divergent ways. Edward's rejection of the English state church and his dabbling in heresy implied one use of god-family rhetoric; George's support of the Church of the Elizabethan settlement implied quite another. The former, as an heir and patriarch, celebrated the Father's voluntary exercise of power, based on reason and the sacrosanct individual conscience, whereas the latter, the dependent younger brother, hailed the Son's paradoxical achievement of glory through his humble endurance of affliction within the Church. In the audacious motto Lord Herbert wrote for his own portrait, he praised God for demanding nothing more of him than his own upright conscience: "Make me, Eternal Goodness, wholly good:/Myself I'll answer for my hardihood" (qtd. in Bedford, *Defense of Truth*, 146).[14] Meanwhile, George Herbert lauded the redemptive suffering of the Son for the church, "For what Christ once in humblenesse began,/We him in glorie call, *The Sonne of Man*" (*Works*, 168, "The Sonne," ll. 13–14).

The Herberts' theological split began with their Arminian-Calvinist disagreements, and it extended to differences about the institutions of the church and the priesthood, the authority of Scripture, the efficacy of sacraments, the nature of heaven, and the meaning of time. Edward Herbert's *De Veritate* and other philosophical works espouse a natural theology that assert humanity's universal access to salvation, independent of all sects and creeds, based on five *Notitiae Communes* or common notions: (1) There is a God, (2) God should be worshipped, (3) Virtue and piety are the essence of religion, (4) Sins must be repented to be forgiven by God, and (5) Just reward or punishment awaits the soul in an afterlife (Carré, ed., *De Veritate*, 55–57). In December 1622, French Ambassador Edward Herbert dedicated a manuscript of his *De Veritate* to his brother George and his secretary William Boswell "on the understanding that they expunge anything they find theirein that is contrary to good morals or to the true Catholic faith" (Hutchinson, ed., *The Works of George Herbert*, xl). No reply by George to Edward's request has survived, possibly because George could not have reviewed *De Veritate* without assailing the work's major tenets. And so George Held inquired about Edward's motives in requesting his brother's *imprimatur*: "Did the elder Herbert's gesture perhaps grow out of his insensitivity to or disapproval of his brother's ecclesiastical bent?" ("Herbert and His Brothers," 31).

From the beginning to the end of his career, Edward Herbert sharply attacked the prerogatives of the priesthood. In his "State Progress of Ill," Edward jibed at the "sugred Divines" who, having no inheritance themselves, conveniently preached "Humility and Patience is/The way to Heaven," and meddled in the business of those "whom Ambition swayes" (*Poems*, 13, ll. 104–10). In *De Veritate*, he depicted priests as "a crafty and deceitful tribe, prone to avarice, and often ineffective, this is because they have introduced much under the pretext of Religion which has no bearing upon Religion" (294). Similarly, in *A Dialogue Between a Tutor and his Pupil*, he charges that priests invented superstitious cults to enrich themselves and says flatly: "I prefer the philosopher before the priest" (43). And in his late poem, "Restrained Hopes," he again compared the priest to the philosopher:

> Nor do they always best of the Heav'ns deserve,
> Who gaze on't most, but they who do reserve
>   Themselves to know it, since not all that will
>   Climb up into a Steeple or a Hill,
> So well its pow'r and influence observe,
>   As they who study and remark it still.
>
> (Poems, 81, ll. 25–30)

Here again, Cherbury prefers the authority of the philosopher, who is able to put sacred offices into a broader perspective, to that of the priest, who benefits directly from those offices. Climbing "up into a Steeple" or a pulpit, he slyly suggests, does not make a man wise or holy.

Although we do not know how George Herbert reacted to the anticlericism of *De Veritate*, we do know how his contemporary Richard Baxter responded vigorously on his behalf. The well-known Puritan author of *The Saints' Everlasting Rest*, Baxter was a close acquaintance of Sir Henry Herbert and an enthusiastic reader of George Herbert's verse.[15] In the dedicatory epistle of *Some Animadversions on a Tractate De Veritate*, Baxter wrote to Sir Henry that he wished Edward Herbert's soul had been *"possesst"* with the *"fervent ascendent holy* LOVE, *as breatheth in Mr.* G. Herbert's *Poems"* (A3r). Later in the apologetic work, in an apostrophe to Lord Herbert of Cherbury, he directly challenged *De Veritate*'s criticism of the priesthood:

> You had a Brother of your own, so holy a man, as his sincerity was past exception; and so zealous in his Sacred Ministry, as shewed he did not dissemble; And I suppose had it been necessary, you would have so maintained him, that he should not have fled from truth for fear of poverty. (*Some Animadversions*, 164)

By extolling George Herbert's holy example, Baxter was giving the lie, in a way which Lord Herbert's supporters could not easily resist, to the portrayal of priests as "a crafty and deceitful tribe." In their divergent views of the priesthood, the Herbert brothers were also manifesting a paradox of seventeenth century Christianity. Although the clerical office was rising in status and becoming more professional, the anticlericism of the Reformation often cast the parish priest in contempt (Collinson, *The Religion of Protestants*, 113–14).

In his *Country Parson*, George Herbert very much insists upon the dignity of the priest, who serves "in Gods stead to his Parish" (*Works*, 254). Knowing well "the generall ignominy which is cast upon the profession," the country parson "endeavours that none shall despise him" (268). Herbert's model parson exercises his spiritual and legal authority throughout his parish, counseling young men on their vocations, executing the poor laws, converting recusants, reporting noncommunicants to the Bishop, chiding latecomers, and intervening in property disputes. When the priest serves as a nobleman's chaplain, he is to "keep up with the Lord and the Lady of the house, and to preserve a boldness with them and all, even so farre as reproofe to their very face" (226). This professional priest exercises his powers so efficiently that Douglas J. Swartz has described him as the state official who "elaborates" Stuart rule at the local parish level ("Discourse and Direction," 191). It was, indeed, one of the few professions (along with that of a successful courtier), by which a younger brother might wield authority over his elder brother. In "The Priesthood," George Herbert speaks of this office as that "Blest Order, which in power dost so excell," and in which "God doth often vessels make/Of lowly matter for high uses meet" (160–61, ll. 1, 34–35). By "lowly matter," Herbert referred to more than the degenerate status of mankind at large. Later in the poem, he wrote: "The poore do by submission/ What pride [does] by opposition" (ll. 41–42). Thus, Donald Friedman remarks on George Herbert: "He was, to be sure, a younger brother in fact, but as a priest an undoubted 'Heir' of his Father" ("Donne, Herbert, and Vocation," 146).

The Herberts' disagreement about the priesthood implied yet other differences about the church. When George Herbert writes of the church, as in "The British Church," he writes of a discrete state institution with an episcopal polity and a traditional liturgy. It is "The British Church" of the Elizabethan settlement, doubly buttressed by God's grace. Lord Herbert of Cherbury, however, boldly opposes such an institution in his *De Religione Laici*:

> What, namely, shall the layman, encompassed by the terrors of divers churches militant throughout the world, decide as to the best religion? For there is no church that does not breathe threats, none almost that does not deny the possibility of salvation outside its own pale. (87)

On the principle of universal access to salvation, Edward Herbert thus rejected the church George Herbert championed. "What he intended and what he saw to be vitally necessary," according to R. D. Bedford, was his challenge to "the status of the Church's authority" (*The Defense of Truth*, 159). "Authority," Edward Herbert wrote in *De Veritate*, "is a favorite refuge of ignorance" (241). To the extent that Edward Herbert entertained an ideal of the church, it was "so literally and determinedly 'catholic' that it becomes a vague and amorphous concept to which it is difficult to give any precise content" (*The Defense of Truth*, 160). His church embraced the virtuous and pious, but it profferred little to them in the way of doctrine, liturgy, and church polity.

These opposite understandings of the church are demonstrated forcefully in Edward Herbert's "Echo in a Church" and George Herbert's "Heaven." While both poems originate as sacred parodies of the Sidneyan echo poems of *The Arcadia*, they resound with theological differences. In past commentary on the poems, critics have been content merely to recognize the poems' likenesses. G. C. Moore Smith considered the resemblance of the poems so remarkable that he exclaimed: "This poem ['Echo in a Church'] might well have been written by George Herbert" (Moore Smith, ed., *The Poems*, 154). Mary Ellen Rickey later made a fuller account of the poems' similarities:

> This form seems particularly effective for a religious dialogue: the poet's supplications are made at some length; he is answered briefly but clearly, the nature of the echo-answers serving to set them off from the human speech of the piece. Evidently George Herbert found the genre effective for the purposes of devotional verse, for one of *The Temple*'s last poems, *Heaven*, follows much the same plan. Like *Echo in a Church*, it represents the poet as doubtful at the beginning of the dialogue as to the identity of the echo, becoming convinced only after

an answer or two that the source of the replies is divine.
("Rhymecraft," 507)

Rickey noted further similarities in the poems' stanza forms
and narratives, but neither Moore Smith nor she commented
on the different theological trajectories of the Herberts'
echoes.

Like George Herbert's "The Collar," Edward Herbert's "Echo
in a Church" features a distracted speaker, who airs his confused thoughts before recognizing God's voice. Yet the speaker
of "The Collar" is a disheartened priest, who rebelliously
strikes the communion table and mocks the communion wine.
When he finally hears the peremptory voice of his Father rep-
rimanding him, "Child!," he replies, "My Lord," accepting
again his role as a humble son and servant. As John R. Roberts
describes it, "The Collar" is a "calling poem" in which the
priest is impelled to "surrender himself in Christlike obedience" to his vocation ("Me Thoughts," 197 ff.). The speaker
of Cherbury's "Echo in a Church," however, makes no such
childlike surrender to Christ and his sacraments. Rather, the
effect of the poem is quite the reverse. It is to emphasize that a
transcendent God cannot be circumscribed by any priestly
or saintly confessor, ecclesiastical function, or institutional
church.

Edward Herbert's poem opens with the speaker seeking
to "discharge/the burden" of his sins in a confession. "Conscience," he wrote in *De Veritate*, "tells us that our crimes may
be washed away by true penitence" (298). Calling penitence
"the most universal and most easily procurable sacrament of
nature," he warned explicitly about the misappropriation of
penance by priests: "Nor finally let priests promise that sins
will be remitted by a transaction of little moment . . . for they
would be forcing themselves upon the tribunal of God, and
seizing upon His throne, snatching His inscrutable judgments
into their own domain" (*De Religione Laici*, 111). Edward

Herbert's "Echo in a Church" dramatizes this theological principle by answering three profound questions: Where are sins forgiven?, Who forgives them?, and How are they forgiven? The setting of "Echo in a Church" might be either in an English church or in a Roman church with a confessional, such as Edward Herbert must have visited in his long sojourns in Italy and France in the 1610s and 1620s. In his "Praecepta & Consilia," he advised his grandsons to see foreign cities and, "what religions thrive there" (*Poems*, 111, ll. 153–54). Roman confession was clearly the principal "transaction of little moment" that he censured in *De Religione Laici* as an unwarranted priestly interference in the universal sacrament of penitence, but the ecclesiastical blessings and sacraments of the Church of England were also subject to his criticism.

Edward Herbert's "Echo in a Church" gains its effects largely through the mystery surrounding the setting and speakers, a mystery probed by a theological inquiry with a surprise ending. The confused and weary speaker, arriving at a church, begins the inquiry:

> Where shall my troubled soul, at large
> > Discharge
> The burden of her sins, oh where?
> > *Echo* Here.
>
> > Whence comes this voice I hear?
> > Who doth this grace afford?
> > If it be thou, O Lord,
>
> Say, if thou hear my prayers when I call.
> > *Echo* All.
> And wilt thou pity grant when I do cry?
> > *Echo* I.
>
> Then though I fall,
> > Thy Grace will my defects supply,
> > But who will keep my soul from ill,

> Quench bad desires, reform my Will?
> *Echo* I will.
>
> O may that will and voice be blest,
> Which yields such comforts unto one distrest,
> More blessed yet, would'st thou thy self unmask,
> Or tell, at least, who undertakes this task.
> *Echo* Ask.
>
> Then quickly speak,
> Since now with crying I am grown so weak,
> I shall want force even to crave thy name,
> O speak before I wholly weary am.
> *Echo* I am.
>
> (*Poems*, 47–48, ll. 1–26)

The mysterious questions, "Where shall my troubled soul, at large/Discharge/The Burden of her sins, oh where?" (ll. 1–3), "Whence comes this voice I hear?" (l. 5), and "Who will keep my soul from ill/Quench bad desires, reform my Will?" (ll. 14–15), and the even stranger requests, "thy self unmask" and "thy name/O speak" (19, 24–25), make sense in only one context. This context is of a spiritually distressed pilgrim, wandering into a church, and seeking to confess his sins through either a human or angelic mediator.[16] The speaker assumes the "Lord" of line 7 to be a mediator who "undertakes this task" of hearing confessions (l. 20), and so he presses him further to "unmask" his identity and divulge his "name." These are requests that one can make properly (although boldly) of a priest, angel, or saint, but not of a transcendent God. When the speaker unwittingly asks the name of God, as Moses asked the name of the God of the burning bush, he receives the same awesome and incomprehensible answer, "I am that I am" (KJV, Exodus 3.14). The speaker is confronting a transcendent God, who cannot be constrained at all by mortal names, scholastic definitions, dogmatic creeds, or human institutions.

The sudden revelation of the transcendent God in the final

line of Edward Herbert's poem is replete with theological implications. It suggests that the place for confession is not lim-
ited to any church "built of clay or stone or living rock or
even of marble," but is in the internal space of the conscience,
what he called the "recesses of the soul," or the "human mind
informed by the Common Notions" (*De Veritate*, 303–04).
When the echo responds "here" in line 5, it answers from this
internal space, although the speaker mistakes the reply to
mean the external space of the church. The echo's further
answers, and especially the "I am" of line 26, imply that it is
the transcendent God alone, without the mediation of a priest,
angel, or saint, that forgives sin. Here, Edward Herbert is pressing Protestant anticlericism to the limits of natural theology,
holding the conscience as absolutely autonomous and sacrosanct, brooking no mediation. Rather extravagantly, Edward
Herbert hoped that the natural theology of "*De Veritate* might
help to bring about a reconciliation between the English
and Roman Churches" (Bedford, *The Defense of Truth*, 135).
While the echo of George's "The Collar" remands the speaker
to his ecclesiastical function in the English Church, the echo
of Edward's poem calls its speaker away from the thought
that the true church is "that which fights beneath any one
particular standard, or is comprised in one organisation" (*De
Veritate*, 303).

Although the poetic form of George Herbert's "Heaven" is
similar to "Echo in a Church," the poem's echoes make a different theological point. Whereas Edward Herbert's verses begin
in an institutional setting and turns the reader away from it,
toward natural theology, George's verses begins in the Ovidian
silvae and the Sidneian Arcadia and turn back dogmatically
toward Christian scripture and the church, which interprets
scripture. These are the "holy leaves" that "still abide" and
that "impart the matter" of salvation "wholly" within the
church. The speaker of the poem is, as Helen Vendler calls
him, something of a "doubting Thomas," who must be

persuaded heavenward by the indefatigable Echo. The speaker asks ten decasyllabic questions and receives ten mono- and bisyllabic replies:

> O who will show me those delights on high?
> > *Echo.*   I.
>
> Thou Echo, thou art mortall, all men know.
> > *Echo.*   No.
>
> Wert thou not born among the trees and leaves?
> > *Echo.*   Leaves.
>
> And are there any leaves, that still abide?
> > *Echo.*   Bide.
>
> What leaves are they? impart the matter wholly.
> > *Echo.*   Holy.
>
> Are holy leaves the Echo then of blisse?
> > *Echo.*   Yes.
>
> Then tell me, what is that supreme delight?
> > *Echo.*   Light.
>
> Light to the minde: what shall the will enjoy?
> > *Echo.*   Joy.
>
> But are there cares and businesse with the pleasure?
> > *Echo.*   Leisure.
>
> Light, joy, and leisure; but shall they persever?
> > *Echo.*   Ever.
>
> > > > (*Works*, 188, ll. 1–20)

The gentle regularity of Echo's replies, as Vendler says in *The Poetry of George Herbert*, "acts out that patience of God with his 'child' . . ., or rather, that frowardness in the 'child' necessitating God's patience" (226). The reassuring parental voice of the echo enjoins the child to find contentment in God's word. The first six rhymes suggest that the Bible is the divinely inspired source that reveals "those delights on high" as completely as human beings can grasp such ineffable things. "Holy leaves" correspond to the most profound human desires: they are the echoes of bliss and blessing. In other words, the way to heaven is fully revealed in the church's sacred scriptures, and the living breath of Holy Spirit echoes through these vital "leaves."

Elsewhere, George Herbert says of the "Holy Scriptures" that "heav'n lies flat in thee," and "This book of starres lights to eternall blisse" (*Works*, 58). Thoroughly Protestant in his regard for scripture, he assumes with Luther "that the soul can do without anything except the Word of God and that where the Word of God is missing there is no help at all for the soul." (*Martin Luther: Selections*, 54). This is the Reformation tenet of *sola scriptura*: "The ground of faith and the means by which God's grace is communicated is the Holy Scripture" (Veith, *Reformation Spirituality*, 25). In his *Country Parson*, in fact, he uses the most elemental language, the metaphor of a sucking infant, to describe the priest's fundamental reliance on scripture: "The chief and top of his knowledge consists in the book of books, the storehouse and magazene of life and comfort, the holy Scriptures. There he sucks, and lives" (*Works*, 228). While critics of *The Temple* often dispute theological particulars, they largely agree upon the centrality of biblical references and typology to Herbert's poetry.

For his part, Edward Herbert believed only the universally accepted "common notions" were essential to salvation, and he viewed the Bible as an instructive book that had long been abused by ecclesiasts. *De Veritate* broaches this subject cautiously: "But if carelessness or the passage of time has allowed to creep into a sacred or profane book any passage which maligns God or calls in question those divine attributes which are universally recognised, why should we not agree either to amend the work—and this has been done before—or to charge its interpreters with error . . .?" (316). Since the Scriptures were mediated by fallible human beings and were subject to the same manipulations as other historical narratives, Edward Herbert was prompted to ask the troubling question, "What in the Bible is the very word of God"? (*De Religione Laici*, 101).

As it contained within it the germ of modern Biblical criticism, Edward Herbert's question was so troubling that Richard Baxter countered it with 17 vociferous arguments. Baxter bristled: "These are things. . . . Which God would not *permit* to be done to deceive them [i.e., Christians] in so high a matter; Because he is the Omnipotent, Omniscient, Gracious Governour of the world; And if these Testimonies were not of God, it were impossible to know any Testimony to be of God" (*More Reasons*, 149). In responding to such arguments, Edward Herbert acknowledged that all scriptural narratives are matters of possibility, rather than of certainty, and all are subject to rational critique. Baxter assessed quite accurately that in Lord Herbert's philosophy "it were impossible to know any [revealed] Testimony to be of God." Whereas the Bible permitted George Herbert to mount to heaven on "bended knee" (*Works*, 58), it presented uncertainties and obstacles to Edward Herbert's intellectual freedom. Around these obstacles, he stepped carefully but unapologetically. In a sense, Cherbury's anti-biblicism anticipated young William Wordsworth's exuberant advice to a friend more than a century later: "Close up those barren leaves" and "Let Nature be your Teacher."

Even though both George and Edward Herbert professed belief in an afterlife, their visions of heaven differed as much as their attitudes toward scripture. In the Latin hexameters of Cherbury's "De Vita coelesti," one of his latest and most speculative poems, heaven was the wish-fulfillment of an isolated soul: "I forsake the rude company of this crazed age,/ As I breathe out the infernal breezes and breathe in the heavenly ones" (*Poems*, 103, ll. 10–11; my translation). As in the Elysian fields, virtuous pagans roam in Cherbury's heaven: "And then we will be able to see their faces/And view their brilliance and radiant brows" (105, ll. 73–74). Donne had asked similarly in his "Satire 3" whether one would "Meet blind philosophers in heaven, whose merit/Of strict life may be imputed faith . . .?" (*Complete English Poems*, 161, ll. 12–13).

Lord Herbert answered a resounding "yes" to Donne's question, but without mentioning the Christian theology of imputed grace.

As Edward Herbert's pure spirit ascended alone to the rewards of heaven, it also contributed its private store ("dotem") of virtue to God.

> Cùm segnes Animas, Caelum quas indit ab ortu,
> Exacuat tantm labor, ac industria nostra,
> Ac demum poliat Doctrina, & moribus illis,
> Vt redeant pulchrae, dotem Caeloque reportent . . .

> Since only our toil and diligence may forge
> The passive souls that heaven imparts at birth,
> Refining them then with doctrine and manners,
> So they return beautiful and carry riches to heaven . . .
>
> *(Poems*, 104, ll. 33–36)

The passage, perhaps alluding to the Parable of the Talents in Matthew 25, is Arminian, even almost Pelagian, in its emphasis on individual merit. Rossi says of the theology of the poem: "Here [Edward] Herbert manifests his faith in free will . . . Grace is not a gratuitous gift, but payment and reward for our free efforts" *(La Vita*, 3: 106).

The rewards Edward Herbert anticipates in heaven comprise all the pleasures that a Jacobean gallant could ask for. These heavenly joys include those of free movement and acquisition,

> And if freedom is desired, you can run through
> The most admirable spots under numberless skies
> And pluck here and there the pleasures of any place.
>
> *(Poems*, 104, ll. 56–58)

divine contemplation and statecraft,

> But if we desire higher contemplation, then
> The escritoires of heaven lie exposed to us.
>
> (105, ll. 75–76)

amorous dalliance,

> But if we delight more in heavenly love,
> Then we dissolve into flames that lap and caress
> One another . . .

(105, ll. 82–84)

and music and theatre:

> And if we wish to laud God, He lauds us,
> And the celestial choir harmonizes, and heaven
> Resounds with the sweet modulation . . .
> The whole frame of heaven becomes as a theatre.

(ll. 88–90, 92).

Only missing from this celestial pleasure-palace are the joys of domestic affection. If Lord Herbert wished to see his wife Mary, his children, parents, or siblings in heaven, he did not say so in "De Vita coelesti." As in his Platonic love verses, Cherbury's beatific vision is of a reciprocal love between free spirits, unencumbered by kinship dependencies. Rossi says this vision is characterized by the individualistic principles of Eudemonism and Epicureanism (*La Vita*, 3: 108). In any case, this heaven is a very privileged place, like a gentleman's closet or library, a place for narcissistic self-approval: "So in the divine light/(As in a mirror) one may know the soul completely,/And may compose a beautiful appearance for one's self" (*Poems*, 104, ll. 53–55). In his heaven, the soul is painfully pleased with itself and its surroundings, basking in golden clouds of complacence.

By contrast, George Herbert envisions the heavenly banquet in "Love III" as a domestic ritual of submission. This family ritual begins with a poor guest who is unworthy of the attentions of the master of the house, but who nevertheless obtains them.

> Love bade me welcome: yet my soul drew back,
>   Guiltie of dust and sinne.

But quick-ey'd Love, observing me grow slack
    From my first entrance in,
Drew nearer to me, sweetly questioning,
    If I lack'd any thing.

A guest, I answer'd, worthy to be here:
    Love said, You shall be he.
I the unkinde, ungratefull? Ah my deare,
    I cannot look on thee.
Love took my hand, and smiling did reply,
    Who made the eyes but I?

Truth Lord, but I have marr'd them: let my shame
    Go where it doth deserve.
And know you not, says Love, who bore the blame?
    My deare, then I will serve.
You must sit down, sayes Love, and taste my meat:
    So I did sit and eat.
                  (*Works*, 188–89, ll. 1–18)

Unlike Edward Herbert's resplendent soul, which mounts to the heavens with wealth and a habit of self-admiration, this soul arrives at the heavenly manor with nothing but dirt on his clothes and shame on his face. The dust bespeaks his poverty and social presumption. The speaker knows he has violated the courtly ideal of cleanliness, which, as Keith Thomas states, "was much concerned with the need to show deference and respect to one's social superiors" (Hamilton and Strier, eds., *Religion, Literature and Politics*, 69). George Ryley, Herbert's seventeenth century commentator, described the poem's speaker as "amazed and hovering there, surprised with the glories of the state," and ashamed of his own unworthiness (*Mr. Herbert's Temple*, 265). The guest's posture and attitude in the opening lines suggest the *Outlandish Proverb*: "When children stand quiet, they have done some ill" (*Works*, 338, no. 504). Thus, while the dialogue of the poem presents a theology of unmerited grace and imputed righteousness, in all other respects it is a domestic drama.

Helen Vendler describes "Love III" as a "social comedy" involving "the domestication, so to speak, of a hesitant guest" (*The Poetry of George Herbert*, 275). Similarly, noting George Herbert's years of dependence upon his kinmen's tables, Schoenfeldt reads the poem brilliantly as a rhetorical contest of manners at a nobleman's table, which the divine host wins by his artful submissiveness. This contest operates, according to Schoenfeldt, by the courtly and Christian rule of Stefano Guazzo: "That the more loftie we are placed, the more lowly wee ought to humble ourselves: which is in deed, the way to rise higher" (Guazzo qtd. in *Prayer and Power*, 217). While the poem assumes a hierarchical social order (a society in which clothes, table places, and table manners make significant differences), it also enacts a ritual transformation of that order, enabling the outsider to take the place of the host.

As the host named Love occupies the social positions of father and heir, he holds his "natural" position at the head of the table. In Overbury's character-portrait, "The Elder Brother" especially gravitated to this position: "The load-stone that drawes him is the upper end of the table" (*The Overburian Characters*, 17). According to the reverse social logic of the poem, however, the outcast speaker is drawn magnetically to the head of the table by the host's solicitude. The host welcomes him from his first step in the door, approaches him closely, takes his hand, and then at last ushers him to his seat. The meal is a eucharistic celebration, drawn in composite fashion from the parables of the humble feasts in the Gospel of Luke: the banquet for the waiting servant, who is served "meat" by the Lord (KJV, Luke 12.37); the parable of the ambitious guest who takes the lowest seat (Luke 14.8); the banquet for the unbidden poor, who displace the rich guests (Luke 14.16); and the banquet for the prodigal son, who asks to be treated as a servant but is embraced by the forgiving father (Luke 15.19).

Thus, in George Herbert's heaven, the family's places

at table are turned around with a vengeance. To the extent that the host insists upon his priority as father ("Who made the eyes but I?") and as only-begotten son ("And know you not, says Love, who bore the blame?"), he also suffers the role of servant, feeding the guest "my meat." "Service is no Inheritance," says one of the *Outlandish Proverbs* (*Works*, 347, no. 792), but it becomes so in Herbert's heaven. In her insightful reading of the lyric, Vendler observed that "the painful distinction between God the Father-Judge and God the Son-Redeemer vanishes here," and one can add that the painful distinction between the eldest and younger brothers does as well (*The Poetry of George Herbert*, 274). For the poet-priest, heaven was a place where the privileges of the heir are dispensed to others, unmerited, a place where the outcast becomes the heir by submitting to the host. Again, in Calvin's words, the younger son knows he does not "deserve the right of the first-born," but he "ingratiates himself with his father," and receives the blessing of "our first-born brother, Christ." Stanley Fish's well-known comment in *The Living Temple*, "Love's smile is like his sweetness; it sugars a bitter pill," does not fully appreciate the keen appetite of the speaker for a place at table, but it does intimate the bitter family conflict latent in the poem (133).

The profound wishes of the speaker of "Love III" are those that Freud characterized as the Family Romance, a stage in which a young child idealizes the parents intensely and experiences acute sibling rivalries. In this stage, Freud wrote, "a younger child is very specially inclined to use imaginative stories . . . in order to rob those born before him of their prerogatives" (*Complete Psychological Works*, 9: 240). These "imaginative stories" include attributing fictitious love affairs to one's mother and "the replacement of both parents or of the father alone with grander people" (240). Another variant of the Family Romance occurs when the fantasizing child is recognized as legitimate while his sibling rivals are "elimated

by being bastardized" (240). In "Love III," the heir's prerogatives are imagined as his "meat," his body and blood, which
the gracious father gives to the submissive son, fulfilling his
sensual desires and his deepest wish of taking his brother's
seat at the table. Once unworthy, he is recognized as legitimate,
figuratively consuming and literally replacing the heir, his
rival. George Herbert's heaven is certainly the place for familial love, but there is no room at the intimate table of "Love III"
for another seat.

The most elusive subject of the Herbert brothers' dialogue
is time. George and Edward Herbert's writings represent a series of contrasting emblems of secular and sacramental time,
of what Jacques LeGoff called the *"temps de l'Eglise"* and the
"temps du marchand" (qtd. in Quinones, *The Renaissance
Discovery of Time*, 6). To revise LeGoff slightly, one might
speak of the "time of the priest" and the "time of the philosopher." In striking contrast to George's "Time," "Church
Monuments," and "In Solarium," Lord Herbert's philosophical writings and poems "To His Watch When He Could Not
Sleep" and "For a Dyal" stand as unorthodox emblems of
fatality, cosmic regulation, human regimentation, and modernity. Whereas the speakers of George's lyrics are able to
surrender anxieties about time to God, who is both the eternal Son and the diurnal sun, the isolated individual in Lord
Herbert's lyrics cannot surrender his apprehensions to anyone else. He owns time, but time owns him, just as surely as
his pocket watch ticks away his life.

Like Shakespeare in "When I do count the clock that tells
the time," Edward Herbert was fascinated by the Renaissance
invention of the clock and its serene mechanical functioning
amid the frenzy of life. The universe seemed to Edward
Herbert, as it would later to Boyle and Newton, "a great piece
of clockwork," and God was the clockmaster, who was to
be known by reason and analogy rather than by revelation.
What was to become the deist's icon of God as the eternal

clockmaker appears in the thirteenth chapter of *De Religione Gentilium*, in which Edward Herbert disputed Lucretius's belief in the accidental character of the universe.

> So others of this Sect attribute all things to Chance and Fortune, according to which Doctrine I cannot apprehend, how there could be any Kind, species, or indeed any agreeable Series of things; for if any Person that hath not forfeited the use of Reason, shall observe a Watch, shewing the Hours exactly, for a Day and a night together, will presently conclude it the product of Art and Labour; how much rather, who does but contemplate the vast Machine of this World, performing its Motions so regularly, not for 24 Hours only, but so many Ages, will pronounce it to proceed from an All Wise and Powerful Author. (*The Ancient Religion*, 255)[17]

This passage is imbued with the Reformation insistence on God's minute providence, but it is also evocative of the reasoning of post-Newtonian religion and anticipates later doubts concerning the creation. While the argument for God's existence from design and the Epicurean emphasis on chance were ancient, Lord Herbert's formulation anticipates the modern skeptic's doubts about the eternal clockmaker. It is, after all, against this utterly crazed man ("ecquis plane demens") that Herbert makes his case with a conspicuously modern analogy for God's existence. Furthermore, if one accepts the clockmaker argument, as Edward Herbert proposes, one is left with an abstract author of a distressingly deterministic creation. The clock emblem is one of mechanical regulation and fatality, newly derived, as John Kerrigan put it, from "the springs, coils, and pendula of renaissance machinery" (Kerrigan, ed., *Shakespeare's Sonnets*, 34).

The clock's association with fate and modern regimentation is enacted in Lord Herbert's lyrics "To His Watch When He Could Not Sleep" and "To a Dyal." In "To his Watch," he addresses his watch's dial with strange curiosity and tenderness.

Uncessant Minutes, whil'st you move you tell
  The time that tells our life, which though it run
  Never so fast or farr, you'r new begun
Short steps shall overtake; for though life well

May scape his own Account, it shall not yours,
  You are Death's Auditors, that both divide
And summ what ere that life inspir'd endures
  Past a beginning, and through you we bide

The doom of Fate, whose unrecall'd Decree
  You date, bring, execute; making what's new
  Ill and good, old, for as we die in you,
You die in Time, Time in Eternity.

                               (*Poems*, 1, ll. 1–12)

Cleanth Brooks said of this poem that it "opens brilliantly and closes with some resonant lines" but that he had "to admit defeat" in understanding it (*Historical Evidence*, 81). The greatest difficulty comes in the second stanza, where Herbert seems to say that although life itself may transcend the effects of passing time ("May scape his [i.e., its] own Account"), no living being can avoid the reckoning of "Death's Auditors," the ticking minutes. The newly begun minutes, taking their "short steps" around the dial, count the remainder and total of every life, and effect the unalterable sentences of fate. The pocket-watch gives to the individual an isolated and internal consciousness of his measured life, but it presents no external power to which he can resort for salvation.

As the speaker moves toward his death each minute, the minutes and time itself proceed to their consummations. These are the three climactic deaths of natural decay (in which the individual dies), social change (in which the individual's memory is obliterated), and cosmic cataclysm (in which time itself ends). The poem's distinctive form—three quatrains, with alternating Petrarchan and Shakespearean rhyme, and with several trios of parallel phrases—accents the three deaths and gives the verse a symmetrical but static quality. Edward

Herbert's identification with the dying minutes suggests an early modern sense of time as an individual and precious but fateful commodity. Again, he owns time, but time owns him. As Kerrigan put it in his introduction to *Shakespeare's Sonnets*, "If, in the middle ages, time was natural and ecclesiastical, in the sixteenth century, it became increasingly private yet impersonal, a source at once of piety and alienation" (37).

Edward Herbert expressed the same conflicting feelings of piety and alienation toward time in one of his finest Latin verses, his elegiac lines "For a Dyal." Again, Lord Herbert addresses a clock that he associates with his own stoical bearing as a philosopher:

> Discurrens dubiae placidus compendia vitae,
> > Excipiens tacito gaudia tuta sinu,
> Praeteritis laetare bonis, nec saeva futuri
> > Exagitet miseros cura prematve dies:
> Omnis in adversum ruit hora volatque retrorsum
> > Et velut exhorrens jam peritura fugit.
> Dum numerano dolet, dumque addens subtrahit, illa,
> > Quae vitae ratio, calculus atque tuae.
>
> > (*Poems*, 89; ll. 1–8)

> Tranquil dial, running through the sums of a doubtful life,
> > Gathering safe pleasures in your quiet breast,
> Rejoice in the good things that are past, nor let fierce care
> > For the future harry nor harass our wretched days.
> Every hour rushes onward and flies back, and as if shuddering
> > And just about to die, it flees. While counting up,
> It ticks off, and while adding, it subtracts those digits
> > That are the sum-total and reckoning of your life.
>
> > (My translation)

The multiple ironies of Herbert's Latin poem are difficult to render into English, yet still presciently modern. The *compendia* of line 1 refer both to the "summations" or abridgements of a life (OLD, *compendium*, 4a), and to the "shortcuts" of the digits that the watch's hand follows around the dial (OLD, *compendium*, 3a). The adjective *dubiae* implies that the life of clock's rotations is full of peril, comprising many hourly deaths. The poet's life too, which is conflated with the dial's, is also uncertain and vexed, bounded as it is by mechanical measures. The watch seems to contain both quiet pleasures and murmuring noises in its *sinus*, the fold of its breasts—a clever pun, based on the fold of the Roman toga. Its agitations are hidden beneath the tranquil face and are only occasionally revealed in the shuddering of its hands.

While the serene dial of Edward Herbert's watch epitomizes modern self-regulation and autonomy, it is a starkly mechanical emblem, which values life rigidly as a *ratio* and *calculus*. In these poems, Lord Herbert addresses his watch in a nighttime revery during a fit of insomnia—a typically modern moment of angst, punctuated by the watch's ticking hand. Underlying Lord Herbert's stoical admiration for his timepiece is a deep anxiety that was becoming commonplace throughout Western Europe, especially in Protestant countries. Writing of the "worldly asceticism" of seventeenth century Protestants, Max Weber observed apprehensions were rising about lost and wasted time. "It does not yet hold, with Franklin, that time is money," wrote Weber in *The Protestant Ethic*, "but the proposition is true in a certain spiritual sense. It is infinitely valuable because every hour lost is lost to labour for the glory of God" (158). Concerning English Protestants of the period, Kerrigan adds: "In innumerable treatises, the 'spending' of time and money were equated, and the 'wasting' of both was opposed to a 'saving' which included the soul" (*Shakespeare's Sonnets*, 36). Without the securities of a church or savior, Lord Herbert's philosophy may well have intensified these apprehensions, leading to a more painstaking accounting of time.

Although George Herbert did not share his brother Edward's fascination with pocket watches, he too expressed anxieties about time. "The disease which I am troubled with now," George wrote to his brother Henry, "is the shortness of time"

(*Works*, 365). George Herbert's *Outlandish Proverbs* warn emphatically of the waste of time: "Law sutes consume time, and mony . . ." (347, no. 776); "Time undermines us" (351, no. 923); and "He that hath time and looks for better time, time comes that he repents himself of time" (359, no. 1102). In his proverb-laden "Church-Porch," he admonishes the young courtier to regulate his soul as he would a timepiece: "If with thy watch, that [thy soul] too/Be down, then winde up both" (24, ll. 454–55). Along with this sense of the preciousness of each passing moment came other unfocused anxieties about time, related to the gradual loss of the orthodox liturgical calendar as a sacramental frame for human history.

For George Herbert the priest, who called his country parson "a Lover of old Customes," the secular erosion of liturgical time represented spiritual desolation. In his enigmatic emblem poem "Hope," he not only turns back, but gives back the secular clock in exchange for a Christian symbol. The ingenuous speaker of the poem describes the exchange of a timepiece for a sacramental emblem: "I gave to Hope a watch of mine: but he/An anchor gave to me" (*Works*, 121). One could not hold onto a pocket watch with the same absolute conviction with which one grasped the Christian anchor. Donne wrote in his "Obsequies to the Lord Harrington" of the nagging inconsistencies of both "small clocks" and "great clocks": "Yet, as in great clocks, which in steeples chime,/Plac'd to informe whole townes, to'imploy their time,/An error doth more harme, being generall,/When, small clocks faults, only'on the wearer fall" (*The Epithalamions*, 71, ll. 143–46). And Pope summed up this new anxiety tersely in his *Essay on Criticism*: "'Tis with our *Judgments* as our *Watches*, none/Go just *alike*, yet each believes his own" (*The Poetry*, 38, ll. 9–10).

When George Herbert described a timepiece as a sacred emblem of the soul, he chose the ancient *solarium*, or sundial, and the hourglass, instead of the modern clock. His "In Solarium," begins:

Coniugium Caeli Terraéque haec machina praestat;
　Debetur Caelo lumen, & vmbra solo:
Sic Hominis moles animâque & corpore constat. . . .
(*Works*, 417, ll. 1–3)

This instrument displays the bridal of the earth and sky;
　The light belongs to heaven, and the shadow to earth:
So the magnitude of man rests in both body and spirit. . . .
(My translation)[18]

The sundial, unlike the mechanical clock, is attuned to the diurnal rhythms of nature and to heaven's blessing of the earth. Thus, it becomes a sacred emblem for the human personality, composed equally of flesh and spirit. Christ, as both man and God, the perfect Sundial, becomes the true measure of human worth, of *Hominis moles*, and the instrument of salvation. As such, this sacred clock, with its dependence on the church and sacraments, differs from the mechanical dial of Edward Herbert's poems, the emblem of secular time and the autonomous individual.

When George Herbert writes of chronological time in "Church Monuments," he depicts not a ticking watch, but an hourglass. Bowing at the sanctified fixture of a church tomb in order to meditate and "take acquaintance of this heap of dust," the speaker imagines it as an hourglass. The tomb, filled with the sand of human decay, represents an extraordinary kind of time-piece, one that collapses upon itself as it tells of time passing: "Flesh is but the glasse, which holds the dust/ That measures all our time; which also shall/Be crumbled into dust" (*Works*, 65, ll. 20–22). The "heap of dust" or hourglass of the tomb is also a reflective glass, mirroring the "heap of dust" which is the speaker himself. The monument is a powerful, but traditional, Christian *memento mori*: a reminder that the speaker and all historical traces of his existence will dissolve in time. As in Edward Herbert's poem, the speaker dies in time, and time dies in eternity, but here the death occurs in

a sanctified space, in the vault of a church, and promises resurrection at the end of human time. George Herbert imagines
this resurrection humorously in "Dooms-day": "Summon all
the dust to rise,/Till it stirre, and rubbe the eyes;/While this
member jogs the other,/Each one whispring, *Live you brother?*"
(186, ll. 3–6).

George Herbert's two long historical poems on the progress
of warfare and the westward movement of the church, "Triumphus Mortis" and "The Church Militant," both suggest that
human history aggravates evil and would lead to our self-
annihilation, were it not for the action of divine grace. In "The
Church Militant," he asserts that the church "shall ev'ry yeare
decrease and fade;/Till such a darknesse do the world invade/
At Christs last coming, as his first did finde" (*Works*, 196,
229–31). Thus, Deborah Shuger finds: "There is no progress,
meaning, or fulfillment within the temporal order in either
'The Church Militant' or (often) 'The Church'" (*Habits of
Thought*, 114), and Schoenfeldt comments, "In [George] Herbert's imagination, history stalks religion as relentlessly as
sin stalks the Church" (Roberts, ed., *New Perspectives*, 89).
Indeed, the sacred emblems of *The Temple* imply a rejection
of secular, chronological time as a measure of human life.

Nowhere is this rejection clearer than in the serio-comic
poem "Time," a pastiche of Father Time imagery with a spoof
of human presumptions about salvation history. Richard
Strier describes the poem well as a "comic piece in which
the speaker, a saintly naif [is] lecturing time for its slackness"
(*Love Known*, 122–23).

> Meeting with Time, Slack thing, said I,
>   Thy sithe is dull; whet it for shame.
> No marvell Sir, he did replie,
>   If it at length deserve some blame:
>   But where one man would have me grinde it,
>   Twentie for one too sharp do finde it.

Perhaps some such of old did passe,
Who above all things lov'd this life;
To whom thy sithe a hatchet was,
Which now is but a pruning-knife.
   Christs coming hath made man thy debter,
   Since by thy cutting he grows better.

And in his blessing thou art blest:
For where thou onely wert before
An executioner at best;
Thou art a gard'ner now, and more,
   An usher to convey our souls
   Beyond the utmost starres and poles.

And this is that makes life so long,
While it detains us from our God.
Ev'n pleasures here increase the wrong,
And length of dayes lengthen the rod.
   Who wants the place, where God doth dwell,
   Partakes already half of hell.

Of what strange length must that needs be,
Which ev'n eternitie excludes!
Thus farre Time heard me patiently:
Then chafing said, This man deludes:
   What do I here before his doore?
   He doth not crave lesse time, but more.

(*Works*, 122, ll. 1–30)

The speaker's ostentatiously pious complaint is that Father Time is not rigorous and mechanical enough—he is slack in his timely duties, and his deadly scythe has become rather dull in cutting the threads of life. Time's jocular but precise answer, accented with the phrases "at length" and "Twentie for one," points out the narrator's obsession with chronological time.

In the ensuing homily, the speaker laboriously relates a distinction between Old Testament and New Testament dispensations, in which Time has been transformed from an executioner into a gardener. The narrator's flawed theological argument fails to convince Father Time, however. The failure appears clearly in the fourth stanza in which the speaker concludes absurdly that life on earth is "already half of hell" and "length of dayes lengthen the rod." Here, he appears to mistake *chronos*, the determinate progress of the hours, for *chairos*, God's intervention in history and salvation of humankind. As Father Time informs him, the narrator needs more *chronos*, not less, to realize the *chairos* of God's saving grace. In contrast, when the speaker of "The Priesthood" thinks of time, it is of *chairos*. He throws himself at his Lord's feet, awaiting an act of both courtly and divine grace: "There will I lie, untill my Maker seek/For some mean stuffe whereon to show his skill:/*Then is my time*" (*Works*, 161, ll. 37 39, my emphasis).

Although Edward and George Herbert certainly knew one another's poetry, they made few direct comments upon each other's work. In his autobiography, Edward tersely mentioned George's writings: "Some of . . . [his] English works are extant; which, though they be rare in their kind, yet are far short of expressing those perfections he had in the Greek and Latin tongue, and all divine and human literature" (11). The brief and rather dismissive note conceals the fact that the Herberts' poems speak insistently to one another in a family dialogue: about their positions of heir and dependent son; about salvation by submission and independent action; about the blessing of the church, and about the abuses of it; and about time as a sacramental order and as an individual recognition of destiny.

Strangely enough, while George Herbert's lyrics are much better known than Edward's, it may be Edward's poems on his watch that embody modern spiritual life most acutely. As Michael Bristol astutely points out, "The fact of . . . [Lord Herbert's] 'marginality' can be a bit puzzling in that his ideas anticipate many of the widely shared norms (and contradictions) of contemporary liberal political culture" ("Sacred

Literature," 16). While few critics will agree with G. C. Moore Smith that "in poetic feeling and art Edward Herbert soars above his brother George" (*Poems*, xvii), perhaps the recognition of the family dialogues in the Herberts' writings, first apprehended by Margaret Fuller, may yield new ground in criticism of their poetry. By attending to these dialogues, one might hear not only the theological music of the spheres, but also the wrangling of the peers—that is, the family conflicts that animate both Herberts' poetry.

6 Tempests in the Blood

ء

Thomas Herbert's "The Storme . . . from Plimmouth"

> Lightning was all our light, and it rained more
> Than if the sun had drunk the sea before.
> (John Donne, "The Storme," ll. 43–44)

For truly, it was more likely that the mountaines should haue beene rent in sunder from the top to the bottome, and cast headlong into the sea, by these vnnaturall winds; then that we, by any helpe or cunning of man, should free the life of any one amongst vs.

Notwithstanding the same God of mercy which delivered *Ionas* out of the Whales belly, and heareth all those that call vpon him faithfully, in their distresse; looked downe from heauen, beheld our teares, and heard our humble petitions, ioyned with holy vowes. Euen God . . . did so wonderfully free vs, and make our way open before vs, as it were by his holy Angels still guiding and conducting vs. . . .

(Sir Francis Drake, *The World Encompassed*)

There was no mistaking the significance of English sailors in the early modern world of discovery and colonization. They were the instrument and symbol of an emergent nationalism, which pitted English ships against the French, Spanish, Portuguese, and Dutch in the contests of trade, piracy, colonizing, and maritime warfare. The defeat of the Armada, Drake's circumnavigation, the sacking of Cadiz, and the Virginian voyages were points of honor closely allied with religion in Elizabethan and Jacobean England. So Geoffrey Whitney's emblem "Auxilio diuino" on God's providence pictured a divine hand pulling Drake's *Golden Hinde* by velvet cords around the world: "God was on his side,/. . . his shaken shippe did guide" (*A Choice of Emblemes*, 203, ll. 5–6). Likewise, the medal Elizabeth commissioned to commemorate the defeat of the Spanish Armada read: "*Flavit Jehovah et dissipati sunt.* The Lord blew and they were scattered" (Adams, *The Land and the Literature of England*, 159). The Atlantic storms that tossed ships became not only the symbols of spiritual crisis, as in Donne's "The Storme," but also the emblems of God's destruction of his enemy and deliverance of his chosen. In other words, England's naval successes proved its manifest destiny as a colonial power, or as Sir Francis Bacon put it: "To be master of the sea is an abridgement [i.e., epitome] of monarchy" (qtd. in Lloyd, *The Nation and the Navy*, 35).

The importance of the sea and storms in British political myth was not lost on George Herbert, who, like most of his contemporaries, celebrated the channel as England's great defensive wall. His "British Church" was "double-moated" by water and by God's grace (*Works*, 110, ll. 28–30), and in "In pacem Brittanicam," he thanked God for England's insular security:

> Naufragij causa est alijs mare, roboris Anglo,
> > Et quae corrumpit moenia, murus aqua est.
> Nempe hìc Religio floret, regina quietis,
> > Túque super nostras, Christe, moueris aquas.
>
> (411, ll. 5–8)

The sea shipwrecks others, but strengthens England,
  And water, which breaks ramparts, is our wall.
Surely religion flourishes here, the queen of peace,
  And you, Christ, have moved upon our waters.

(My translation)

The rhetoric of these poems was more Jacobean than Elizabethan, emphasizing God's protection of peaceful England rather than the destruction of England's maritime rivals. Still, the verses do express an obvious pride in England's sea power, a pride that was nourished by George Herbert's association with John Donne, a veteran of the Cadiz expedition of 1596, and his relationship with his youngest brother, Thomas.

The writings of the last and most enigmatic member of the Herbert family, Captain Thomas Herbert, have never been carefully examined or compared to George Herbert's poetry. At least one work, "The Storme ... from Plimmouth," the only poem we know with any certainty that Thomas Herbert wrote, bears a distinctive relation to George's poetry of emblems and stormy inner weather (see appendix C).[1] While the Herbert brothers wrote in very different poetic registers, they both experienced what Henry Vaughan called "tempests in [the] blood."

Thomas Herbert was the last of Magdalen's ten children by Richard Herbert. Donne said in her funeral sermon that Magdalen was married young to her first husband and "multiplied into ten *Children; Iob's* number; and *Iob's* distribution, (as shee, her selfe would very often remember) *seven sonnes*, and *three daughters*" (8: 87). She was fortunate to see all ten of her children survive to adulthood and, after the death of her first husband, Richard, to marry Sir John Danvers in 1609. Richard Herbert, esq., died in October of 1595, when Magdalen was two months pregnant with Thomas, and she later suffered the deaths of three sons and a daughter before her own death in 1627.[2] The experience of a broken family, fragmented by the death of a spouse or children, was all too common during this period. Thomas Herbert, the posthumous child, was baptized in the Parish Church in Montgomery, Wales, on 15 May 1597, but moved with his family repeatedly in his early life— to his grandmother Newport's house in Eyton, Shropshire, in 1597, to Oxford in 1599, and to Charing Cross early in 1601 (Edward, Lord Herbert, *Autobiography*, 12; Charles, *A Life*, 31–33).

Meanwhile, Magdalen Herbert sought to assure the patrimonies of her younger children, which were promised by the late Richard Herbert and eventually secured in an arbitration award that bound Edward Herbert to pay annuities to his younger brothers. As a posthumous child, Thomas's claim to inheritance was the most precarious. Magdalen's second demand of her son Edward in their negotiations involved Thomas. Her account of the arbitration, beginning "The case betwene my sonne and me is this," reads: "Secondly for my sonnes to have thos Annuities wch their father gave them, made vpp 40$^£$ a yere duringe their lives, and my yongest sonne [i.e. Thomas] who was vnborne at the tyme of the makinge these annuities to have the like" (Surrey Record Office, Loseley Manuscripts, L.M. 2014/103). Fortunately for Thomas, Magdalen's second demand was met in large measure, and her youngest son's name was scrawled in a cramped hand alongside his brothers' names in the "arbitration award by George More, Herbert Crofte and John Morice, knights, between Magdalen Herbert, widow, and her son Ed. Herberte knight," preserved in the Surrey Record Office (Loseley Manuscripts, L.M. 349/7).

At the busy and prosperous house at Charing Cross, Thomas began his education as a gentleman. In the *Kitchin Booke* kept by Magdalen and her steward John Gorse from 11 April to 4 September 1601, Thomas, aged four, is recorded among the gentlemen in attendance at table. According to the *Kitchin Booke*, Magdalen Herbert maintained a very large table, regularly feeding 14 gentlemen and gentlewomen, 14 servants, and frequent guests, such as schoolmasters, musicians, and pastors. The household greatly decreased in July as she and most of the children and servants retired to the country, although young Thomas and Henry stayed at Charing Cross, with the steward Gorse and four other servants (see chapter 2 and appendix A). Thomas would not remain at home for long, however, proving to be the most peripatetic member of a family that often ventured abroad. In his *Country Parson*, George Herbert advised that the younger son of a nobleman might "travel into *Germany*, and *France*, . . . observing the Artifices, and Manufactures there" (*Works*, 278). All of the Herbert brothers except George traveled in Europe, and Thomas did so from an especially tender age.

In his autobiography, Edward Herbert says that his younger brother Thomas, "being brought up a while at school, was sent as a page to Sir Edward Cecil, lord-general of his Majesty's auxiliary forces to the princes in Germany, and was particularly at the siege of Juliers, A. D. 1610" (12). Amy M. Charles further speculated that Sir George More helped obtain the post of page for Thomas when he was only six years of age. In a letter dated 3 December 1603, Edward Herbert expressed thanks to Sir George More for assisting "my little brother," perhaps referring to this matter (Charles, *A Life*, 45–46). The details of Thomas's early schooling and where and when he joined Cecil's troops in Germany are unknown, but it is very likely that he had left England before Magdalen was married to Sir John Danvers in February 1609. His advancement to a military career was rapid, but it was by no means exceptional for a younger son of a noble family. John Earle's contemporary character sketch in *Microcosmography* presented "The Younger Brother" with three career choices: "the Ministry," "the King's highway," or "the Low Countries . . ., where he dies without a shirt" (23). While George and possibly Charles Herbert decided on the first career alternative, Thomas, Richard, and William all chose the third, the latter two brothers dying in the warfare on the continent. It was probably in the 1610s, when all of his brothers roved abroad, that George Herbert advised the noble youth of "The Church-Porch": ". . . if souldier,/Chase brave employments with a naked sword/Throughout the world" (*Works*, 10, ll. 87–89).

The highlights of Thomas Herbert's military and naval career are related splendidly in Edward, Lord Herbert of Cherbury's *Autobiography*, at greater length than any of his brother's lives, including George's. Edward begins his record of Thomas's military successes with his young brother's bold entrance into the siege of Juliers under Edward Cecil and Prince Christian of Anhalt's command, "where he [i.e. Thomas] showed such forwardness, as no man in that great army before him was more adventurous on all occasions" (10). From Edward's larger-than-life account, Thomas Herbert emerges as a brave soldier, a monumental naval hero, and a sadly neglected office-seeker. Since this account stands as the basis for all later digests of Thomas Herbert's life, it is worth quoting at some length:

> . . . he went to the East Indies, under the command of Captain Joseph, who, in his way, thither, meeting with a great Spanish [i.e., Portugese] ship, was unfortunately killed in fight with them; whereupon, his men being disheartened, my brother Thomas encouraged them to revenge the loss, and renewed the fight in that manner . . ., that they forced the Spanish ship to run aground. . . . After which time, he, with the rest of the fleet, came to Surat, and from thence, went with the merchants to the Great Mogul; where, after he had stayed about a twelvemonth, he returned with the same fleet back again to England. After this, he went in the navy which King James sent to Algiers, under the command of Sir Robert Mansel . . .; it was his hap to meet with a ship, which he took . . ., which, it was thought, saved the whole fleet from perishing. He conducted, also, Count Mansfeld to the Low Countries. . . . After this, he commanded one of the ships that were sent to bring the prince from Spain. . . .

After he had brought the prince safely home, he was appointed to go with one of the king's ships to the Narrow Seas. He also fought divers times with great courage and success, with divers men in single fight, sometimes hurting and disarming his adversary, and sometimes driving him away. After all these proofs given of himself, he expected some great command; but finding himself, as he thought, undervalued, he retired to a private and melancholy life . . .; in which sullen humour having lived many years, he died and was buried in London, in St. Martin's near Charing Cross. . . . (12–14)

This family legend of the brave captain was based in fact, but was undoubtedly embellished by Edward Herbert's quixotic pride in his family's military heritage. Lord Herbert challenged more than a few of his opponents to duels, and later blustered to his grandsons, "You should remember that none in the long line of your ancestors feared a fair combat" (*Poems*, 116; my translation). The disappointing end of Thomas's life also appealed strongly to Edward's regret over his own failed career as French ambassador. As George Held observed in "Herbert and His Brothers": "How apt these words would be in describing the fate of Edward Herbert himself, denied preferment after his recall from Paris in 1624 and retired to his castle for much of the remainder of his life" (24).

Other documents substantiate a small handful of facts about Thomas Herbert's naval career. A "Mr. Harbert," assumed to be Thomas, sailed on the East Indian Company's expedition to Persia in the spring of 1617. The commander of the fleet, General Benjamin Joseph, was killed in March of 1617 in "a dangerous fight with a Portugal carack" (Saintsbury and Fortescue, eds., *Calendar of State Papers*, 22–23). On 3 November 1617, the English envoy Thomas Roe reported that "Mr. Harbert, weary of the progress, is bound for England" (70) and on 6 December, Roe wished, "Thanks [to] all who use Harbert . . . kindly" (84). A list of "Captaines that goeth for Algiers" among the Herbert papers in the Public Record

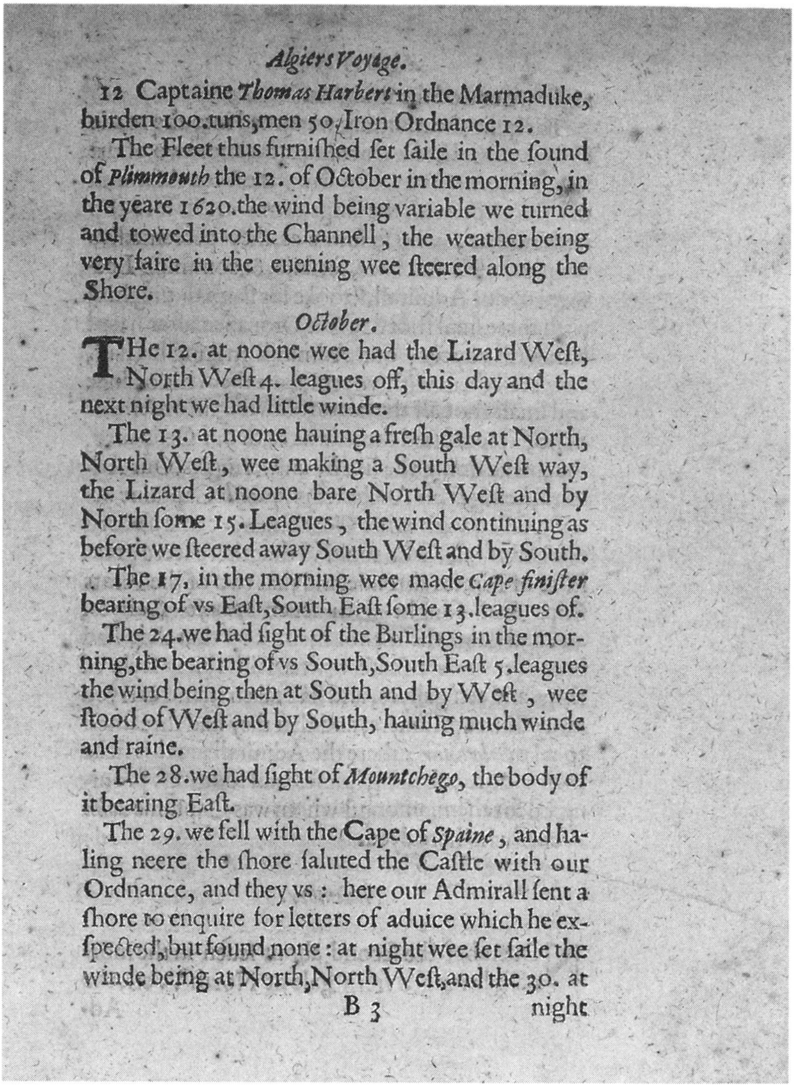

Algiers Voyage.

12 Captaine *Thomas Harbert* in the Marmaduke, burden 100.tuns, men 50, Iron Ordnance 12.

The Fleet thus furnifhed fet faile in the found of *Plimmouth* the 12. of October in the morning, in the yeare 1620.the wind being variable we turned and towed into the Channell, the weather being very faire in the euening wee fteered along the Shore.

October.

THe 12. at noone wee had the Lizard Weft, North Weft 4. leagues off, this day and the next night we had little winde.

The 13. at noone hauing a frefh gale at North, North Weft, wee making a South Weft way, the Lizard at noone bare North Weft and by North fome 15. Leagues, the wind continuing as before we fteered away South Weft and by South.

The 17. in the morning wee made *Cape finifter* bearing of vs Eaft, South Eaft fome 13.leagues of.

The 24.we had fight of the Burlings in the morning,the bearing of vs South, South Eaft 5.leagues the wind being then at South and by Weft, wee ftood of Weft and by South, hauing much winde and raine.

The 28.we had fight of *Mountchego*, the body of it bearing Eaft.

The 29. we fell with the Cape of *Spaine*, and haling neere the fhore faluted the Caftle with our Ordnance, and they vs : here our Admirall fent a fhore to enquire for letters of aduice which he exfpected, but found none : at night wee fet faile the winde being at North,North Weft,and the 30. at

B 3　　　　　　night

Figure 5

Page from John Button's *Algiers Voyage*, 1621. By permission of the Folger Shakespeare Library, Washington, D.C.

Office also corroborates Thomas Herbert's service on Mansell's expedition against the Dey Pirates in 1620–1621 (PRO 30/53/ 10, fol. 47). Likewise, Walton, in his *Life of Herbert*, wrote: "The seventh son was *Thomas*, who being made captain of a ship in that fleet with which Sir *Robert Mansel* was sent against *Algiers*, did there shew a fortunate and true English valor" (262).

In John Button's published journal of the expedition, Thomas is listed as the captain of the *Marmaduke*, a merchant ship of "burden 100.tuns, men 50. Iron Ordnance 12" (see figure 5) (*Algiers voyage*, B3r). From Button, we also learn that Thomas Herbert, like so many of the sailors, suffered serious illness while the fleet pursued pirates in the Mediterranean: "The 27. [of January 1621] the Admirall with the rest of the fleet set sayle, leauing the Marmaduke behind, whose Captaine [Herbert] and Master were both sicke a shore" (D1r). There is nothing in Button's account to either confirm or deny Edward Herbert's claim that Thomas participated in the English capture of the lone great prize of the expedition, a rich merchant ship, upon 2 June 1621. Button's journal, slightly abridged, was given greater currency in Samuel Purchas's *Hakluytus Posthumus or Purchas his pilgrimes* in 1625, and served as a source for eighteenth and nineteenth century historical accounts of the Algiers Expedition. In September 1625, Herbert's naval career reached its pinnacle, when the Duke of Buckingham appointed him Captain of the *Dreadnought* (Bruce, ed., *Calendar of State Papers*, 111). Amy M. Charles also insisted "there can be little doubt" that a young English nobleman, referred to variously as "Ensign Harbert," "Auntient Harbert," and "Mr. George Herbert" in letters of the Venetian archives, and who barely escaped hanging in a mutiny in Venice in 1618, was actually Thomas Herbert (*A Life*, 224–27).

These few references and the vivid seascape and nautical lore of "The Storme . . . from Plimmouth," a manuscript poem signed "Capt. T. Herbert," and found among the Powis Papers in the National Library of Wales, jointly testify to Thomas Herbert's colorful naval career (see appendix C). What happened after Herbert's captaincy of the *Dreadnought* in 1625 is much less clear. Sidney Lee conjectured that Thomas "apparently died midway between 1626 and 1642" (*Autobiography*, 14, n. 2). It is certain that Thomas Herbert was dead by 14 June 1643, when Edward wrote to his brother Henry, "And here I must remember that of all of us, there remains now but you and I to brother it" (Warner, ed., *Epistolary Curiosities*, 30). As Lee pointed out and as I have confirmed, the parish register of St. Martin-in-the-Field's parish does not list Thomas Herbert's burial at anytime between 1625 and 1644. The omission of his name from the register is unfortunate since it bears significantly upon the attribution of eight satirical pamphlets to Captain Thomas Herbert (Kitto, ed., *The Registers*).[3]

From 1638 to 1641, a certain Thomas Herbert, referred to in the British Museum catalog as "Thomas Herbert, verse writer," wrote and published eight tracts. In his *Dictionary of National Biography* article on "Thomas Herbert (1597–1642?)," James McMullen Rigg concluded that George Herbert's brother Thomas Herbert was "probably the author of the following trifles":

> 1. "Stripping, Whipping, and Pumping . . .," London, 1638, 8vo.
> 2. "Keep within compasse Dick and Robin . . .," 1641, 12mo.
> 3. "An elegie upon the death of Thomas, Earle of Strafford," (heroic couplet), London, 1641; 4to. 4. "Newes newly discovered in a pleasant dialogue betwixt Papa the false pope and Benedict an honest fryer . . .," London, 1641, 12mo. 5. "An answer to the most envious, scandalous, and libellous Pamphlet, entituled Mercuries Message . . ." (heroic couplet), London, 1641, 4to. 6. "A Reply in the Defence of the Oxford Petition, with a declaration of the Academians teares for the decay of learning . . .," London 1641, 4to. 7. "Vox Secunda Populi. Or the Commons Gratitude to the most Honourable Philip, Earle of

Pembroke . . .," London, 1641, 4to. . . . 8. "Newes out of Isling-
ton; or a Dialogue very merry and pleasant between a knavish
Projector and honest Clod the Ploughman, with certaine songs,"
London, 1641, 12mo. . . . (Stephen and Lee, eds., *Dictionary of
National Biography*, 9: 666)

Based upon these attributions, Amy M. Charles also inferred
that Captain Thomas Herbert was "brought up in learning"
and at the end of his life "turned to writing satiric and scurrilous verse" (*A Life*, 46). Yet a careful examination of these pamphlets reveals that most, if not all of them, could not have
been written by Captain Thomas Herbert, George Herbert's
brother.

The most self-revealing of these tracts, *An Answer to . . .
Mercuries Message* (1641), expresses pity for Laud's fall, and
though never justifying Laud, supports episcopacy against the
menacing rhetoric of *Mercuries Message*, a tract that mocks
Laud as one of the "Vsurping Prelates [who] shall/Rule us in
pride no more." However, we learn most about the verse writer
Thomas Herbert not from his own satires, but from the attack
of his pamphleteering opponent, writing under the psuedonym
of Mercurius, in *Mercuries Message Defended, Against the
vain, foolish, simple, and absurd cavils of Thomas Herbert a
ridiculous Ballad-maker*, another tract printed in London in
1641. Opening his satire in *ad hominem* fashion, Mercurius
refers to a chance meeting with his adversary Herbert. He says
that he had supposed Thomas Herbert might be "some hanger
on at the Episcopall palace in Lambeth" or "some brave op-
poser," until he met Herbert one day and found himself to be
"mightily . . . mistaken" (3). He claims to have been passing
"through a stinking Alley," when, "in a blinde alehouse, I heard
a crew of roaring Ballad-singers trouling out a merry Ballad
called, *The more knaves the better company*" (3). Then,

> And one amongst the rest cried out, Well sung *Herbert*, who as
> it seems, bore up the base amongst them, and in that deboist

manner consumeth his time, and when his money is spent, (as for the most part it is six or seven times a week) writes a new merry book, a good godly Ballad, or some such excellent piece of stuffe even as the droppings of the spigot inliveneth his muddy muse, to put his feeble purse in fresh stocke again: looking in at the name *Herbert*, and seeing such a poore ragged companion, I tooke him rather to be some dung-hill rakers page, than a lackey to the Muses. And so thought to passe by, untill upon better enquiry I was certainly informed that he was the Authour of that much applauded Answer. (3–4)

Although it is tempting to think of the rakish ballad-singer as Captain Thomas Herbert at the end of a disappointing and dissolute life, other references urge against this conclusion. The Mercurius writer later refers to the author of *An Answer* as a young man: "some young *Gregory Nonsence*, that might have been a scholar had he not run away from *Cambridge* when he should have been whipt for his knavery: and came up to *London* to write scurrilous pamphlets for halfe a crowne a piece" (10). In 1641, if still alive, Captain Thomas Herbert was no young man: nor had he come recently from Cambridge. The Cambridge *Book of Matriculations and Degrees* and the records of *Admissions to Trinity College* both list a Thomas Herbert, who matriculated as a sizar in Michaelmas term, 1639, but did not graduate (Venn and Venn, eds., 340; Ball and Venn, eds., 367). This young man *might* have been "Thomas Herbert, the ballad-maker," but he certainly was not Captain Thomas Herbert. Finally, in his *Answer*, the verse writer Thomas Herbert provided a crucial piece of evidence about his identity. Anticipating that Mercurius would charge him with flattering Archbishop Laud, the ballad-maker produced this revealing couplet: "No *Canterburian* I, though Kentish borne,/I shun his actions, and his censure scorne" (*An Answer*, 5). Thus, it seems certain that "Herbert, the balladmaker," author of *An Answer, Keep within Compasse, News Out of Islington*, and other tracts, was a young man born in

Kent—and not in Montgomery, where the elder Captain Thomas Herbert was born.

If Captain Thomas Herbert was not a scribbler of "scurrilous tracts," what did he do after forsaking his career as a sea captain? Charles has suggested that Thomas served briefly as a secretary to his brother Sir Henry Herbert in 1637, and witnessed a bond between Sir Ralph Clare and Sir Henry in 1640 ("Sir Henry Herbert," 4). One "Master Thomas Herbert, deputy to Sir Henry Herbert," did make entries in the Stationer's Register on 22 March, 25 March, 13 April, and 22 April 1637 (Arber, ed., 4: 350, 355, 356). Also, the bond between Clare and Sir Henry Herbert in May 1640, now in the National Library of Wales, was "Sealed & deliver'd in the p'sence of. Tho. Herbert" (NLW Ms. 5299E). One cannot be utterly certain, however, that this Thomas Herbert was Sir Henry's brother, the Captain. During the 1630s, Sir Henry Herbert also maintained a very cordial relationship with his cousin Sir Thomas Herbert (1606–1682), son of Christopher Herbert of York.

Like Sir Henry Herbert, who became Master of the Revels through the agency of the Earl of Pembroke, his cousin Sir Thomas depended on the patronage of William and Philip Herbert. According to Anthony à Wood, this Sir Thomas Herbert spent the 1630s in "the converse of the muses," publishing his travel narrative, *A Relation of Some Years Travaile*, in 1634, and producing an enlarged second edition, *Some Yeares Travels into Divers Parts*, in 1638 (*Athenae Oxoniensis*, 4: coll. 15). For his cousin's first volume, Sir Henry wrote a commendatory verse of 34 lines, beginning, "No sooner welcome home from trauell, then/Cosen, thou dost put forth to Sea agen." The second voyage that cousin Thomas was taking, it seems, was not only a voyage into print but also into patronage. Both editions of his travels included lavish dedications to Philip Herbert, Fourth Earl of Pembroke, and in 1631 Sir Thomas confided to Thomas, Lord Fairfax, "My Lord of Pembroke will,

I hope, be my friend in an occasion that I go about" (Johnson, ed., *Fairfax Correspondence*, 1: 239).

In this literary period of his life, Sir Thomas's close relationship with Henry Herbert is testified to in a letter from Lord Scudamore.[4] On 29 August 1640, Scudamore wrote to Henry Herbert, "Your cosen Mr. Tho. Herbert and his wife are both returned in health last night. Hee is now with me, presents you his service, and desires pardon for not writing this day" (Warner, ed., *Epistolary Curiosities*, 27). So it is uncertain whether the Thomas Herbert mentioned in the Stationer's Register and the bond of 1640 is Henry Herbert's brother or cousin, and he may very well be the latter. Unless more evidence about Captain Herbert's later career comes to light, all one can know of it is that he lived in London and probably died in the 1630s or 1640s, and certainly before 14 June 1643.

The manuscript poem "The Storme . . . from Plimmouth" therefore remains the most engaging and significant record of Captain Thomas's life, the one that distinguishes him both as a man of letters and as a man of the sea, and the one that allies him most closely to his brother poets and his family's friend John Donne. The manuscript was listed in the appendix of W. J. Smith's *Herbert Correspondence* (359) in 1963 and was mentioned by Amy M. Charles in 1982 ("Sir Henry Herbert," 1, n. 2), but the poem itself has never been edited or discussed at length. The manuscript, dated circa 1620–1640 by Smith, was long preserved among the papers at Powis Castle, with letters of Edward Herbert of Cherbury and other Herberts, before the papers were deposited in the National Library of Wales, in 1933 and 1937 by the Fourth Earl of Powis, and in 1959 by the Fifth Earl of Powis. What Smith says of the Powis papers in general also describes "The Storme" manuscript in particular: "Neither the exact descents nor the precise movements of these letters can now readily be established" (*Herbert Correspondence*, 1). While the exact provenance of the manuscript has not been determined, the script, paper, narrative and emblematic content, as well as the signature "Capt. T. Herbert" and the proximity to other Herbert family letters all support Professor Charles's attribution of the poem to Thomas Herbert, George Herbert's brother.

"The Storme . . . from Plimmouth" is a fair copy, slightly corrected and almost surely in the author's hand, of a nearly completed poem in triplets, with 26 stanzas and 76 lines. It was written neatly on good linen paper, on a loose sheet approximately 40 centimeters long, folded to make two folio leaves, each 20 centimeters wide and 31 centimeters tall. Sometime after the manuscript was written, it was folded twice again, presumably for storage or for inclusion in a packet of letters. Over time, the loose manuscript has become tattered at the edges, but no words appear to have been lost, and legibility is good throughout. The first leaf clearly bears a watermark of a French Pot design, inscribed with the letters GRO and headed with a crescent: it is very similar but not identical to another French Pot illustrated in W. A. Churchill's *Watermarks in Paper* (Plate 469).[5]

The script of "The Storme . . . from Plimmouth" is in a strong italic hand; the stanzas are clearly numbered, with a light score mark after most of the stanzas and a pronounced score after the final stanza and before the author's signature. Marginal notes accompany stanzas 1, 9, 18, 23, and 26, and a final note offers an emblem for the poem (see appendix C). Only stanza 24, reading, "It breaks . . . upp," is incomplete, although the phrasing in other stanzas is occasionally rough and somewhat broken. Corrections of single words were made by the author in stanzas 2, 14, and 23. In all, the manuscript poem gives the impression of a careful composition, to which the author could sign his name with mingled pride and irritation, still not satisfied he had found the right words for every stanza.

"The Storme . . . from Plimmouth" vividly renders a near

shipwreck with a wide palette of literary and maritime allusions. The poem employs ample nautical lore and frequent seascapes, an Ovidian simile, some Virgilian winds and omens, some Donnean cosmological conflict, a pious Latin tag, and a final sacred emblem with both religious and political implications. Thomas Herbert may have known Donne's verse epistles, "The Storm" and "The Calm," copies of which remain among the Herbert family manuscript poems in the National Library of Wales (NLW Ms. 5308E). Indeed, his "Storme" belongs within a contemporary tradition of English sea poems that includes Donne's lyrics, Thomas James's "Lines on His Companions Who Died in the Northern Seas," Nicholas Murford's "The Storm and Calm," and William Hammond's "The Boat." These are verses that graphically recounted maritime experience and transformed it into religious and political allegory. Thomas Herbert's "Storme" is also broadly related to many popular emblems of ships, seas, and storms, such as Geoffrey Whitney's "The shippe, that long vppon the sea," Henry Peacham's "Of orient hew, a Rainebow," and George Herbert's "The Storm." And while Thomas depicts the tempest with less psychological insight than his brother, the end of his poem concurs with the opening lines of George's "The Bag": "Storms are the triumph of his art:/Well may he close his eyes, but not his heart" (*Works*, 151, ll. 5–6).

Unlike George Herbert's short lyrics of internal tumult, however, Thomas's longer narrative poem begins and ends at precise geographical coordinates with political associations. The title words appear with a large gap between the paired words "The Storme" and "from Plimmouth," and thus is rendered "The Storme . . . from Plimmouth." The ellipsis in the title allows the second pair to form a phrase with the first line of the poem: "from Plimmouth/Anchor we wayd North . . ." Almost as if writing a nautical logbook in the poem and accompanying notes, Thomas Herbert records the direction of the wind (north and by east), the steering and course of the ship (south and west, "towards the North Cape in Spaine"), the precise latitude (50.20), and even the islands and rock formations encountered. The mysterious "hard bishopps, clarks, Sad Scilla left behind" of line 3 refer to the extreme western rocks of the Scilly Islands, named on maps as "The Bishop and His Clerks," and well-known to English sailors for the danger of shipwreck they presented (Quixley, ed., *Antique Maps*, Maps 16 and 25).[6] The narrative ends, after a fierce tempest at "the Center of the three seas in the bay of Biscay," with a miraculous landing at La Coruña, at "the groine" of "Cape Finisterrae," "lat. 43.30." These precise and recurrent notations of place mark the poem as authentic maritime reportage—a "true" story of the sea. A political undercurrent also underlies Thomas's description of the battling waves—"A surly Spanish Don," a French "Mounsr" [i.e., Mounsieur], and "The British"—in the stormy Bay of Biscay. Clearly, the ship's landing at La Coruña had political associations for England.

The deliverance of the ship at La Coruña and the emblem's assertion that the ship is "never sinking wth a Rainbow horning her" seem especially fraught with political significance. La Coruña was, after all, the port at which the Spanish Armada had rallied after setting sail from Lisbon in 1588, and it was the city that Sir Francis Drake had partially sacked and burned in 1589. Although the English officially maintained peace on the seas with Spain throughout most of James I and Charles I's reigns, Spain was still considered England's great national enemy, as events in the Thirty Years' War bore out (Clowes, *The Royal Navy*, 2: 391, 549). In theological and emblematic literature, Noah's rainbow-crested ark prefigured the afflicted, but victorious church: "With flood and weather th' Arke is tost,/So is the Church but nothing lost,/For as the pitch the ship doth keepe,/So faith preserueth in perils deepe" (Willet, *Sacrorum Emblematum Una Centura*, D1v). Likewise, in "The Storme . . . from Plimmouth," the ark seems to promise the deliverance of the English church and nation from their enemies. Indeed, the names of royal ships in Elizabeth's and James's naval expeditions carried the same Biblical symbolism. Her Majesty's ships that repelled the Spanish Armada included the *Ark Royal*, the *Rainbow*, and the *Elizabeth Jonas*. Captain Thomas Herbert would have known the *Rainbow* well, since it was rebuilt in James's reign and sailed alongside the *Marmaduke* on the Algiers mission in 1620–1621.

The dates of Thomas Herbert's poem and the events recounted in it are both uncertain, although they are probably between 1617 and 1625, during his tenure as a sea captain. The poem's detailed reportage also suggests "The Storme . . . from Plimmouth" was written soon after the titular "storme." While Herbert's ships sailed from Plymouth on the embassy to Persia in 1617 and the Algiers expedition of 1620–1621, no such terrible storm was reported on either voyage. Sudden and severe storms were themselves fairly common in the Bay of Biscay, and may have occurred at any time during Herbert's captaincy.

Whatever its date, Thomas Herbert's verse displays a mastery of nautical lore and terminology that his brother George never attempted. As a watchful sea captain, Thomas details the destruction of his ship, almost piece by piece. There is the loss of the main topmast and topgallant mast, and the rending of the catharping in stanza 17; the washing off of the bowsprit, cathead, and davit in stanza 19; the stripping of the grating and the breaking of three leaks and two fissures in the bow in stanza 20; and finally the knocking down of the bulwarks and the raking of the hawses by a loose cannon in stanza 22. The poet applies nautical terms vividly and precisely. For example, in stanza 21 he says that the ship was "brought vpon careen to lye" by the winds, referring to the positioning of a ship on its side, usually when turned over for repair and caulking (OED, careen, 1). Or, to take another example, Herbert's description of the "irksome calme" in stanza 5, in which his ship, "feeling no helme," "rockt this, that way," closely resembles Sir Henry Mainwaring's account of the "flat calm" in *The Seaman's Dictionary* (1623):

> A calm is more troublesome to a seafaring man than a storm . . . In some places, as in the Straits, when it is an extraordinary great storm . . ., on the sudden there will be no wind, but a flat calm, yet an extraordinary billow which is wonderous troublesome and dangerous; for then having no use of sail to keep her steady on a side, the great sea will make a ship roll so . . . she will be in danger to roll her masts by the board, or herself under water. (*The Life and Works of Sir Henry Mainwaring*, 2: 114)

However, while the deadly calm follows the storm in Mainwaring's account and in Donne's "The Calm," in Herbert's poem it is just one of a series of "Presages" of the coming disaster.

The mythological machinery and "Presages" of the poem combine standard classical allusions with curious closeups of sea life. On the whole, the effect is more fantastic than fearful. In stanzas 7–8, the Aeollian winds, through "faire persawsion" of the gods, as in book 1 of *The Aeneid*, break out of their prison and begin a meteorological "mutiny." A shoal of writhing fish "with brinish eye," a flock of "lowring" sea birds, and a bizarre herd of porpoise all serve as omens of the storm. The most distinctive of these harbingers are the porpoise, which mount one another "at leapfroggs" and accompany their play with "grunting woefull" (l. 26). The porpoise's ability to predict storms was apparently well-known to sailors in Herbert's time. Sir Kenelm Digby remarked similarly in his *Journal of a Voyage to the Mediterranean*: "I neuer yet saw store of porposes playing, but soone a storme ensewed, for I haue not seene greater abundance then to day, and att night wee had foule weather" (9). Herbert alludes to yet another curious piece of sea lore in stanza 23, when the auspicious appearance of the Gemini stars Castor and Pollux, shining beneath the "fantastique glowing" of St. Elmo's fire, foretells the salvation of the ship (ll. 67–69). In order to magnify these spectral and ominous effects in the poem, Herbert also writes several Donnean lines of meteorological conflict: "So a dire meteor to mortalls does appeare,/A fell presaging and disasterous yeare,/darting its maligne influence angular" (ll. 40–42). Despite all these omens, however, "The Storme . . . from Plimmouth" has little of the dread and hellish atmosphere of Donne's "Storm" or the pained soul-searching of George Herbert's "Storm."

Rather, Captain Thomas Herbert's trademark as a poet is the utterly self-assured voice he uses to concoct his nationalistic myth. This unremitting proud voice sounds in the first Ovidian simile of the poem. In the second stanza, Herbert's ship appears "proudly mounted on the Oceans backe," its canvas smiling, the deck hands singing, the seas themselves laughing "for ioy" (ll. 4–6). In the third stanza, Herbert compares the ship to Jove, disguised as a bull, absconding with the Tyrian Princess Europa, as in book 2 of *The Metamorphoses*:

> So amorous Joue in maiesty did ride,
> The sea gods, nymphs, faire Venus tend the bride,
> from Asia sporting, now to Europes side.
>
> (ll. 7–9)

Here the solecism of a Jove mounting the sea, rather than the bull being mounted on the sea by Europa, goes almost unnoticed, as the poet exults in the regal majesty of his ship—lord of all it surveys. Nor does this pride appear undue, as the storm seems not so much God's punishment for sin as a sign of his favor to the English ship and nation. From "amorous Jove" the ship is next metamorphosed into Noah's ark, the vessel in which God saves a holy remnant of humankind. Like the Jovian bull at the beginning of the poem, the sacred ark is also resplendent and horned: "A Shippe never sinking wth a

Rainbow *horning* her" (my emphasis). And Thomas Herbert
is the captain of both the profane and the sacred ship, equally
at ease with classical majesty and dalliance and with Christian piety in service of country. Even the pious motto that the
rainbow bears in stanza 25, "Quid Ni si pereo?," "What [is
there to fear?] unless I pass away?," promises God's blessing
to Herbert for "many a yeare" for faithfully enduring the storm.

The poetic voice that resounds proudly in "The Storme . . .
from Plimmouth" differs tellingly from the quieter but more
troubled voice of George Herbert's poetry. Both poets employed
some of the same elements—storms, rainbows, arks, tokens
of God's power and deliverance—but to very different ends.
Aldous Huxley sensed keenly the meteorological "instabil-
ity" in George Herbert's poetry: "Frost, sunshine, hopeless
drought, and refreshing rains succeed one another with bewil-
dering rapidity. Herbert is the poet of this inner weather" (*Texts
and Pretexts*, 13). In the most extended and brilliant study of
George Herbert's storm imagery, Michael C. Schoenfeldt comments that "Herbert's spiritual meteorology is not perpetu-
ally stormy, but tempests seem always to be approaching or
departing." Schoenfeldt finds that Herbert uses tempests to
represent God's (and likewise the King's) terrifying power over
his creatures and simultaneous love for them, illustrating the
"appurtenances of Stuart rule not only at its most physically
cruel but also at its most gloriously idealized" (*Prayer and
Power*, 142–43). Both Herbert brothers associated storms with
God's power over the nations, George Herbert marvelling in
"The Bag": "Though windes and waves assault my keel,/He
doth preserve it: he doth steer,/Ev'n when the boat seems most
to reel" (151, ll. 2–4). But the poet of *The Temple* concentrated
on the "inner weather" of an afflicted soul, whereas Captain
Thomas Herbert focused on the "outer weather" of navigation and political events.

This contrast between outer weather and inner weather
becomes clearer upon examining more of George Herbert's
lyrics. "Affliction V" begins and ends with the symbols of the

ark and the rainbow that Thomas Herbert used in "The Storme . . . from Plimmouth":

> My God, I read this day,
>   That planted Paradise was not so firm,
> As was and is thy floting Ark; whose stay
> And anchor thou art onely, to confirm
>   And strengthen it in ev'ry age,
>   When waves do rise, and tempests rage.
>
> *   *   *   *
>
>   Affliction then is ours;
> We are the trees, whom shaking fastens more,
> While blustring windes destroy the wanton bowres,
> And ruffle all their curious knots and store.
>   My God, so temper joy and wo,
>   That thy bright beams may tame thy bow.
>
> (*Works*, 97, ll. 1–6, 19–24)

Not only are George Herbert's lines more exquisitely witty—with the allusions to courtly knot gardens and the delicate pun on "bow"—but also more internally directed than his brother's. Whereas Thomas Herbert thinks of his ship's condition, George Herbert thinks of his soul's condition, which suffers and benefits from affliction, like the seasoned timber of "Vertue." Here, the Ark is not the English church or nation, but the lone, faithful soul, tossed by spiritual tempests, but saved by God "in ev'ry age." By contrast, in the poem "Miserie," the soul without God as anchor, is: "A sick toss'd vessel, dashing on each thing;/Nay, his own shelf:/My God, I mean my self" (*Works*, 102, ll. 76–78). The storm, for George Herbert, is not an external test of seamanship and divine favor, but an internal assault upon sin that results in purifying tears. In "The Storm," he declares: "Poets have wrong'd poore storms: such dayes are best;/They purge the aire without, within the breast" (132, ll. 17–18).

Although Thomas and George Herbert used the emblems of storms and arks in quite different poetic registers, storms were for both brothers the triumphs of their distinctive arts. Thomas's art was sailing merchant and military ships in search of preferment and in service of a national cause—an art to which he once lent a pen in his one surviving poem. While the family legend of Captain Herbert was undoubtedly embellished by his brother Edward, "The Storme . . . from Plimmouth" shows that Thomas Herbert promoted his own legend as he elaborated the English maritime myth. He was, like his ship, "proudly mounted on the Oceans back."

George Herbert's art—serving as "God's courtier" and his mother's literary surrogate—was of a subtler kind, involving moral introspection and a fine sensitivity to social nuance and gesture. If, as Pearlman contends, George Herbert struggled with and ultimately rejected the military heritage of his family, Thomas Herbert's career may have epitomized for George that aggressive tradition. Surely, as the lyric "Denial" suggests, the poet-priest must have sometimes been reminded of his brother's martial exploits: "My bent thoughts, like a brittle bow,/Did flie asunder./Each took his way . . ./Some to the warres and thunder/Of alarms" (80, ll. 6–10). In July 1627, upon the death of Magdalen Herbert, George Herbert wrote explicitly about the military conflicts that concerned his brother. While the Catholic General Tilly was poised to fight in Holland and Buckingham was leading a naval expedition to relieve Protestants in La Rochelle, George claimed that a cloudburst of tears for his mother occluded all other sights. In the ninth elegy of *Memoriae Matris Sacrum*, he grieved:

> While the King prepares a fleet for these great exploits,
>   Yet we weep. Only this matter occupies your children.
> Look, the fleet is about to set sail, blaming the slack winds,
>   But if it waits for rain, our tears have supplied the waters.
> Tilly turns to the Dutch, the French turn to the Sea,
>   We to mourning: This is the only signal of our leaders.
>   (*Works*, 427, ll. 7–12, my translation)

Here, George Herbert did not so much repudiate England's (or his family's) naval ambitions, as plead a temporary indifference to them, while the entire clan joined in a regenerative rain and swell of tears for their mother. Finally, in the image of the rain, the lines suggest that family matters of military honor and religious piety suffused both George and Thomas Herbert's respective arts.

7 Religion on Tiptoe

≈

Sir John Danvers, the Virginia Company, and "The Church Militant"

Christian names, surnames, place names:
Brafferton, called after a manor-
house in Yorkshire, whose rents had been
    bequeathed by Robert Boyle,
a man of learning and great piety,
to bring the infidels of Virginia,
across the water, out of their
    dark and miserable
ignorance to true religion. . . .

(Amy Clampitt, "Matoaka")

George Herbert did not live long enough to hear himself
proclaimed a prophet or hear the scruples over the publication of *The Temple* because of the notorious couplet in "The
Church Militant": "Religion stands on tip-toe in our land,/
Readie to passe to the *American* strand" (*Works*, 196, ll. 235–
36). According to Izaak Walton, when the Cambridge Vice-
Chancellor reviewed the book for licensing in 1633, he "would
by no means allow the two so much noted Verses . . . to be
printed; and Mr. *Farrer* [sic] would by no means allow the Book
to be printed, and want them." Upon Nicholas Ferrar's insistence, the Vice-Chancellor conceded the point, saying that he
knew Herbert was "a Divine Poet," but he hoped "*the World
will not take him to be an inspired Prophet*" (Walton, *The
Lives*, 315). Another of Herbert's early biographers, Barnabas
Oley, remarked similarly on the passage from line 235 to line
258 in the poem: "Shal I say, I hope, or Fear Mr. *Herbert's
lines* should be verified?. . . . I pray God he may prove a true
prophet for *poor America*, not against *poor England*" (Patrides,
ed., *George Herbert*, 77).

Confirming the fears of Oley and the Vice-Chancellor,
reforming ministers, pamphleteers, and religious writers
throughout the seventeenth century regarded the poem as an
ominous prophecy of the decline of the English Church. In
1635, the Puritan lecturer Samuel Ward of Ipswich received
Archbishop Laud's ecclesiastical censure for preaching "that
Religion and the Gospel stood on tiptoes ready to be gone" (qtd.
in William Prynne, *Canterburies Doome*, 361). And worse,
"For taking Herbert to be an Inspired Prophet," writes Elizabeth Clarke, "Samuel Ward was arrested and died a lingering
death in prison" (*Theory and Theology*, 12). Following Ward,
several generations of writers and preachers considered Herbert as a prophet of England's impending religious collapse.
They included Richard Baxter in *The Saints Everlasting Rest*
(1650), Thomas Hall in *A Practical and Polemical Commentary* (1658), John Aubrey in his *Brief Lives* (1669), the verse

writer of another "Church Militant" in *Adversus Impia* (1674), Henry Vaughan in "To Christian Religion" in *Thalia Rediviva* (1678), the tract writer of *Prophecys Concerning the Return of Popery into England, Scotland and Ireland* (1682), Baxter again in *Obedient Patience in General* (1683), the author of *An Enquiry After Religion* (1691), and George Ryley in *Mr. Herbert's Temple and Church Militant Explained and Improved* (1715). In *The Mount of Olives* (1652), Vaughan, Herbert's most zealous pupil and imitator, called his poetic master "a most glorious true Saint, and a Seer," and referred to "The Church Militant" as one of "his incomparable prophetick Poems" (*The Works of Henry Vaughan*, 186).[1]

"The Church Militant" was not only Herbert's most topical and controversial poem, but it was also one of his most popular. Robert H. Ray's study of Herbert allusions in the seventeenth century found that among Herbert's poems only "The Church-porch" was cited more frequently than "The Church Militant" ("Herbert's Seventeenth-Century Reputation," 4). The reception of the poem in the twentieth century, however, has differed strikingly from its popularity in the seventeenth. In *The Living Temple*, Stanley Fish summarizes the dissatisfaction with which many critics have responded to the final poem of *The Temple*: "Perfect, complete, and climactic is what many readers would like *The Temple* to be, but 'The Church Militant,' pessimistic, inconclusive, and anticlimactic, is an impediment that those same readers feel obliged either to distort or remove" (144). Perhaps in part because of the critical disfavor toward the poem, Amy M. Charles described "The Church Militant" as an "early poem," dating it well before the spring of 1619, when George Herbert's eldest brother Edward was appointed French Ambassador (*The Williams Manuscript*, xxi).

With a few notable exceptions, critics in the twentieth century have viewed "The Church Militant" as disjoined from the other poems of *The Temple*. George Herbert Palmer commented that the poem might be "an altogether detached piece" (Palmer, ed., *The English Works*, 3: 305); Hutchinson said it "stands apart . . . from the lyrical poems"of "The Church" (*Works*, 543); Stanley Fish wrote that "it does not seem to be a fit conclusion to the poems that precede it" (*The Living Temple*, 143); Lee Ann Johnson called the poem "a separate entity" ("The Relationship of 'The Church Militant,'" 201); and Deborah K. Shuger considered "The Church Militant" as one of three discontinuous parts of *The Temple* (*Habits of Thought*, 91–119). Perhaps Louis L. Martz summed up best, in *The Poetry of Meditation*, what has become the critical consensus: "And certainly 'The Church Militant,' in many respects may seem to represent a rather desperate effort to salvage, if only by way of appendix, a very early poem" (289). The poem is, indeed, an appendix, and it might be described as an earlier verse, but not as juvenalia. The question then to be asked is: What sort of appendix is "The Church Militant," and why is it appended to "The Church"?

The argument of this chapter, which dates the poem from 1619 to 1622, suggests that "The Church Militant" represented George Herbert's first uncertain movement away from a career at court, and that Herbert did not meditate that step by himself, but with Sir John Danvers, the Ferrars, and other members of the Virginia Company. All of them anticipated that Christian religion would spread to America through the missionary efforts of the company; and all feared the Protestant losses in the Thirty Years' War would have disastrous results for the Church of England. All of them used their relations and allies in the Virginia Company to prosper their careers, and all were disaffected from the court by the struggles and dissolution of the company. It is not surprising, then, that when Herbert gave his literary manuscripts to Edmund Duncon to deliver to Nicholas Ferrar, he included an earlier poem, "by way of appendix," that exhibited his own courtly and religious hopes and his own disillusionment. Nor is it surprising that Nicholas Ferrar insisted upon the uncensored publication of "The Church Militant" and testified in his preface to Herbert's "independencie" and willingness to forsake "State-employments" (*Works*, 3–5). Nicholas Ferrar, the man whom Herbert called "My Exceeding Dear Brother," was also closely tied to the Earl of Pembroke, the Marquis of Hamilton, the Bishop of Lincoln, and Sir John Danvers—that is, to the Sandys faction of the Virginia Company. He was more than a "spiritual brother," but a close family ally whose career took the same path as Herbert's, from eminence in "State-employments" to religious retreat.

In late September 1619, when George Herbert was suing for his loftiest political office, the post of Cambridge University Orator, he wrote to his stepfather, Sir John Danvers, in thanks for his manifold "Favours" in advancing his prospects. In particular, Herbert thanked him for delivering a commendatory letter on his behalf to the outgoing orator, Sir Francis Nethersole, and for writing a commendatory letter to John Williams, the Bishop of Lincoln. While serving as deputy orator in Nethersole's absence, Herbert was occupied in writing a long Latin address, and protested that he could not find time to visit his family in London, "for my *Cambridge* necessities are stronger to tye me here, than yours to *London*" (*Works*, 369). These necessities must have been very strong, indeed, since Danvers was undertaking his most intensive service with the Virginia Company, sitting on the ruling council and more than a dozen committees, working in close concert with John and Nicholas Ferrar, Sir Edwin Sandys, and the Earl of Southampton to commence the first large-scale migration to Virginia. When Herbert wrote to Danvers, "I hope I shall get this place without all your *London* helps, of which I am very proud," he was almost certainly speaking of the courtly connections that his stepfather maintained as an influential member of the company (*Works*, 370).

How does "The Church Militant" reflect the Virginia

Company's business? The question is difficult to answer because of the poem's grand historical and apocalyptic argument, but it is certainly closely related to the activities of Danvers. As a member of the Virginia Company closely associated with the Ferrars, Sandys, and Southampton, and as a member of the Sidney-Herbert clan, termed by Malcolmson the "Herbert family coterie" ("George Herbert and Coterie Verse," 159), John Danvers was a key figure in George Herbert's political and religious careers (see figure 6). Of George Herbert's 19 surviving letters in English, six were written to Danvers, three to Danvers's close friend Nicholas Ferrar, and one to Arthur Woodnoth, who lived for a time with Danvers as his financial agent. In 1629, Herbert married Jane Danvers, a relative of Sir John, continuing his intimacy with his stepfather even after his mother Magdalen's death in 1627. Woodnoth was to serve as the executor and Danvers as the overseer of George Herbert's will in 1633, and it is clear from Daniel Doerksen's work on the Ferrar papers that both Woodnoth and Danvers sought to influence the publication of the first edition of *The Temple* in 1633 ("Nicholas Ferrar, Arthur Woodnoth, and the Publication," 24–25). Because of Danvers's later infamy as a member of the Long Parliament and as one of those regicides who signed Charles I's death-warrant, his close relations to George Herbert and the Ferrars were somewhat minimized by Izaak Walton and occluded by some of the succeeding biographers.

From surviving letters and records, however, one glimpses Danvers's powerful influence, as a successful exponent of the first large-scale migration from England to Virginia, on George Herbert. F. E. Hutchinson hinted at this connection between "The Church Militant" and the Great Migration when he observed that "The allusions to the hopes of evangelizing the American colonies bear some relation to the projects of Ferrar and other members of the Virginia Company" (*Works*, 543). Richard Strier noted likewise: "Herbert's time was also that

Figure 6

Sir John Danvers. From a drawing in the collection of
Robert Stearne Tighe, Esq. Printed in Thane's *British Autography*.
By permission of the Syndics of Cambridge University Library, Cambridge.

of the beginning of the Great Migration, a fact on which he commented suggestively in his vision of religion 'readie to passe to the *American* strand'" (*Love Known*, 85). While Strier was probably referring to "the Great Migration" to New England, which began officially with John Winthrop in 1630, the Virginia Company's shipments in the 1620s were early harbingers of the coming exodus. The ambitious colonization project that Sandys, the Ferrars, and Danvers undertook in the spring of 1619 and continued through the summer of 1622 was the first tiptoe movement of the Church of England to the new world, impelled by an evangelical fervor in the Sandys faction of the Virginia Company.

The movement was "tiptoe" in several senses. It was not only a temporary movement, which would recommence later (the largest part coming in the 1640s and 1650s), but it was also a tentative movement, with many and contrary implications for the English church and crown. "The Church Militant" performed a dangerous ballet upon matters that James I considered his special prerogatives, his *arcana imperii*. The poem stood tiptoe between the hopes of George Herbert's family faction on the Virginia Company and the fears of the King that Sandys's efforts to increase emigration to Virginia might damage the entire venture and harm English relations with Spain. In that tiptoe position, the poem took a brave step forward, a step very much like Herbert would take in becoming the rector of the tiny parish church in Bemerton. Thus, however alien "The Church Militant" seems to our sensibilities today, Herbert's apocalyptic poem was extremely pertinent to its contemporary audience.

The Virginia Company was first chartered by James I in 1606 to colonize the North American coast and to "tende to the glorie of His Divine Majestie [i.e., God] in propagating of Christian religion to suche people as yet live in darkenesse and miserable ignorance of the true knowledge and worshippe of God" (Bemiss, ed., *The Three Charters*, 2). Some of the early chapters in the colony's history are well known—particularly Captain John Smith's voyage in 1607, his supposed deliverance from the Powhatans by the Indian princess Pocahontas, her marriage to John Rolfe and voyage to England in 1616, the notorious "Starving Time" of the Winter of 1609–1610, the military government of Sir Thomas Gates and Sir Thomas Dale, and the growing market for tobacco (despite King James's *Counterblaste to Tobacco* in 1604) as a valuable commodity. Two more charters were granted the Virginia Company, in 1609 and 1612, and with the establishment of a lottery for the company in 1612, new capital enabled the further growth of the colony.

The leading officials of the Virginia Company at this time were Sir Thomas Smith and other large London merchants, who were understandably cautious, considering the early disasters as well as the Spanish Ambassador Gondamar's protests about English privateering in the New World. In 1612, while trying to publicize the mercantile hopes for the plantation, the Reverend Robert Johnson still recalled the "ill and odious wound of Virginea, which settled so deepe a scarre in the mindes of many" (*The New Life of Virginea*, D3v). That conservative attitude toward colonization and tenderness towards the King's prerogatives dominated the Virginia Company's policy until the spring of 1619, when Sir Edwin Sandys became Treasurer and John Ferrar was appointed Deputy.

The government of the Virginia Company under Sandys, Southampton, and the Ferrars represented the interests of smaller investors and aristocratic patrons, who, as Wesley F. Craven noted, "added Virginia to the patronage of men of letters, to the support of charities, and to their social activities as one more object for the devotion of their wealth and leisure" (*The Dissolution of the Virginia Company*, 27, 42). These investors eagerly explored the possibilities of new industries in Virginia, made the evangelization of the natives an urgent priority, demanded a careful examination of the company's accounts, and promoted a wholesale increase in the number of laborers, servants, wives, and ministers sent to Virginia.

Historical accounts of the final years of the Virginia Company, before its dissolution in 1624, have differed strikingly. Whig historians such as Edward D. Neill in *History of the Virginia Company of London* and Alexander Brown in *The Genesis of the United States* viewed the Sandys-Southampton faction as a force for democratic government and Puritan religion in Virginia, which King James and his followers rejected (Malcolm, "Hobbes, Sandys, and the Virginia Company," 307). In his influential *Dissolution of the Virginia Company*, however, Craven argued that individual economic interests, rather than political differences, underlay the disputes between the company's three factions—headed, respectively, by Smith and the Alderman Robert Johnson; Sandys and Southampton; and the Earl of Warwick and Sir Nathaniel Rich (24 ff.). For Craven, whose analysis of the Virginia Company begins with the charges of Sandys's opponents, the colony's government after 1619 was an unrelenting disaster. Recently, David Ransome, Karen Ordahl Kupperman, and other scholars have contested Craven's history of the company, arguing that the Sandys-Southampton administration was more provident and the last years of the Virginia Company more positive than Craven allowed. According to this view, Sandys, Southampton, and the Ferrars, inspired by missionary zeal and nationalistic motives, commenced the first stage of the "Great Migration" to North America in 1619, which proceeded steadily until reports of the "Great Massacre" and the storm over the company's tobacco contract doomed the venture (Kupperman, "The Founding Years of Virginia," 105–06; Ransome, "Wives for Virginia," 3–18; Ransome, "'Shipt for Virginia,'" 443–58).

Clearly, George Herbert's family members and allies were deeply involved in the affairs of the Virginia Company. Apart from Danvers, the Ferrars, and Woodnoth, Herbert's patrons and family allies in the company included: William Herbert,

Earl of Pembroke; Ludowick Stuart, Duke of Lennox and Richmond; James Hamilton, Marquis of Hamilton; John Williams, Bishop of Lincoln; Sir Francis Bacon; Sir Edward Herbert, his cousin, the attorney-general; Sir Robert Harley; Sir George More; Sir Herbert Croft; Sir Walter Chute; Sir Francis Wolley; and, of course, the Dean of St. Paul's, John Donne. In 1609, Donne sought the post of secretary to the Governor of the Virginia colony, Sir Thomas Gates, and though his suit failed he was later admitted as a member (Bald, *John Donne: A Life*, 162). In late October 1622, Sir John Danvers, Sir Philip Cary, Mr. Bing, and Nicholas Ferrar were delegated to invite Donne to preach a sermon to the company, and on 6 November, Danvers reported that "the Deanes Answeare was verie fauourable and respectiue of the Companie" (Kingsbury, ed., *The Record*, 2: 114, 119). Donne delivered the sermon on 13 November 1622, at St. Michael's Church, Cornhill, to an audience of some 300 members. His passionate missionary sermon lauded the efforts of Sandys and the Ferrars to evangelize the Powhatans: "You shall have made this *Iland*, which is but as the *Suburbs* of the old world, a Bridge, a Gallery to the new; to ioyne all to that world that shall never grow old, the Kingdome of heaven" (*Sermons*, 4: 280-81).[2]

Since the colonization of Virginia went through several stages and the Virginia Company several administrations during George Herbert's lifetime, it is important to know as precisely as possible when "The Church Militant" was written. As is the case with so much of George Herbert's English poetry, "The Church Militant" has not been dated with exactness and critics have found few definitive clues in the poem's topical allusions. Herbert's editor, F. E. Hutchinson, posited that the poem was written before 1624. Hutchinson made this judgment based on three pieces of evidence: the poem's references to France and Spain, which suggested that "Herbert was at work upon it before Prince Charles exchanged the hope of a Spanish for a French betrothal"; the allusions to the evangelism of America, which fit with "the projects of Ferrar and other members of the Virginia Company"; and the poem's "anti-Roman animus," which, he said was "characteristic of Herbert's early and more controversial mind" (*Works*, 543).

Although Hutchinson stated a definite and reasonal *terminus ad quem* for "The Church Militant"—that it was written before 1624, when all hope for the Spanish Match was lost and when the Virginia Company was dissolved—he did not specify a *terminus a quo* (or first possible date) for the poem. Thus, Ted-Larry Pebworth refers to Hutchinson's dating of the poem in "the early 1620s" (Wilcox and Todd, eds., *George Herbert: Sacred and Profane*, 145), and Amy Charles cites Hutchinson in proposing that "The Church-Militant" was probably written before 1618 or at least before 1619 (*Williams Manuscript*, xxi). What, then, is the first possible date for the composition of the poem?

Study of the Virginia Company migrations suggests that "Religion" was "tip-toe . . ./Readie to passe to the *American* strand" at only one brief period in the company's history: from the spring of 1619 through the summer of 1622. While I cannot establish definitively a date for the poem—any more than could Hutchinson, Pebworth, or Charles—I suggest that Herbert's family involvement in the Virginia Company strongly recommends these dates, between the commencement of the Sandys-Southampton migrations to the Chesapeake in 1619 and before the news of the "Great Massacre" brought a storm of criticism in the late summer of 1622 and the Virginia Company lurched toward its inevitable dissolution. The date of the poem itself is not as significant as its brave espousal—whatever the cost—of the missionary ethic of Sandys and Danvers's faction of the company.

Although "the conversion and reduccion of the [native] people in those partes unto the true worshipp of God and Christian religion" was a clearly stated goal of the Virginia

Company's Charters of 1606, 1609 and 1612, the goal was far from realized during Sir Thomas Smith's administration (Bemiss, ed., *The Three Charters*, 54). Smith's experience as a merchant and investor—as a leading figure in the Haberdashers and Skinners Companies, the Governor of the Muscovy Company, and Governor of the East India Company—encouraged him to consider Virginia foremost as another mercantile venture. Likewise, "the merchants who followed Smith's leadership regarded Virginia as merely one other of their numerous commercial ventures" (Craven, *The Dissolution*, 25–26). The great struggles of the first colonists, first to survive on the American coast, and second to return profits to the company, also discouraged Smith's administration from undertaking large migrations and ambitious missionary efforts. One of the first and most energetic of Virginia ministers, Rev. Alexander Whitaker in *Good Newes from Virginia*, urged others to join him in 1613, "since his haruest heere is great, but *the labourers few*" (44, my emphasis). In fact, one of the Sandys faction's central complaints about Smith's administration of the company was that after 12 years of his government there were only "Three Ministers in orders, & Two wthout" in Virginia (Kingsbury, ed., *The Records*, 4: 321). In his stinging indictment entitled *Sir Thomas Smith's Misgovernment of the Virginia Company*, Nicholas Ferrar scornfully cited Smith's alleged statement of 1622, that, "as for the convertinge of ye Infidells it was a thinge impossible they being ye Cursed race of Cham" (12).

While the mission to the Chesapeake tribes certainly began under Smith through the efforts of Whitaker and others, that mission did not advance far until 1616. It was in June of that year that England welcomed North America's most famous convert to Christianity, the Indian princess Matoaka, better known as Pocahontas, now baptized Rebecca and married to John Rolfe. The company allowed her the ample sum of £4 per week for her maintenance, her portrait was taken by

Simon von de Passe, and she had an audience at Whitehall with King James. In all, the Virginia Company made an allowance of more than £150 to Mrs. Rolfe to assist in the conversion of natives to Christianity (Ransome, "Pocahontas," 87). The support of Matoaka indicated the company's "eagerness to convert the native inhabitants of Virginia to Christianity" (88), and it gave a princess's face to its missionary enterprise. The Rolfes' visit was funded by a missionary collection in local parishes, which was authorized by James I for the building of churches and a college for native children in Virginia. In a warrant dated 10 March 1617, Sandys, who was at the center of the effort, expressed the company's hope that the Rolfes would "imploy their best endevours to the winning of that People to the knowledge of God" and would "set forward the buisines of building a Colledg in Virginia for the trayneing up of those heathen Children in true religion" (Ransome, ed., *Ferrar Papers*, Reel 1, No. 72).

During the Sandys-Southampton administration, efforts to evangelize the Indians were intensified through the transport of clergy, the building of churches, and the promotion of the college at Henrico. Perry Miller wrote that "Sandys inspired a sort of religious revival" ("The Religious Impulse," 507), but it would be more accurate to say that Sandys and his followers gave prominence to the original missionary goal of the company. On 17 May 1620, the counsel of the company declared that:

> in euery Burrough there be prouided and placed at the least one godly and learned Minister, to be chosen in each particular *Plantation*, by the seuerall Aduenturers and Planters; And for the foure ancient *Burroughs*, to be prouided and nominated by vs, and our Successors. (Kingsbury, ed., *The Records*, 3: 276)

Private plantations like Martin's Hundred were allowed to choose their own clergy, but the Counsel approved ministers for the boroughs of James City (Jamestown), Henrico, Charles

City, and Elizabeth City, as well as for the college. During the Sandys and Southampton years, "there were sent more then eight able Ministers" to Virginia alone (4: 522). Ministers sent to both Virginia and Bermuda between 1618 and 1624 included: Rev. Mr. Barnard, Rev. William Bennett, Rev. Richard Bolton, Rev. Mr. Hopkins, Rev. Robert Paulett, Rev. Greville Pooley, Rev. Robert Staples, Rev. Mr. Starkey, Rev. Mr. Stockton, Rev. Thomas White, and Rev. Hant Wyatt. (3: 76, 401, 485; 4: 119, 402; Ransome, "Shipt for Virginia," 451–52)

As well as sending clergy, the leaders of the company also transported religious books, liturgical vessels, and other supplies for churches, for which they solicited contributions. On 20 July 1619, "towe [i.e., two] great church bibles" and two copies of *The Book of Common Prayer* were donated, probably for the college in Henrico. At about the same time, an anonymous donor contributed a communion set with a velvet "carpet" and a linen tablecloth for the college (Ransome, "Shipt for Virginia," 453; Kingsbury, ed., *The Records*, 1: 247–48). In outfitting the Virginian voyages, the Deputy John Ferrar considered the spiritual as well as the material needs of the colony. A bill submitted to Deputy Ferrar in 1620 shows that he purchased 126 religious books for the company, including Bibles, psalters, 50 catechisms, a "servis book larg," and various books of pratical piety ("Shipt for Virginia," 455–56).

The mission to the natives also benefitted from the charitable donations between 1619 and 1622. A few notable examples illustrate the public support for the Virginian mission: upon his death in 1619, Nicholas Ferrar, Sr., bequeathed £300 to the company for the college in Henrico; upon his death in 1621, the preacher Mr. Bargrave gave his library, valued at 100 marks, to the college; in the autumn of 1621, members of the East India Company, persuaded by the Rev. Patrick Copland, contributed £125 toward the construction of a free school for children in Charles City; in November of 1621, a donor contributed 40 shillings for a sermon to be preached to the company; in January of 1622, another benefactor gave "a large Church Bible, the Comon prayer booke, Vrsinus Catichisme and a smale Bible richly imbroydered" to the college; and upon his death in 1622, George Ruggle bequeathed £100 to the college.[3] In the early 1620s, "Religion" was standing up expectantly in the Virginia Company and proceeding forward toward America more eagerly than it would for at least a decade.

The missionary efforts of Sandys and his followers found their last and most eloquent expression in Donne's sermon of November 1622. As attempts to evangelize the natives were already being questioned and curtailed, Donne admonished the company to continue its Godly mission: "O, if you would be as ready to hearken at the returne of a *Ship*, how many *Indians* were converted to *Christ Iesus*, as what Trees, or druggs, or Dyes that Ship had brought, then you were in your right way, and not till then" (*Sermons*, 4: 269). After the Indian uprising of 1622, the Virginia colonists' attitude toward the native inhabitants had shifted abruptly, from "Save the Infidels" to "Exterminate the Brutes." Then, proposing a campaign of burn and pursue, the secretary of the Virginia Company, Edward Waterhouse, hoped that "their [the natives'] ruine or subjection [may] be soone effected" (*A Declaration of the State of the Colony in Virginia*, 24).

Inasmuch as the Church of England represented both its ministers and its people, one could not say that it was "on tiptoe in our land,/Readie to passe to the *American* strand" until at least 1619. There were only about 400 colonists in Virginia in 1618 before the waves of new emigration began. The plantation had been on the brink of financial collapse and depopulation before its charter was reformed in 1618, giving colonists the rights to "hold land, trade independently, and participate in government" (Perry, *The Formation of a Society*, 17–19). Sandys, who helped engineer these reforms, was then elected treasurer in April of 1619, and John Ferrar was elected deputy, the new leaders giving "a new impetus to the peopling of Virginia" (Ransome, "Shipt for Virginia," 445). Between 1619 and 1624, some 4,000 immigrants arrived in Virginia, the bulk of them coming in the years 1620–1622. In fact, the population of the colony had increased to nearly 2,000 by the end of 1621 (Craven, *The Dissolution*, 96; Kingsbury, ed., *The Records*, 4: 520). In their defense against the charges of Smith's faction, Sandys and his followers declared that "wth a Third part of the mony, and in a fourth part of ye tyme, wee brought the Plantation to . . . four tymes the nomber of Men that Sr Thomas Smith lefte it in, and in all other parts in comparably better" (Kingsbury, ed., 4: 524). No longer simply a corporation of hired laborers under the direction of the company's officials, Virginia emerged under Sandys's wing as a fledgling colony with its own institutions and culture.

Not only did members of the Sandys faction encourage the emigration, but they also emigrated themselves. The best known examples are Sir Edwin Sandys's brother George and niece Cecily Bray, who both arrived in Virginia in 1621; the Ferrars' brother William, who traveled with Sir George Yeardley in early 1619 but died soon after; and the Ferrars' cousin William, who arrived in 1618.[1] Futhermore, George Herbert also had family relations and friends on the voyages. From Sir John Danvers's letter in July 1620 to his stepson Edward, then the English Ambassador to France, one can establish that Danvers played an important role in outfitting and recruiting the Virginian voyages.

Danvers's entire letter of 27 July 1620, which is preserved in the Public Record Office, is dedicated to his attempt to procure French wine dressers, silkworm experts, and silkworm "seeds" for the Virginia Company's voyages in the autumn of the year. The tone of the letter is urgent, ending with the wish that "the same hast[e] I haue written in will cause this beare[r] noe long date in comming." The letter also indicates Danvers's willingness to expend his own resources and to call on his own family members for the success of the voyages. He wrote of ships that were soon to embark:

> Ships being setting out about those times & a frend of Mine an Extraordinary worthy honest man goes in the first shipp thither & there means to reside as thire Com[m]ander in that State[.] in the second goes some other worthy men as Captaine Chester a great sea Captaine & a brother of S[r] John Brow[n] w[th] divers of my acquaintance. wee shall send allsoe in October. Soe that noe time betweene this & that will be amiss. you may assure they shall be vsed very well & whatsoever you please to promise or dispurse for their wages[,] entertainment, or for their voyage hither shall be duly performed & discharged according as your Letters shall direct though it be to double their vsuall wages. . . . I have sent you herein inclosed a Letter (fro[m] one [who] serves me as butler) unto his father who is a greate Nourisher of Silk wormes & skilld about Choice of Vine Plants. Who I presume will be induced to offer to doe you service heerin, and I have sent you books & such declarations as wee give abroad whereby you may discover our hopes & somewhat perceaue you may doe an acceptable pleasure to many & alsoe assist to soe glorious a worke. (PRO 30/53/3)[5]

From the letter, one detects Danvers's nationalistic pride in the company's ventures—"soe glorious a worke"—and also his willingness to call on his stepsons, servants, and acquaintances in equipping and staffing the voyages. The Sir John Brown that Danvers mentions was George Herbert's brother-in-law, the husband of his sister Frances, and a close friend to Danvers. Later, Brown named Danvers the godfather of his "sonn & Heire," and upon Danvers's advice sent his young son to Little Gidding for schooling in 1631 (Ransome, ed., *The Ferrar Papers*, Reel 4, No. 821). The "frend of Mine," that Danvers spoke of, who "there means to reside as thire Com-[m]ander in that State" was almost certainly Captain Thomas Nuce, who had been appointed deputy to the governor for the company's common lands in May 1620. Upon Nuce's death in 1623, Danvers would appeal to the council to aid Nuce's widow (Craven, *The Dissolution*, 165; Kingsbury, ed., *The Records*, 1: 349; 2: 457, 466).

The energetic tone of Danvers's letter to Edward Herbert is also important, insofar as it expresses his optimism that the Virginian emigration would result in "so glorious a worke." Amy M. Charles asserted that "The Church Militant" was probably written before the Sandys administration, since. . . .

> The difficulties and the declining fortunes of the Virginia Company between 1618 and 1624, when the dissolution occurred, would scarcely encourage any steady hope, and Herbert could hardly have escaped knowing of the great disappointment his stepfather . . . shared during these years with numerous other members of the company to whom the colony represented in significant measure an effort to spread religion (*The Williams Manuscript*, xxi)

Here, Charles's reasoning—that Herbert would not write, "Religion stands on tip-toe in our land" when the company's religious mission was failing—is sound, but her chronology is mistaken. For one, Danvers's letter in July 1620 suggests that his hopes were still buoyant for all facets of the colonization.[6]

Danvers, like Sandys and the Ferrars, maintained his hopes for the religious mission at least until the news of the Indian uprising of 1622 forced an abrupt change in policy. During Sandys's administration, Danvers worked on many of the company's most contentious and taxing committees—including the committee for auditing Sir Thomas Smith's accounts, the committee for censuring Alderman Johnson, the committee for drawing up a tobacco contract, and the committee for establishing the college—and he attended the frequent council meetings at the Ferrars' house on St. Sithe's Lane. Yet he remained hopeful about the venture until the company's last days. Like Sandys and the Ferrars, Danvers anticipated that the arrival of wives in Virginia would make the Colony more stable and prosperous, and he subscribed 16 pounds for the transport of young women in the *Marmaduke, Warwick,* and *Tiger* in 1621 (Ransome, "Wives for Virginia," 8).

Danvers also, along with Sandys and the Ferrars, hoped to profit from a tobacco monopoly granted to the company, and he spoke to Buckingham "att Theobalds concerning Virginia busines" early in 1620 with such profits in mind. His surviving letter, to George Villiers on 2 February 1619/1620, begged the patronage of Buckingham and the King that he be "admitted an vndertaker" in "the Customs of Virginia" (Bodleian Library, Ms. Add. D 110, fol. 237r). That project of the tobacco contract did not fail utterly until the company met with King James and the Privy Council in April of 1623. Then, the fate of the Virginia Company itself was sealed and Danvers was bitterly disappointed.[7]

The great expectations for the Virginia colony in the early 1620s were epitomized by the Reverend Patrick Copland, who in his sermon *Virginia's God Be Thanked* depicted the colonists building a new society like a busy hive of bees. He imagined the colony as it buzzed with industry in March 1621:

> Seing, I say, that now all former difficulties (which much hindered the progresse of your noble Plantation) are removed, and in a maner ouercome: And that your people in your Colony (through Gods mercy) were all in good health, euery one busied in their Vocations, as Bees in their Hiues, at the setting sayle of your Ship the *Concord* from *Virginia* in March last. O what miracles are these? (10)

Similarly, Arthur Woodnoth, in a tract dedicated to Danvers, presented the progress of the Sandys-Southampton administration as extraordinarily hopeful in the early 1620s. He boasted:

> And now was likewise so great a complyance in this pious work, and moneys came in so plentifully . . ., as seemed almost to

> promise as well as to invite a great part of the Nation to with-
> draw themselves from an oppressing unto a more free govern-
> ment establishing in *Virginia*; whither great store of shipping was
> engaged and even in readinesse. . . . (*A Short Collection*, 8–9).

Even Wesley F. Craven, who discounted Woodnoth's tract and
took a bleak view of the last years of the company, acknowledged that the "leaders in the colony seem to have been more
optimistic during the winter of 1621–1622 than at any time
before" (*The Dissolution*, 195).

The date of "The Church Militant" and its relation to the
Virginia Company are important not simply as notations in a
chronology. They signal a crux in George Herbert's career, the
point at which he took his first tiptoe step toward the ministry. To Herbert, as to the Ferrars, Woodnoth, and Danvers, the
mission to the New World became a lifelong concern. George
Herbert, until his death, preserved a measure of hope for the
mission to America, including "The Church Militant" in the
Bodleian manuscript of *The Temple*, and mentioning the "new
Plantations" in *The Country Parson*. He asked: "But if the
young Gallant think these Courses dull . . ., where can he busie
himself better, then in those new Plantations, and discoveryes,
which are not only a noble, but also as they may be handled, a
religious imployment?" (*Works*, 278).

In fact, Herbert's decision to include the long apocalyptic
poem in the Bodleian manuscript very well may have reflected
the efforts of Danvers and the Ferrars to revive the Virginia
Company in the early 1630s. In a letter dated 24 May 1631, apparently at the behest of the King, the Earl of Dorset requested
that Attorney General Heath prepare a bill appointing Danvers, Nicholas and John Ferrar, and others to a commission
"for advising upon some course for establishing the advancement of the plantation of Virginia." On 25 November 1631,
Danvers and other commissioners met and "thought fit to
proceed upon the digest of a new patent for re-establishing a
Company." King Charles and his Privy Council, however,

decided otherwise, concluding that the formation of a company would be damaging to the King's interests (Saintsbury, ed., *Calendar of State Papers, Colonial Series, 1574–1660,* 130, 136).[8]

Likewise, Nicholas Ferrar's insistence to the Vice-Chancellor of Cambridge in 1633 that he must allow "The Church Militant" to be printed with the tiptoe couplet suggested Ferrar's own continuing passion for the evangelization of America. Concerning his brother Nicholas, John Ferrar cited Patrick Copland's speculation that "NF [Nicholas Ferrar] would in ye end leave all ye old world & go to Virginia in ye New world & employ those excellent rare gifts y^t God had given him" (*A Life of Nicholas Ferrar,* 61). Likewise, Woodnoth and Danvers also maintained longtime interests in the New World, especially Bermuda. Woodnoth served as the deputy governor of the Somers Island Company in 1644, and Danvers served as its governor in 1651. After attending a meeting of the company at Danvers's Chelsea House in July 1651, the poet George Wither wrote to him: "I need not illustrate this [the significance of the colonies] unto you, nor have I written to provoke you to those prosecutions, which may conduce to the well being of the *Sommer Islands* or *Virginia;* for you have sufficiently testified many ways your zeal therein" (Danvers, *Copy of a Humble Petition,* 27).

What makes "The Church Militant" an extraordinary poem is not its topicality, or its grand historical view, or even its apocalyptic conclusion, since George Herbert wrote other poems with those features. Ted-Larry Pebworth notes the common apocalyptic argument in "The Church Militant" and the two poems to Elizabeth Stuart, Queen of Bohemia, which were apparently written some time between 1621 and 1622 ("George Herbert's Poems," 113). The eschatological argument and dark tone of "The Church Militant" also appear in Herbert's Latin progress poems, "Triumphus Mortis" and

"Triumphus Christiani," written between 1618 and 1623 (Hovey, "'Inventa Bellica,'" 276). Rather, what makes "The Church Militant" an extraordinary, albeit conflicted, poem is its sudden, unexpected step forward, away from Stuart courtly politics toward a more autonomous view of the church and the life of the individual Christian. It is a poem that begins as a paean to the English church and monarch, but turns to intense fear and an appalling prophecy of the decline of religion in England. It is a poem, in short, that reflects George Herbert's willingness to withdraw from his career at court, if necessary, in order to satisfy his religious vocation.

In his courtly poems of the early 1620s—the poems to the Queen of Bohemia, "Triumphus Mortis," and other Latin poems to the King in *Musae Responsoriae* and *Lucus*—George Herbert conjoined the English church and crown. Very much in this vein, he wrote to Danvers in October 1619 about his hopes for the office of Cambridge University Orator: "This dignity, hath no such earthiness in it, but it may very well be joined with Heaven" (*Works*, 370). In "George Herbert's Apocalypticism," Pebworth reads "The Church Militant" as another example of the "doubleness of his [Herbert's] thought—his constant consciousness of the interplay of the sacred and the profane—and its unity in a vision that collapses such distinctions together" (Wilcox and Todd, eds., *George Herbert: Sacred and Profane*, 150). Pebworth is referring not only to Herbert's apocalyptic poems, but also to his religio-political commentaries such as "The British Church." "The Church Militant" certainly begins with this double vision of God and king, but the poem abruptly diverges from it in the tiptoe couplet, turning away from praise of the English church to a dire prophecy of its decline.

"The Church Militant" opens with a praise of God's providence that sounds, by no coincidence, very much like the praise of a sovereign king. The speaker prays to his all-powerful lord:

> Almightie Lord, who from thy glorious throne
> Seest and rulest all things ev'n as one:
> The smallest ant or atome knows thy power,
> Known also to each minute of an houre:
> Much more do Common-weals acknowledge thee,
> And wrap their policies in thy decree,
> Complying with thy counsels, doing nought
> Which doth not meet with an eternall thought.
> But above all, thy Church and Spouse doth prove
> Not the decrees of power, but bands of love.
>
> (Works, 190, ll. 1–10)

This praise of God's omniscience and "decrees of power" over creatures and commonwealths, which is only exceeded by his "bands of love" for his Church, might equally be addressed to an earthly sovereign, such as James I. Schoenfeldt cites this passage in suggesting that God's divine examination of the speaker in *The Temple* is very much like that of the Stuart monarch's surveillance of his subjects (*Prayer and Power*, 135–36). Herbert had, after all, praised King James in very similar terms in poems like "Ad Regem":

> Since thousands of matters ever beset your mind,
>   And the world depends upon your power. . . .
>
> (Works, 385, ll. 1–2; my translation)

Hence, the refrain repeated throughout "The Church Militant," "*How deare to me, O God, thy counsels are!/Who may with thee compare?*" (191, ll. 47–48.) is not so simple a rhetorical question as one might suppose. For better or worse, the King's *arcana imperii*, his politic designs and secret counsels, did in ways compare to God's providence. Noting that "Herbert's sweeping assertion [about commonwealths] . . . does not accord with the actual sordidness found throughout the history of power politics," Raymond A. Anselment describes the opening of the poem as highly ironic ("George Herbert and the Metamorphoses," 302). Yet, at this point in the poem, the formal compliment seems entirely genuine: it is not until later that one is struck by the sordidness of human politics.

This concurrence of the language of divine and secular praise in the opening of "The Church Militant" was a staple of Stuart royal encomia. And the poem's satire of the Roman church and the Pope, and its praise of the English church were commonplaces of Jacobean courtly literature. The ever-westward movement of the gospel in "The Church Militant" seems to find its *ne plus ultra*, its outermost boundary, in England. The poet writes of how the English church and crown has surpassed Europe's Holy Roman Empire:

> *Spain* in the Empire shar'd with *Germanie*,
> But *England* in the higher victorie:
> Giving the Church a crown to keep her state,
> And not go lesse then she had done of late.
> *Constantines* British line meant this of old,
> And did this mysterie wrap up and fold
> Within a sheet of paper, which was rent
> From times great Chronicle, and hither sent.
> Thus both the Church and Sunne together ran
> Unto the farthest old meridian.
>
> (*Works*, 192, ll. 89–98)

Here, the speaker trumps up the familiar political mythology of Constantine's British birth and his legendary donation of Roman lands and temporal powers to the Church. The church and throne of England are, thus far in the poem, the farthest ambit of spiritual and temporal power.

The next major movement of the poem, in which the speaker describes Sin's dogged pursuit of Religion westward, also reiterates Stuart political propaganda.[9] The brunt of this description is to savage the Pope as a pious and self-indulgent fraud:

> Sinne being not able to extirpate quite
> The Churches here, bravely resolv'd one night

To be a Church-man too, and wear a Mitre:
The old debauched ruffian would turn writer.
I saw him in his studie, where he sate
Busie in controversies sprung of late.
A gown and pen became him wondrous well:
His grave aspect had more of heav'n then hell:
Onely there was a handsome picture by,
To which he lent a corner of his eye. . . .
So now being Priest he plainly did professe
To make a jest of Christs three offices. . . .

       *   *   *   *

And having conquer'd, did so strangely rule,
That the whole world did seem but the Popes mule.
As new and old *Rome* did one Empire twist;
So both together are one Antichrist.
            (*Works*, 194–96, ll. 161–70, 173–74, 203–06)

Notwithstanding its precedents in Luther, this sniggering portrait of the Pope as a dilettantish theologian and Antichrist is a political hatchet job. One might be surprised to find such a crude polemical caricature in George Herbert's poetry—that is, unless one had read his Latin poetry. In "Papae Titulus," he mocked Urban VIII's pretensions as a poet and he again allied the Pope with the Antichrist:

Who the Antichrist is we can stop asking: the Pope
  Is neither God nor Man: Christ was both.
            (*Works*, ll. 1–2, my translation)

Equating Rome with Babylon and the Pope with the Antichrist was only too common in Reformation apologetics, and almost *de rigueur* in Jacobean England. Nicholas Ferrar himself, when confronted with charges of papacy, protested, "I as verily believe the Pope to be Antichrist as any article in my faith" (qtd. in Gardiner, *History of England*, 7: 264). Herbert's antipapal caricature, intended to show his patriotic allegiance to the Church of England, was therefore an extremely common, almost trite, form of political propaganda.

In its predictions of human degeneration, of the persecution of the true church, and of the rise of an Antichrist and false church, "The Church Militant" was reworking some of King James's favorite polemical materials. As James VI of Scotland, he had written *A Fruitfull Meditation* upon the twentieth chapter of the Book of Revelation and had made the same predictions. Both Herbert and King James saw the Protestant church as necessarily militant, in a state of siege. James wrote:

> There shall arise an Antichrist and enemie to God and his Church: hee shall bee head of a false and hypocriticall church: hee shall claime a supreme power in earth: he shall vsurpe the power of God: he shall deceiue men with abusing locusts: he shall persecute the faithfull: none shall bee found that dare openly resist him: In the end, feeling his kingdome decay, and the trew Church beginning to prosper, he shall by a new sort of deceiuing spirits, gather together the Kings of the earth in great multitudes like the sands of the Sea, and by ioyning or at least suffering of that other great open enemy, he shall with these numbers compasse the campes of the faithfull . . . but victorie shal he not haue . . . (qtd. in Tuveson, *Millenium and Utopia*, 53).

King James, like Herbert, viewed the religious wars of Europe as the fulfillment of New Testament prophecy. Yet, while James proclaimed that the Antichrist, his "deceiuing spirits" (the Jesuits), and the other great enemies (Spain and the Hapsburg Empire) would not have victory in Europe, Herbert suggested otherwise in "The Church Militant." To its great credit, the poem does not end with the facile reification of England and the demonization of other churches and rulers. Instead, it takes a dangerous step forward into political criticism.

In the final major movement of the poem, the reader discovers that the English church and state are by no means the *ne plus ultra*: God will draw Empire, the Arts, and Religion

inevitably farther westward to America, and Sin will dominate England, as it has the rest of Europe. The progress of the
one church westward predictably follows the commonplace
idea of the inevitable progress of the arts and of empire. These
rhetorical *topoi* of *translatio imperii* and *translatio studii* were
already well established in the seventeenth century, and were
made even more famous by Bishop George Berkeley in the
eighteenth: "Westward the Course of Empire takes its Way"
(Cochrane, "Bishop Berkeley," 310). Donne also described the
Church as a chariot moving "in that communicable motion,
circularly; It began in the East, it came to us, and is passing
now, shining out now, in the farthest West" (*Sermons*, 6: 173).
Yet, Donne's lines are not nearly so cutting as Herbert's. There
was an almost unspeakable fear expressed in "The Church
Militant," the fear of England's spiritual extinction, which set
the poem apart and inspired Herbert's contemporary reputation as a prophet.

In the conclusion of the poem, Herbert inverted the worn
antipapist rhetoric of the Antichrist into a potent challenge
to the English church and monarch.

> Religion stands on tip-toe in our land,
> Readie to passe to the *American* strand.
> When height of malice, and prodigious lusts,
> Impudent sinning, witchcrafts, and distrusts
> (The marks of future bane) shall fill our cup
> Unto the brimme, and make our measure up;
> When *Sein* shall swallow *Tiber*, and the *Thames*
> By letting in them both pollutes her streams:
> When *Italie* of us shall have her will,
> And all her calender of sinnes fulfill;
> Whereby one may foretell, what sinnes next yeare
> Shall both in *France* and *England* domineer:
> Then shall Religion to *America* flee:
> They have their times of Gospel, ev'n as we.
>
> (*Works*, 196–97, ll. 235–48)

The prophecy that succeeds the famous couplet is of nothing less than the ruin of English religion: the spread of papacy through France to England, the accompanying spiritual desolation of the nation, and true religion's abandonment of England altogether. Unlike the poems to Elizabeth of Bohemia, this apocalyptic argument was a chilling reproach to the Stuart church and state.

If Stephen Greenblatt is right that atheism in this period was "almost always thinkable only as the thought of another" and was "one of the characteristic marks of otherness" (Dollimore and Sinfield, eds., *Political Shakespeare*, 19), then Herbert's poem was deeply subversive. At this time, only a radical poem would prophesy the transformation of the English church into its demonic other, the Whore of Babylon. The "prodigious lusts,/Impudent sinning, witchcrafts, and distrusts" (197, ll. 237–38) that the poem predicts are the products of spiritual exhaustion and atheism, and perhaps it is notable that Herbert's country parson expected to find papists and atheists in his rural parish (*Works*, 282). Shunting aside the stock royalist and nationalist rhetoric, "The Church Militant" firmly predicts God's utter abandonment of England's national church. Unlike the fiery tone of separatist diatribes against the English church, Herbert's tone is deliberately cold-blooded, bespeaking fear and bitter disillusionment rather than revolutionary fervor.

This fear, which Thomas Fuller called the "Feare of Losing the Old Light," was prevalent throughout the seventeenth century, especially in the turbulent years of the civil wars and the commonwealth. Since Fuller was a close friend of Danvers and an admirer of George Herbert, his sermon preached at Exeter in 1646 seems an apt commentary on many of Herbert's lines.[10] Like Herbert, Fuller understood the westward course of the church as an eschatological certainty, based on his interpretation of the Book of Revelation. As the scriptural sources of his belief, Fuller cites Revelation 2.5 (an admonition to the Church of Ephesus to repent or lose the "Candlestick" of the Gospel) and Revelation 6.2 (the victorious progress of the White Horse of the Christian Church). According to Fuller, the movement of the White Horse is "a Progressive . . . motion, like the Sun in the Firmament," and the Candlestick "is observed to have a favourable inclination to verge more and more Westward. This putteth us in some hopes of America" (*Feare of Losing the Old Light*, 10, 12). The dark side of this hope was the fear that England, like the Church of Ephesus, would lose its own Christian religion, never to regain it: "wee hitherto cannot finde a Countrey, from which the Gospel did totally depart, to which it ever afterwards returned" (10).

Like Herbert, Fuller feared that England would lose the gospel by making the foolish bargain of its faith for colonial profits in America. In fact, Fuller in *Feare of Losing the Old Light* and Herbert in "The Church Militant" expressed this fear with the same mercantile metaphor:

> Onely God forbid we should make so bad a bargaine, as wholly to exchange our Gospel for their Gold, our Saviour for their Silver, fetch thence *lignum Vitae*, and deprive our selves of the *Tree of life* in liew thereof. (*Feare*, 13)

> My God, thou dost prepare for them a way
> By carrying first their gold from them away . . .
> We think we rob them, but we think amisse:
> We are more poore, and they more rich by this.
> Thou wilt revenge their quarrell, making grace
> To pay our debts, and leave her ancient place
> To go to them, while that which now their nation
> But lends to us, shall be our desolation.
>
> (*Works*, 197, ll. 249–50, 253–58)

If the comparison between Fuller and Herbert illustrates their common scriptural sources and apocalyptic imagery of light and darkness, it also delimits the deep pessimism of "The

Church Militant." Fuller merely acknowledged the public fear of "losing the old light"; Herbert took England's loss of faith as a foregone conclusion. Fuller prayed for a public repentance and renewal of the English church; Herbert prayed for the Son to come in judgment and consummate the church's westward circuit. Fuller wished to avert the end, Herbert to summon it. Sin's conquests were, as Herbert said in "L'Envoy," "dayly spread[ing]" (199, l. 8), casting Europe in darkness and hastening the Day of Judgment.

The prophetic conclusion of "The Church Militant" is all the more surprising, given its place in Herbert's career. The likely date of the poem puts it in the midst of Herbert's career as orator at Cambridge, at the same time or soon after he wrote his *Musae Responsoriae* in support of the Jacobean Church, very near the time he was writing Latin epigrams to King James and celebrating the British peace as god-sent (in "In pacem Britannicam"), and before he addressed Latin orations to the Hapsburg ambassadors in February of 1623, to King James in March of 1623, and to Prince Charles in October of 1623. In other words, in the midst of his manifold efforts at ceremonial flattery and in a poem that begins with such politic rhetoric, George Herbert expressed doubts about whether the "dignity"of political office might "be joined with Heaven." Or, as he protested in "Submission": "Perhaps great places and thy praise/Do not so well agree" (95, ll. 15–16). It is little wonder that, while Herbert circulated other Latin and English courtly poems, he held tightly onto "The Church Militant" until his death. It is also little wonder that he entrusted the manuscript of the poem, with the rest of the *Temple* manuscript, to John Danvers's friends Nicholas Ferrar and Arthur Woodnoth. Through their experiences with the Virginia Company, they too expressed a passion for the mission to America, and they too concluded their careers with pessimism about worldly government.

There was no single event which determined Herbert's retreat to the rural parish of Bemerton in 1630. Walton suggested that the deaths of Herbert's courtly patrons—the Duke of Lennox and the Marquis of Hamilton in 1624, and King James in 1625—ended Herbert's "court hopes" (*The Lives*, 276). Joseph Summers and Amy Charles also mentioned Herbert's oration to Prince Charles in October 1623, the dissolution of the Virginia Company in 1624, and Edward Herbert's recall as French Ambassador in 1624 as decisive events in Herbert's departure from court (Summers, *George Herbert*, 39–44; Charles, *A Life*, 104–18). Probably all of these events and others contributed to a decision which Herbert, always struggling over his vocation, made over the course of a decade. Some of the same events also led to Nicholas Ferrar's decision to enter the diaconate and begin his religious community at Little Gidding in 1625. The evidence of "The Church Militant" suggests that even when he was publicly employed as "God's courtier," Herbert questioned whether that service could be sanctified, and whether darkness was not already vitiating the English church and crown.

"Religion" was "on tip-toe" not only for George Herbert, but also for many members of his family and literary coterie, who walked unhappily away from Whitehall in 1624 and 1625. This family connection does not make "The Church Militant"a graceful poem—it will still sound leaden to most readers, whose ears are not tuned to seventeenth century religious polemics. Recognizing the relation betweeen Herbert's career aspirations and the mission of the Virginia Company, however, does make the poem a more fitting appendix to *The Temple*. The domestic struggle with vocation that runs so unmistakably through *The Temple*—from the familial advice of "The Church-porch" to the intimate colloquy of "Love III"—also forms the subtext of "The Church Militant." Inasmuch as it partakes of Herbert's vocational struggles, "The Church Militant" is riven with contradiction: it is a courtly poem that

rejects the court, an idealistic poem that expresses deep pessimism, and a religious monition that voices worldly concerns.
In the end, it is an instance of the human conflict that resounds throughout *The Temple*, counterposing divine aspirations and fleshly needs as delicately as any sacred artwork of
the Renaissance.

Appendix A

Magdalen Herbert's Table Guests

The following list represents John Gorse's entries of guests for "Dinner" and "Supper" (and "Drinking," in lieu of Supper on 11 April) as well as Magdalen Herbert's entries of "the names and nomber of my howshoulde" in her *Kitchin Booke*, 1601. Because of the abbreviated nature of Gorse's entries and the incomplete records of the many Herbert family relatives and servants, this list should be considered a close estimate rather than a precise accounting of persons. One cannot know, for example, whether the four blank entries on 25 June, 3 July, 5 July, and 6 July represent one, two, three, four, or any distinct individuals beyond those already mentioned by name in the book. Again, I am grateful to John Herbert, the Earl of Powis for allowing me to study the *Kitchin Booke* at the National Library of Wales, Aberystwyth, during the summer of 1996.

1.–2. [?] Unnamed guests for supper on 25 June and for dinner on 3 July, 5 July, and 6 July

3. Mr. ap Anton

4. Mr. ap Anton's brother

5. Mr. John Barker

6. Mr. Barker's man

7. Richard Barnett, Serving Man

8. Mr. Bird of Queen's Chapel

9. Mr. John Bithell [?]

10. A Boy that Came with Horses

11. Mrs. Bridges

12. Lady Bromley
13. Lady Bromley's woman
14.–15. Two of Her Own [Lady Bromley's]
16. William Brooke
17. Mrs. Brooke
18. Dr. Bull
19. Dr. Bull's man
20. Mr. [   ] Cooke: guest for supper on 27 June and 28 June
21. Mr. Edward Cooke
22. Mr. Edward Cooke's boy
23. Mr. Edward Cooke's sister
24. Mrs. Francis Cooke
25. Mr. John Cooke
26. Mr. Coxe
27. Mr. Coxe's man
28. Mr. Davies
29. Mr. Deane of Westminster
30.–31. Mr. Deane's Footman/Mr. Deane's Men
32. Mrs. Elizabeth Detten, Gentlewoman
33.–34. Two Strangers that Came unto Mrs. Detten
35. Frances Doughtie, Chambermaid
36. A Dyer that Brought Stockings
37. The Embroiderer/ An Imbroiderer
38. Parson Evans
39. Hugh Fell, one of Wolley's men
40. Mr. Fisher
41. Mr. Fisher's man
42. Mr. Galliger
43. Mr. Greville
44. John Gorse, Steward
45. Mr. Harris
46. Mr. Harris's daughter
47. Mr. Harris's wife
48. Mr. Robert Harley
49. Mr. Harley's man
50. Mr. Harper/Parson Harper
51.–52. A Blinde harper and his boy
53. Henry Heath, Serving Man
54. Mr. Will Heather
55.–56. Two of Mr. Heather's boys
57. Mr. Herbert of [   ]
58. Charles Herbert, Gentleman
59. Footman of Charles Herbert

60. Mr. Edward Herbert, Gentleman

61. Elizabeth Herbert, Gentlewoman

62. Frances Herbert, Gentlewoman

63. George Herbert, Gentleman

64. Henry Herbert, Gentleman

65. Margaret Herbert, Gentlewoman

66. Mrs. Magdalen Herbert

67. Mrs. Mary Herbert, wife to Edward Herbert

68. Mr. Myles Herbert

69. Richard Herbert, Gentleman

70. Thomas Herbert, Gentleman

71. Mr. Walter Herbert

72. William Herbert, Gentleman

73. Edward Heywood, Serving Man

74. Mr. Higgins, the Apothecary

75. Katherine Higgins, Chambermaid

76. Brother to Katherine Higgins

77. Mr. Ireland

78. Mr. Ireland's brother

79. Mr. Jones

80. Mr. Jones's Wife

81. Mr. Jones's man

82. Humphrey Jones, Serving Man

83. Mr. Edward Langley

84. Mr. Vayne Langley

85. Mr. George Lawley

86. Mr. Lawley's man

87. Mr. Thomas Lawley

88. Mrs. Lloyd

89. Mrs. Lloyd's woman

90. Mr. Charles Lloyd

91. Footman/Messenger of Charles Lloyd

92. Mr. Jenkin Lloyd

93. John Lloyd, Mr. Williams's man (cf. 144)

94. Lewys Lloyd

95. Jane Manneringe, Chambermaid

96. Thomas Manneringe, Serving Man

97. Mr. Michell

98. Mr. William Morgan

99. William Morris, Serving Man

100. Mr. Morrice/Captain Morris

101.–102. Two Bayliffs from Monmouthshire

103. Sir Robert Needham

104. Richard Newport

105. Mr. John Nicholles/ Mr. Nicholas

106. Mr. Nichollsonne

107. William Norbury, Serving Man

108. Henry Old

109.–110. Two of Henry Old's friends

111. Mr. Edward ap Olliver

112. Son of Edward ap Olliver

113. Richard ap Olliver

114. Son of Richard ap Olliver

115. Mr. George Owen

116. Mr. George Owen's man Mr. Parrot

117. Mr. Phellisplace/ Captain Fellysplace or Fettisplace

118. Mr. Phillips the Schoolmaster

119. [ ] Powell: guest for dinner on 14 June

120. Mr. Reece Powell

121. A Porter that Came with Coales

122. Mr. Richard Pryce

123.–124. Two of Mr. Pryce's men

125. David Rogers

126. Nurse Rose

127. Nurse Rose's son

128. Mr. Rosse

129. William Rosser

130. Mr. Salter

131. Mr. Shutte/Shute

132. Mrs. Shutte

133. Mr. Smallman/ Smaleman

134. William Speak

135. Mr. Threllwall

136. Mr. Threllwall's Wife

137. Doctor Turner

138.–139. Dr. Turner's Two Men

140. Doctor Turner's Wife

141. Jone Vaughan, Nurse

142. Vickers the Messenger

143. Wamsley the Taylor

144. Frances Warner, Serving Man

145. Mr. Wentworth

146. Mr. Wentworth's man

147. Edward Whittingham, Serving Man

148. Mr. Williams of Newport
149. Mr. Williams's boy
150. Mr. Williams's man
151. Mr. Williams of the Queen's Stable
152. Mr. Henry Williams
153. William Williams
154. William Williams's Bayliff
155. William, the Footman from Montgomery
156. The wynde Instrument maker
157. Mr. Wolley
158. Mr. Wolley's man
159. Mrs. Wolley
160. Mr. Wood the Preacher
161. Mr. Wrentner
162. Mr. Wrentner's man

Appendix B

Henry Herbert's Devotional Writings

Views of Sir Henry Herbert's religious character have been understandably influenced by the attribution to him of two devotional collections of prayers. The first is entitled *The Broken Heart*, which was written in 1621 and survives in a manuscript in the Bodleian Library, and the second is entitled *Herbert's Golden Harpe*, which survives in manuscripts in the Bodleian and Huntington Libraries, and which has been edited and published by Professor Chauncey Wood of McMaster University. Based upon these attributions, Amy M. Charles conceived the young Sir Henry Herbert to be a man with "serious . . . religious interests" ("Sir Henry Herbert," 12); Susan Anne Dawson speaks of "the intensity of faith which must have been a common bond in Henry's circle of family and friend" (*Sir Henry Herbert*, 140); Wood says that "Henry's devotional treatises are not from the head but from the heart, indeed from a broken heart, and from a soul that feels at once the desire for God and the frustration of that desire by postlapsarian disease" (*Herbert's Golden Harpe*, xiv); and N. W. Bawcutt refers to Sir Henry's "strain of genuine and rather melancholy piety," which "befits the brother of George Herbert" (Bawcutt, ed., *The Control and Censorship*, 1). If, indeed, *The Broken Heart* and *Golden Harpe* were written by Sir Henry Herbert, the Master of Revels, these would be reasonable conclusions, but an investigation of the Bodleian and Huntington manuscripts suggests that they very well may have been written by another Henry Herbert.

The case for the authorship of the Bodleian and Huntington has never been made at length, and appears to rest upon tradition and two dubious assumptions: first, that any Henry Herbert writing from 1621–1623 is probably Sir Henry Herbert, George Herbert's brother; and second, that one of the manuscripts is in Sir Henry's hand. Concerning the first point, it should be obvious from the confusions between George's brother the Captain Thomas Herbert, his cousin Sir Thomas Herbert of York, and the versewriter and pamphleteer from Kent named Thomas Herbert, that *Herbert* was an extremely common name in the seventeenth century. Our Sir Henry Herbert, Master of Revels, might be confused with the colonel Sir Henry Herbert, who fought in Holland in the 1620s and 1630s; with Henry, Lord Herbert of Chepstow, son of the Earl of Worcester; with the parliamentarian soldier, Henry Herbert of Coldbrook; and with the many lesser Henry Herberts (Bawcutt, ed., *The Control and Censorship*, 110–11, n. 6).

Second, and more importantly, in spite of Amy M. Charles's assertion that the Bodleian Manuscript of *Herbert's Golden Harpe* is in the hand of Sir Henry, George's brother, none of the three manuscripts offers an example of his distinctively slanted script (see figures 7 and 8). In the summer of 1995, Professor Wood forwarded copies of these three devotional manuscripts along with three known examples of Sir Henry's autograph to Dr. Peter Beal, deputy director of the Department of Printed Books and Manuscripts at Sotheby's. Beal concluded that the three devotional manuscripts are in three different hands, and none of them is Sir Henry's. In his response to Wood on 8 August 1995, Beal went on to ask: "I take it there is no question that this work *IS* by Henry Herbert, brother of the poet George, and not some other Henry Herbert (Herberts are all over the place)?" In fact, what Beal is suggesting seems to be the most probable scenario: that another Henry Herbert is responsible for the three manuscripts.

Not only are none of the three manuscripts in our Sir Henry's hand, but also the manuscript of *The Broken Heart* (MS. Don

f. 26), written in a very minute hand and often corrected, has the distinctive appearance of an autograph (or holograph) manuscript. Indeed, the Bodleian's *Broken Heart* was originally catalogued by Ms. Margaret Crum, who had a lifetime of experience with seventeenth century manuscripts, as an autograph manuscript, and she also concluded that the Bodleian *Golden Harpe* (MS. Don. f. 27) was a copy. The current Bodleian *Summary Catalogue* describes MS. Don. f. 26 as a "Holograph fair copy of devotions of Sir Henry Herbert," and MS. Don f. 27 as a "Contemporary copy in an unidentified hand of devotions of Sir Henry Herbert" (Clapinson and Rogers, eds., 1: 165). Given Dr. Beal's suggestion that another Henry Herbert might well have been the author of the devotions, the Bodleian cataloguers appear to have been correct about every detail of the manuscripts, with the exception of the "Sir" in "Sir Henry Herbert."

Of course, this conclusion about the attribution of these texts does not negate the value of Professor Wood's recent edition of *Herbert's Golden Harpe*, which is a remarkable example of an important seventeenth century devotional genre, no matter who is the author. Nor does it necessarily prove that Sir Henry was any less pious a man. In light of the manuscript evidence, however, the understanding of Sir Henry Herbert's religious beliefs should be based on other, more certain texts.

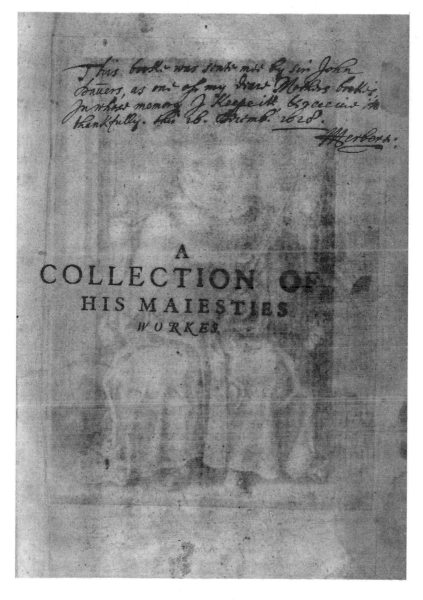

Figure 7

Example of Sir Henry Herbert's handwriting from the title page of
King James I's *Works*, 1616. By permission of the
Houghton Library, Harvard University.

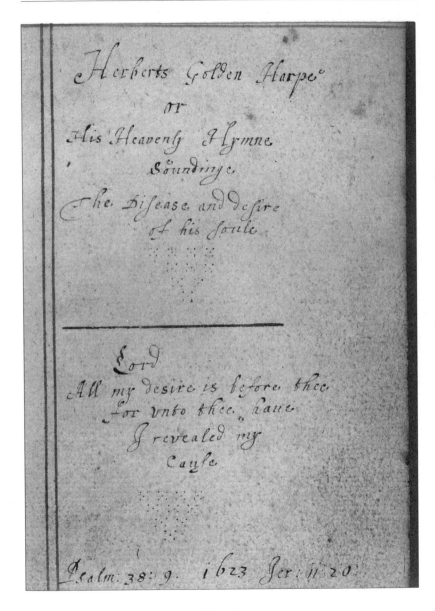

Figure 8

Title page of *Herberts Golden Harpe* (MS. Don f. 27). By permission of
the Bodleian Library, Oxford. The handwriting is clearly not that of
Sir Henry Herbert; compare with figure 7.

Appendix C

Thomas Herbert's "The Storme . . . from Plimmouth"

The Storme . . . from Plimmouth.

Land at
latitude[1]
of 50.20
towards
the
North
Cape in
Spaine.
Rocks
upon the
Coast.

1. Anchor wee wayd North and by East the wind,
    Steerd South and by West; Lye and to Seamen kind,
    hard bishopps, clarks; Sad Scilla left behind.[2]

2. And proudly mounted on the Oceans backe,
    Smile did the canuas, men sung, aboard no lacke,   5
    The foaming seas for ioy did laugh and cracke.[3]

3. So amorous Ioue in maiesty did ride,
    The sea gods, nymphs, faire Venus tend the bride,
    from Asia sporting, now to Europes side.

4. Depressd wee had some foure degrees of Pole,   10
    Sails flappe unto the mast, seas smoth as boule.
    The elements were at truce none did controule.

---

[1] The first line of the marginal note is faint, but it is clear that Herbert is recording his latitude, as he does again at the end of the poem. The ship is southwest of its port of departure, Plymouth.

[2] "Sad Scilla" refers to the rocky Isles of Scilly off Landsend; the "hard bishopps" and "clarks" are the western rocks of the islands, where shipwrecks sometimes occurred before the erection of Bishop's Rock Lighthouse in the nineteenth century.

[3] Line 6: "swelling seas" is changed to "foaming seas," a felicitous correction.

5. O irksome calme! The shippe unweildy lay,
   feeling no helme, the compasse bore no sway,
   Her sides did ake and grone, rockt this, that way.   15

6. See! how a lurking breath comes from the West,
   Another circling steales out of the East,
   A Southseas passe, by Northseas is opprest:

7. The mutiny breaks forth, ther forces drew
   to a square body, then to an angle flew,   20
   At last to a streight line, Southwest yt blew.

8. So aged airs wthin a prison chaind,
   In bowels of the Earth, long tyme arraignd,
   by faire perswasion, fredome hath obtaind.

Presages.   9. Looke! The quicke finned porpusse are in heard,   25
   mourning at leapefroggs, grunting woefull heard,
   tumbled one Lee an other ghastly afeard.

10. Out of the deepe a Schoale of fish there flye,
    trembling amazed heave, wth brinish eye,
    Aboard to light, or ventur in the Skye.   30

11. Prophetique birds from liquid bed did hye,
    distracted flew, and lowred in the skye,
    flutter ther various wings in the winds eye.

12. The searching, subtile, stormy boisterous aire,
    loude roar's the wind, long tongued and jarring are,   35
    The cloud's disburdens, spilt ther full dispaire.

13. Wth one consent the heavens all conspire,
    The melancholique sunne did sad retire,
    And planetts, moons, first starres, ther wrath expire.

14. So a dire meteor to mortalls does appeare,[4]   40
    A fell presaging and disasterous yeare,
    darting its maligne influence angular.

15. Now is the Shippe, beatn, tost, on every side,
    Aft and abaft the sea so fiercely glides,
    Like mountaines round about her, steeme abides.   45

16. Heere comes a sea wth grave and stately gale,
    finding resistance, breakes his curbed pale,
    dashing then one, christning the other Wale.

17. Trying wee were, a furious waue did beare
    main topmast by the board, catharping teare,   50
    And groin'd topgallant mast fell downe for feare.

the
Center
of the
three
seas in
the bay
of
Biscay.

18. A surly Spanish Don, comes in the luffe,[5]
    The Mounsr meets him wth a counterbutte,
    The British greets them wth a sturdy cuffe.

19. At hull we lay, a sea wth crabbed looke   55
    (Can the aged seasoned oake his fury brooke)
    The boulesprite, head, Cat, David, Lyon tooke:

20. Yet not content, a rouling wave did make
    Three leakes wthin her bough, two fishurs brake,
    And grating (as with axe) did clearely take,   60

21. And wth impetuous might in holde did hye,

---

[4] Line 40: Herbert changes "age dire" to "a dire," perhaps correcting a slip of the pen. Line 42: "maligne angle" is changed to "maligne influence."

[5] In lines 52–54, Herbert personifies the three seas as battling Spanish, French, and British forces.

The shippe now brought upon careen to lye,
Looking each minute for her destiny.

---

22. So drubbed Canon, its battery doth make,[6]
    The curtains, bulwarks, forte, downe doth breake,   65
    Wth scornefull bullet thorough the hauses rake.

Castor   23. A sullen thickned mist flyes to the skye,[7]
&   Wth many a tapers beamy glaring eye,
Pollux.   fantastique glowing, ready to sinke we spye.

---

24. It breaks ... upp.[8]   70

---

25. Couering our shippe a Rainbow doth appeare
    An arched colour promist many a yeare[9]
    Quid Ni si pereo, doth the motto beare.[10]

---

lat: 26. We pumpt, set saile, our Men to worke do frame,
43.30'   And at the groine wee to an anchor came,   75
Cape   for Our deliverance, prayse His Holy Name.
Finis-
terrae.   Capt. T. Herbert.

The Embleme
A Shippe never sinking wth
a Rainbow horning her.

---

6 "Battery" refers to a loose cannon's battering of the ship's sides (OED, battery, 1).

7 Herbert changes "falls from" to "flyes to the skye."

8 Herbert draws three short lines, a small arc, and two more lines between the words, indicating blanks to be filled in a final draft of the poem.

9 The writer emphasizes the words "colour" and "prayse" in lines 72 and 76, with a backward flourish at the end of each word.

10 The motto, which the rainbow "doth beare," announces "Quid nisi pereo?" or "What [is there to fear?] unless I pass away?" My thanks to Professor Kenneth Lloyd-Jones of Trinity College, Connecticut, for his assistance with the motto.

Notes

Notes to Chapter One

1. Among the most notable works about literary families in early modern England are: Gary Waller, *The Sidney Family Romance*; Mary Ellen Lamb, *Authorship in the Sidney Family Circle*; Michael Brennan, *Literary Patronage in the English Renaissance: The Pembroke Family*; and Germaine Greer, ed., *Kissing the Rod: An Anthology of 17th-Century Women's Verse*.

2. Among the major New Historicist works concerning courtship, the Metaphysical poets, and literary coteries are: Arthur F. Marotti, *John Donne, Coterie Poet*, and *Manuscript, Print, and the English Renaissance Lyric*; Christina Malcolmson, "George Herbert and Coterie Verse"; Marion White Singleton, *God's Courtier*; and Michael C. Schoenfeldt, *Prayer and Power: George Herbert and Renaissance Courtship*.

3. Concerning the concept of privacy in the period, see Ralph A. Houlbrooke (*The English Family*, 23) and Jonathan Goldberg ("Fatherly Authority," 7–8).

4. While Stone's description of marriage patterns in the period is often cited, many contemporary historians have rejected his harsh depiction of early modern parents as having weak emotional bonds to their young children. See Shammas ("Anglo-American Household Government," 108).

5. My translations of Latin are very much indebted to Betty Rose Nagle, Indiana University Professor of Classics, who graciously read and corrected many pages of my translations.

Notes to Chapter Two

1. The translations of Mario M. Rossi's Italian were done by Professor Glenn Steinberg of the College of New Jersey, Trenton.

2. See also Rubin, "'Let your death be my *Iliad*'" (431).

3. See also Harris, "Property, Power, and Personal Relations" (608 ff.).

4. The results of the case are spelled out in "An Arbitration Award by George More, Herbert Crofte and John Morice, knights, between Magdalen Herbert, widow, and her son Ed. Herberte knight," Loseley Manuscripts, L.M. 349/7. The Loseley Manuscripts are property of Mr. J. R. More-Molyneaux of Loseley Park, Guildford. I am grateful to Mr. More-Molyneaux for permitting me to study these manuscripts.

5. I studied the *Kitchin Booke* during the summer of 1996 at the National Library of Wales in Aberystwyth, on temporary loan from John Herbert's, the Earl of Powis's personal library. See appendix A.

6. Magdalen Herbert divided her family into these categories, listing 30 names on the title page of her account book. Her sons William and Charles were omitted from the list, but later rejoined the household.

7. The genealogical information is available in *The Visitation of Shropshire*, Part 2 (29: 374) and Part 3 (30: 438–439).

Notes to Chapter Three

1. Many critics have traced Herbert's influence in the seventeenth century. Among the studies I have consulted in compiling this list of imitations of "The Church-porch" are: Robert H. Ray, *The Herbert Allusion Book*; Raymond A. Anselment, "Seventeenth-Century Adaptations of 'The Church-Porch'"; Helen Wilcox, "Entering *The Temple*"; Barbara Kiefer Lewalski, *Protestant Poetics and the Seventeenth-Century Religious Lyric*; and Robert Ellrodt, "George Herbert and the Religious Lyric."

2. Among the works on advice literature that have contributed to my summary are John E. Mason, *Gentlefolk in the Making* (23–87), W. Lee Ustick, "Advice to a Son" (409–441), Elaine V. Beilin, *Redeeming Eve* (247–285), and Christine W. Sizemore, "Early Seventeenth-Century Advice Books" (41–48).

3. See also Charles H. and Katherine George, *The Protestant Mind of the English Reformation* (117–173).

4. See Wright, "Was George Herbert the Author of *Jacula prudentum*?" (139–144); Hutchinson, ed., *The Works* (572) ; Charles, ed., *The Williams Manuscript* (xxiii).

5. In support of her assertions, Dawson cites Henry's gathering of other proverbs and anecdotes in his commonplace book, and the erasures of the initial G. H. from the Bodleian and British museum copies of the 1640 collection.

6. See also Dawson, *Sir Henry Herbert* (536–538). Dawson

describes the manuscript, noting the provenance it shared with other Herbert papers and referring to it as an "unsigned holograph." Since the manuscript is clearly not in Sir Henry's hand, its apparent status as a holograph manuscript raises questions about the authorship of the verses.

7. Concerning George Herbert's use of Guazzo's proverbs, see Lievsay (1961, 141–144).

8. Professor Malcolmson's study *Heartwork: George Herbert and the Protestant Ethic* is forthcoming from Stanford University Press.

9. For a further discussion of economic issues in Herbert's poetry, see my "'Whence com'st thou . . . so fresh and fine?'" (14–23).

10. Writing to his friend Sir Justinian Isham on 4 March 1671, William Dillingham explained that he preferred "The Church-porch" to the writing of Edward, Lord Herbert of Cherbury: "For indeed S^r; (to tell you the truth) finding that neither his brother of Cherbery, nor any other that I have Seen have so well comprised the *magna moralia* as he had done in his *Perirrhanterium* or Church-porch I have bin so hardie as to assay the rendering of that Poem of his into Latine . . ." (Northamptonshire Record Office, MS. IC 744). Of all of Cherbury's poems that take up "magna moralia" (i.e., important customs and unwritten laws), "Praecepta & Consilia" does so at greatest length, and so Dillingham presumably compared it to "The Church-porch." Far from being fanciful Neolatin pedantry, Dillingham's Latin translation of "The Church-porch" was a serious attempt to dignify George Herbert's poetry with the same scholarly prestige that Lord Herbert's philosophical works enjoyed in the period.

11. For a further account of this episode in Lord Herbert's life, see John Butler, *Lord Herbert of Cherbury (1582–1648)* (449–462)

Notes to Chapter Four

1. Critics have sometimes associated New Historicism so closely with Foucauldian discourse study and poststructuralist attitudes toward authorship as to exclude all biographical contexts from literary analysis. Schoenfeldt notes well that poems like George Herbert's "Affliction I" seem to "invite" biographical speculation (*Prayer and Power*, 70). Without naively confounding biography and lyric expression, I hope to demonstrate significant connections between Henry Herbert's courtly career and George Herbert's courtly poetry.

2. For a more positive view of Weston, see Kevin Sharpe, *The Personal Rule of Charles I* (148–149).

3. See my "Conquering Laurels and Creeping Ivy," *George Herbert Journal* (1–23).

4. For more about the events of Forced Loan, see Sharpe, *The Personal Rule of Charles I* (18 ff.).

5. For more about the rumors of Hamilton's plot, see S. R. Gardiner, *History of England, 1603–1642* (7: 182–184).

6. See also Gottlieb's "Herbert's Political Allegory of 'Humilitie.'"

Notes to Chapter Five

1. Herbert's biographer Amy M. Charles wrote of this remark: "The rueful postscript of this letter speaks volumes. . . . We do not know what the issue was, nor do we need to" (*A Life*, 77).

2. See also Rickey's *Utmost Art* (34–36).

3. For a contrary view, see Keith Wrightson, *English Society, 1580–1600* (110–113).

4. My translations of the Lord Herbert's notoriously difficult Latin verses are deeply indebted to Betty Rose Nagle, Indiana University Professor of Classics, who kindly read and corrected them.

5. See also Mary Norton, "Edward, Lord Herbert of Cherbury" (164).

6. Mary Herbert's father, Sir William Herbert, had stipulated in his will that she marry a man named Herbert in order to inherit the family properties (*Autobiography*, 21–22; Charles, *A Life*, 32).

7. See also Ralph A. Houlbrooke, *The English Family, 1450–1700* (41–45).

8. See also Gene Edward Veith, Jr., "The Religious Wars in George Herbert Criticism" (29). Veith labels George Herbert a "high church Calvinist episcopalian."

9. Concerning these influences on Edward Herbert, see Richard Strier, "Radical Donne" (305), Roy W. Battenhouse, "The Thought of John Donne" (233), and R. D. Bedford, *The Defense of Truth* (146–148).

10. See also Held, "Brother Poets" (30).

11. Concerning Herbert's tendency toward this heresy, see Russell Fraser, "George Herbert's Poetry" (565–566).

12. While little read in the United States, Ellrodt's *Les Poètes Métaphysiques Anglais* contains one of the most thoughtful and thorough accounts of Lord Herbert's poetry.

13. See Orlin, *Private Matters and Public Culture* (86); Stone, *The Family, Sex and Marriage* (152 ff.); Goldberg, "Fatherly Authority: The Politics of Stuart Family Images" (3–32).

14. Bedford notes: "This motto appears in the portrait of Herbert riding the jennet presented to him by the Duke of Montmorency;

Herbert says, 'This Motto by me.' The Translation is Edmund Blunden's" (170).

15. Baxter stayed at Whitehall for a month with Sir Henry Herbert in the autumn of 1633, according to J. D. Alsop, "A Sunday Play Performance at the Caroline Court" (427).

16. The text of the poem printed by Moore-Smith, based on the British Library Add. Ms. 37157, differs significantly from the version of poem, based on another manuscript, printed by Mario M. Rossi in *La Vita* (3: 390–391). In the latter text, the speaker asks directly: "Say art thou God, or but a voice divine," and again: "I must desire thee to acquaint/Whether thou bee the lord, or but some voice/. . . . To comfort mee from Heaven came."

17. For the original Latin text of this passage, see Sidney Lee, ed., *The Autobiography of Edward, Lord Herbert* (xxviii, n. 1). Professor Eugene D. Hill of Mount Holyoke College notes that the use of the clock in the argument for creation's design gained currency in this period, but the notion of God as an indifferent clockmaker, who abandoned his creation, did not come into common use until the eighteenth century.

18. The opening phrase of the Latin poem, "Coniugium Caeli Terraeque," refers to the same idea as the second line of his poem "Vertue," of a sacramental bond, and so I have rendered it in George Herbert's own lovely English phrase as "the bridal of the earth and sky."

Notes to Chapter Six

1. Thomas Herbert, "The Storme . . . from Plimmouth," National Library of Wales, *Herbert Correspondence*, Appendix, No. 34, Powis Castle 476. The manuscript is owned by John Herbert, Lord Powis, and held by the NLW.

2. Her sons Charles and William died in 1617 or soon after; her son Richard, in 1622; and her daughter Margaret Herbert Vaughan, in 1623 (Charles, *A Life*, 15, 28 29, 131).

3. I have also consulted the microfilm records of St. Martin-in-the-Fields, *Register of Burials, 1636–1653*, fols. 1–103, at the Westminster City Archives Center, 10 St. Anne's Street, London.

4. Warner's edition of the letter lists "Lord Scudamore" and "H. Scudamore" as the writer, but Henry Herbert's longtime correspondent John, Viscount Scudamore is almost certainly the writer.

5. The watermark corroborates that the manuscript was written in the early or mid-seventeenth century.

6. Professor David R. Ransome of the Rhode Island School of Design has very much assisted me in interpreting the maritime

allusions in the poem. I am also indebted to Mr. Paul Nutton of Bramley, Hants, for his answers to my inquiries concerning the Isles of Scilly.

Notes to Chapter Seven

1. For a further list of allusions to "The Church Militant," see Robert H. Ray, *The Herbert Allusion Book*, and Kenneth Alan Hovey, "'Wheel'd about . . . into *Amen*'" (71–72). An anonymous tract in the Broughton Collection at Cambridge University Library is not listed by Ray or Hovey; nor is it indexed in the Wing STC: *Prophecys Concerning the Return of Popery into England, Scotland and Ireland by Arch-bishop Vsher, Mr. Herbert*, et al. (3–4).

2. See also Stanley Johnson, "John Donne and the Virginia Company" (127–138) and W. Moelwyn Merchant, "Donne's Sermon to the Virginia Company," *John Donne: Essays in Celebration* (435-453).

3. Concerning these charitable contributions, see: A. L. Maycock, *Nicholas Ferrar of Little Gidding* (79); Neill, *History of the Virginia Company of London* (138–139); and Kingsbury, ed., *The Records of the Virginia Company* (1: 538, 545, 589–590; 2: 136).

4. For accounts of these emigrants, see Ransome, "Wives for Virginia, 1621" (9); Brown, *The Genesis of the United States*, (2: 891, 994); and Jester and Hiden, *Adventurers of Purse and Person* (273-275). The two William Ferrars have been often conflated in histories of early Virginia, as they are in Brown's account.

5. Danvers also adverted to Virginia Company business in a letter to Edward Herbert on 20 November 1614, although the matter did not seem nearly so pressing as in the 1620 letter (PRO 30/53/7).

6. Amy M. Charles also made the argument that George Herbert would not have made "uncomplimentary strictures on the French" in "The Church Militant" while his brother was French Ambassador, to which post Edward was named in 1619. However, this argument exaggerates the effect of lines 241–46 and overlooks the history of migration to Virginia. The poem's prophecy of a return of Papacy to England, "Whereby one may foretell, what sinnes next yeare/Shall both in *France* and *England* domineer" (*Works*, 197, ll. 245–246), was no more anti-French than anti-English, and it was made more likely by the Catholic victory at White Mountain in November of 1620 than it had been before.

7. Joseph Summers says, "The year 1624 seems to mark the beginning of Sir John Danvers's hostility to the Crown" (*George Herbert*, 43). In the Parliament, Danvers joined with Nicholas Ferrar

and Sir Edwin Sandys in laying "the great load" upon the Lord Treasurer Middlesex, and in taking Sir Nathaniel Rich and Spanish Ambassador Gondomar to task for the difficulties of the company (Saintsbury, *Calendar of State Papers, Colonial Series, 1574–1660,* 66–67). Arthur Woodnoth's colorful (albeit often inaccurate) account of the Virginia Company, which was dedicated to Danvers, records the bitterness that Sandys and his followers felt during the failure of the Tobacco contract and the dissolution of the company. Woodnoth quotes King James's opinion that "The Virginia Company was a seminary for a seditious Parliament," and Danvers's and Sandys's parliamentary careers tended to support that opinion (Woodnoth, *A Short Collection,* 4).

8. I am grateful to Professor David R. Ransome of the Rhode Island School of Design for pointing out this possibility to me. His knowledge of the Ferrars and the Virginia Company have very much contributed to this chapter.

9. To be precise, the poem is usually divided into five sections: the planting of religion in the East (ll. 1–48); the progress of the Church from Egypt to England (ll. 49–100); Sin's progress westward, tracing the Church's steps (ll. 101–156); Sin's corruption of the Roman Church (ll. 157–210); and the Gospel's progress westward from England to America (ll. 211–279). See Hovey, "'Wheel'd about . . . into *Amen*'" (71–84). For the purposes of my argument, I am discussing the poem in three sections: the origin and westward progress of the Church (ll. 1–100); Sin's pursuit of the Church (ll. 100–210); and the Church's movement toward America and the Day of Judgment (ll. 211–279).

10. On the fascinating relationship of Herbert and Danvers to Fuller, see Christopher Hodgkins, *Authority, Church, and Society in George Herbert* (210–214).

Bibliography

MANUSCRIPTS

Bodleian Library, Oxford University

1. Herbert, Henry. *The Broken Heart.* 7 April 1621. Ms. Don. f. 26.

2. ———. *Herbert's Golden Harpe or His Heavenly Hymne.* 20 January 1623. Ms. Don. f. 27.

3. Danvers, Sir John. Letter to George Villiers, Marquess of Buckingham. 2 Feb. 1619/1620. Fortescue Papers. Ms. Add. D 110, fol. 237r.

British Library, London

4. Browne, Lady Francis. Letter to Sir Henry Herbert. 28 June 1647. Herbert of Cherbury Papers. Ms. Add. 37,157.

5. Herbert Family Pedigrees. 17th century. Add. Mss. 39,177. 80b, 92b, 101, 114.

6. Herbert, Sir Henry. Letters to John, Viscount Scudamore. Scudamore Papers. Ms. Add. 11043, fols. 80, 93–94, 95–96.

Huntington Library, San Marino, California

7. Herbert, Henry. *Herbert's Golden Harpe or His Heauenlie Hymne.* 20 January 1623. Ms. HM 85.

Jackson Library, University of North Carolina at Greensboro

8. Charles, Amy M. Amy Marie Charles Papers (1965–1984). Eight Boxes Containing Manuscripts, Letters, Typescripts, Photographs, Microfilms, and Other Materials.

Magdalen College Library, Cambridge

9. Danvers, Sir John, John Ferrar, Nicholas Ferrar, Arthur Woodnoth,

et al. *The Ferrar Papers, 1590–1790.* 2280 letters and documents, 126 prints.

National Library of Wales, Aberystwyth

10. Lord Herbert of Cherbury, Edward. *A Dialogue Between a Master and Pupil.* 11 manuscript leaves of treatise. 17th century. NLW 5296E.

11. ———. Herbert Library Catalogue. c. 1637. NLW 5297.

12. Herbert, Sir Henry, et al. Herbert Letters and Papers. 17th century. NLW 5299E.

13. *Latin Verses on the Virtues* (attributed to Sir Henry Herbert). c. 1650. NLW 5300B.

14. Herbert, Sir Henry. *Proverbs and Extracts* ("Outlandishe Proverbs," in the hand of Sir Henry Herbert). 17th century. NLW 5301E.

15. ———. *The Emperor Otho* Manuscript Drama. 17th century. NLW 5302B.

16. Herbert Papers. 17th century. NLW 5303E.

17. Herbert, Captain Thomas. "The Storme . . . from Plimmouth." c. 1620–1640. Powis Castle Papers (see W. J. Smith, ed., *Herbert Correspondence.* Appendix, no. 34, 476).

18. Herbert Family Pedigrees. NLW Ms. 1739B, fols. 33–34.

19. Herbert Family Manuscript Poems, including verses by John Donne. 17th century. NLW 5308E.

Northamptonshire Record Office, Wootton Hall Park, Northampton

20. Dillingham, William to Just. Isham. 4 Mar. 1671/1672. Isham Correspondence, I.C. 744.

Powis Library, Welshpool

21. Herbert, Magdalen. *Kitchin Booke.* 1601. Ms. account book in the possession of John Herbert, Earl of Powis.

Public Record Office, London

22. Herbert, Sir Henry. Will. 1 Jan. 1672/1673. PROB 11/342, fols. 51–59.

23. Lord Herbert of Cherbury, Edward. Will. 1 Aug. 1648. PROB 11/205, fols. 256–58.

24. Herbert, Henry L., 2nd Baron of Cherbury. Will. 2 Feb. 1737/
    1738. PROB 11/692, fols. 303–04.

25. Herbert Family Correspondence. 17th century. PRO 30/53/3.

26. ———. 17th century. PRO 30/53/7.

27. ———. 17th century. PRO 30/53/10.

28. Herbert, Sir Henry. Letters to John, Viscount Scudamore, 1624–
    1671. Masters' Exhibits, Duchess of Norfolk's Deeds. PRO C115/
    N3/8536–8574.

Surrey Record Office, Guildford Muniment Room, Guildford

29. Herbert, Magdalen. Arbitration Award by George More. 4 June
    1604. Loseley Manuscripts, L.M. 349/7.

30. ———. "The case betwene my sonne and me is this . . ." c. 1603.
    Loseley Manuscripts, L.M. 2014/103.

31. ———. Letter to Sir George Moore. 14 March 1607/1608. Loseley
    Manuscripts, L.M. Cor. 4/23.

Westminster City Archives Center, London, 10 St. Anne's Street

32. St. Martin-in-the-Fields. *Register of Burials, 1636–1653.* Micro-
    film.

PRINTED BOOKS AND ARTICLES

Adams, Joseph Quincy, ed. *The Dramatic Records of Sir Henry
    Herbert, Master of the Revels, 1623–1673.* New Haven: Yale Uni-
    versity Press, 1917.

Alsop, J. D. "A Sunday Play Performance at the Caroline Court."
    Notes and Queries 224 (Oct. 1979): 427.

Amussen, Susan Dwyer. *An Ordered Society: Gender and Class in
    Early Modern England.* Oxford: Blackwell, 1988.

Anderson, Judith H. *Biographical Truth: The Representation of His-
    torical Persons in Tudor-Stuart Writing.* New Haven: Yale Uni-
    versity Press, 1984.

Anselment, Raymond A. "'The Church Militant': George Herbert
    and the Metamorphoses of Christian History." *Huntington
    Library Quarterly* 41 (1978): 299–316.

————. "Seventeenth-Century Adaptations of 'The Church-Porch.'" *George Herbert Journal* 5 (1982): 63–69.

Arber, Edward, ed. *A Transcript of the Registers of the Company of Stationers of London: 1554–1640 A.D.* 5 vols. London: Privately Printed, 1875–1877.

Aries, Philippe. Introduction to *A History of Private Life. Passions of the Renaissance.* Edited by Roger Chartier. Cambridge: Harvard University Press, 1989.

Asals, Heather A. R. *Equivocal Prediction: George Herbert's Way to God.* Toronto: University of Toronto Press, 1981.

————. "Magdalene Herbert: Towards a Topos for the Anglican Church." *George Herbert Journal* 1, no. 2 (1978): 1–16.

Aubrey, John. *Aubrey's Brief Lives.* Edited by Oliver Lawson-Dick. London: Mandarin, 1992.

Bald, R. C. *John Donne: A Life.* New York: Oxford University Press, 1970.

Ball, W. W. Rouse, and J. A. Venn, eds. *Admissions to Trinity College, Cambridge, 1546–1700.* London: Macmillan, 1911–1916.

Battenhouse, Roy W. "The Thought of John Donne." *Church History* 9 (1942): 217–48.

Bawcutt, N. W. "The Manuscripts of Lord Herbert of Cherbury's Autobiography." *The Library.* 6th ser. 12 (June 1990): 133–36.

————. "New Revels Documents of Sir George Buc and Sir Henry Herbert, 1619–1662." *Review of English Studies* n.s. 35 (1984): 316–34.

Baxter, Richard. *Poetical Fragments: Heart-Imployments with God and It Self.* London: T. Snowden for B. Simmons, 1681. Wing STC B1349.

————. *Some Animadversions On a Tractate De Veritate.* In *More Reasons for the Christian Religion, and No Reason Against It.* London: Nevil Simmons, 1672. Wing STC B1313.

Bedford, R. D. *The Defense of Truth: Herbert of Cherbury and the Seventeenth Century.* Manchester: Manchester University Press, 1979.

Beilin, Elaine V. *Redeeming Eve: Women Writers of the English Renaissance.* Princeton: Princeton University Press, 1987.

Bemiss, Samuel, ed. *The Three Charters of the Virginia Company of London. With Seven Related Documents; 1606–1621.* Williamsburg, Va.: Virginia 350th Anniversary Celebration Corporation, 1957.

Ben-Amos, Ilana Krausman. *Adolescence and Youth in Early Modern England.* New Haven: Yale University Press, 1994.

Benet, Diana. "Herbert's Experience of Politics and Patronage in 1624." *George Herbert Journal* 10 (1986): 33–45.

———. *Secretary of Praise: The Poetic Vocation of George Herbert.* Columbia: University of Missouri Press, 1984.

Betz, Siegmund A. E. "Francis Osborn's *Advice to a Son.*" *Seventeenth Century Studies: Second Series.* Edited by Robert Shafer. Cincinnati: University of Cincinnati, 1937. Reprint, Freeport, NY: Books for Libraries Press, 1968.

Blackburn, William. "Lady Magdalen Herbert and Her Son George." *The South Atlantic Quarterly* 50 (1951): 378–88.

Blair, Rhonda L. "George Herbert's Greek Poetry." *Philological Quarterly* 64 (1985): 573–84.

Bland, Edward. *The Discovery of New Brittaine.* London: Thomas Harper for John Stephenson, 1651. Wing STC B3155.

Bloch, Chana. *Spelling the Word: George Herbert and the Bible.* California: University of California Press, 1985.

Boswell, James. *The Life of Samuel Johnson, L.L.D.* Modern Library Series. New York: Random House, 1944.

Bowden, Caroline. "Women as intermediaries: an example of the use of literacy in the late sixteenth and early seventeenth centuries." *History of Education* 22, no. 3 (1993): 215–23.

Breen, Timothy Hall. "The Non-Existent Controversy: Puritan and Anglican Attitudes on Work and Wealth, 1600–1640." *Church History* 35 (1966): 273–87.

Brennan, Michael. *Literary Patronage in the English Renaissance: The Pembroke Family.* London: Routledge, 1988.

Bristol, Michael. "Sacred Literature and Profane Religion: The Modernity of Herbert of Cherbury." *The Witness of Times: Manifestations of Ideology in Seventeenth Century England,* 14–33. Edited by Katherine Z. Keller and Gerald J. Schiffhorst. Pittsburgh: Duquesne University Press, 1993.

Brooks, Cleanth. *Historical Evidence and the Reading of Seventeenth-Century Poetry.* Columbia: University of Missouri Press, 1991.

Brown, Alexander. *The Genesis of the United States.* 2 vols. Boston, 1890. Reprint, New York: Russell & Russell, 1964.

Bruce, John, ed. *Calendar of State Papers, Domestic, 1625–1626.* London: Longman, 1858.

———, ed. *Calendar of State Papers, Domestic, 1627–1628.* London: Longman, 1858.

———. "Inquiry into the Genuineness of a Letter Dated February 3rd, 1613 and Signed 'Mary Magdalene Danvers.'" *The Camden Miscellany,* 5: 3–30. London: Camden Society, 1864.

Brydges, Sir Samuel E., ed. *A Biographical Peerage of the Empire of Great Britain.* 4 vols. London: J. Nichols, 1817.

Burke, Kenneth. "On Covery, Re- and Dis-." *Accent* 13 (1953): 218–26.

Burt, Richard, and John Michael Archer, eds. *Enclosure Acts: Sexuality, Property, and Culture in Early Modern England.* Ithaca: Cornell University Press, 1994

Butler, John. *Lord Herbert of Chirbury (1582–1648): An Intellectual Biography.* Lewiston, NY: Edwin Mellen Press, 1990.

Button, John. *Algiers Voyage in a Journall or Briefe Reportary.* London: B. Alsop, 1621. STC 4208.

Carey, John. *John Donne: Life, Mind, and Art.* New York: Oxford University Press, 1981.

Carlson, Eric Josef. *Marriage and the English Reformation.* Oxford: Blackwell, 1994.

Carré, Jacques, ed. *The Crisis of Courtesy: Studies in the Conduct Book in Britain, 1600–1900.* Leiden: E. J. Brill, 1994.

Castiglione, Baldassare. *The Book of the Courtier.* Translated by George Bull. Harmondsworth: Penguin, 1984.

Charles, Amy M. *A Life of George Herbert.* Ithaca: Cornell University Press, 1977.

———. Introduction to *The Williams Manuscript of George Herbert's Poems,* ix–xxxi. Delmar, NY: Scholars' Facsimiles, 1977.

————. "Mrs. Herbert's Kitchin Booke." *English Literary Renaissance* 4 (1974): 164–73.

————. "Sir Henry Herbert: The Master of the Revels as Man of Letters." *Modern Philology* 80 (Aug. 1982): 1–12.

Chartier, Roger, ed. *A History of Private Life.* Vol. 3, *Passions of the Renaissance.* 5 vols. Translated by Arthur Goldhammer, Cambridge: Harvard University Press, 1989.

Churchill, W. A. *Watermarks in Paper in Holland, England, France, Etc., in the XVII and XVIII Centuries and their Interconnection.* Amsterdam: Menno Hertzberger, 1935.

Clampitt, Amy. *A Silence Opens.* New York: Alfred A. Knopf, 1994.

Clapinson, Mary, and T. D. Rogers. *Summary Catalogue of Post-Medieval Western Manuscripts in the Bodleian Library, Oxford.* 3 vols. Oxford: Oxford University Press, 1991.

Clarke, Elizabeth. *Theory and Theology in George Herbert's Poetry: "Divinitie, and Poesie, Met."* Oxford Theological Monographs. Oxford: Oxford University Press, 1997.

Cleaver, Robert, and John Dod. *A Godlie Forme of Household Government: For the Ordering of Private Families.* London: A. Johnson, 1612. STC 5386.

Clowes, William Laird. *The Royal Navy: A History From the Earliest Times to the Present.* 7 vols. London: Sampson Low, Marston and Co., 1897–1903.

Cochrane, Raymond C. "Bishop Berkeley and the Progress of Arts and Learning: Notes on a Literary Convention." *Huntington Library Quarterly* 17 (1954): 229–49.

Cogswell, Thomas. *The Blessed Revolution: English Politics and the Coming of War, 1621–1624.* Cambridge: Cambridge University Press, 1989.

Collinson, Patrick. *The Religion of Protestants: The Church in English Society, 1559–1625.* Oxford: Oxford University Press, 1982.

Cooper, Charles Henry. *The Annals of Cambridge.* 5 vols. Cambridge: Warwick & Co., 1842–1845.

Copland, Patrick. *Virginia's God be Thanked, or A Sermon of Thanksgiving for the Happie successee of the affayres in Virginia this last yeare.* London: Printed by I.D. for William Sheffard and John Bellamie, 1622. STC 5727.

Corbett, Richard. *The Poems of Richard Corbett.* Edited by J. A. W. Bennett and H. R. Trevor-Roper. Oxford: Oxford University Press, 1955.

Cornwallis, Sir William, the Younger. *Essayes.* Edited by Dom Cameron Allen. Baltimore: Johns Hopkins Press, 1946.

Costella, Joan Kuzma. "True Child, Servant, and Guest of his Master: Images of Household Roles in George Herbert's *The Temple.*" *Ball State University Forum* 30 (1989): 39–51.

Craven, Wesley F. *The Dissolution of the Virginia Company: The Failure of a Colonial Experiment.* New York: Oxford University Press, 1932.

———. *The Southern Colonies in the Seventeenth Century, 1607–1689.* Baton Rouge: Louisiana State University Press, 1949.

Cressy, David. *Birth, Marriage, and Death: Ritual, Religion, and the Life-Cycle in Tudor and Stuart England.* Oxford: Oxford University Press, 1997.

———. "Kinship and Kin Interaction in Early Modern England." *Past & Present* no. 113 (1986): 38–67.

Crossman, Samuel. *The Young Mans Culling: Or, The Whole Duty of Youth.* London: Tho. James for Nath. Crouch, 1678. Wing STC C1272.

Cruttwell, Patrick. *The Shakespearean Moment and Its Place in the Poetry of the 17th Century.* New York: Random House, 1960.

Daniel, John J. *The Life of George Herbert of Bemerton.* London: Society for Promoting Christian Knowledge, 1893.

Danvers, Sir John. *Copy of a Humble Petition from the Governor and Company of the Sommer Islands. . . .* London: Printed for Edward Husband, 1651. Wing STC C3201.

Dawson, Susan Anne. *Sir Henry Herbert.* Ph.D. diss., University of Washington, Seattle, 1990. Ann Arbor: UMI, 1990.

Della Casa, Giovanni. *Galateo.* Edited by Konrad Eisenbichler and Kenneth R. Bartlett. Toronto: Center for Reformation and Renaissance Studies, 1986.

———. *Galateo, or A Treatise of The Maners and Behauiours.* Reprint, Amsterdam: Da Capo Press, 1969.

DiCesare, Mario A., and Rigo Mignani. *A Concordance to the*

Complete Writings of George Herbert. Ithaca: Cornell University Press, 1977.

Dickson, Donald R. *The Fountain of Living Waters: The Typology of the Waters of Life in Herbert, Vaughan, and Traherne*. Columbia: University of Missouri Press, 1987.

Diefendorf, Barbara B. "Family Culture, Renaissance Culture." *Renaissance Quarterly* 40 (1987): 661–81.

Digby, Sir Kenelm. *Journal of a Voyage into the Mediterranean*. Edited by John Bruce. Camden Society Publications, no. 96. London, 1868. Reprint, New York: AMS, 1968.

Doebler, Bettie Anne, and Retha Warnicke. "Magdalen Herbert Danvers and Donne's Vision of Comfort." *George Herbert Journal* 10 (1986): 5–22.

Doerksen, Daniel W. *Conforming to the Word: Herbert, Donne, and the English Church before Laud*. Lewisburg: Bucknell University Press, 1997.

———. "Magdalen Herbert's London Church." *Notes and Queries* 232 (Sept. 1987): 302–05.

———. "Nicholas Ferrar, Arthur Woodnoth, and the Publication of George Herbert's *The Temple*, 1633." *George Herbert Journal* 3, nos. 1 and 2 (1980): 22–44.

Dolan, Frances E. *Dangerous Familiars: Representations of Domestic Crime in England, 1550–1700*. Ithaca: Cornell University Press, 1994.

Dollimore, Jonathan, and Alan Sinfield, eds. *Political Shakespeare: New Essays in Cultural Materialism*. Manchester: Manchester University Press, 1985.

Donne, John. *Biathanatos*. Edited by Michael Rudick and M. Pabst Battin. New York: Garland, 1982.

———. *The Complete English Poems*. Edited by A. J. Smith. Harmondsworth: Penguin, 1986.

———. *The Divine Poems*. 2d ed. Edited by Helen Gardner. New York: Clarendon Press, 1978.

———. *The Epithalamions, Anniversaries, and Epicedes*. Edited by W. Milgate. Oxford: Oxford University Press, 1978.

———. *The Sermons of John Donne*. Edited by Evelyn M. Simpson and George R. Potter. 10 vols. Berkeley: University of California Press, 1953–1962.

Donzelot, Jacques. *The Policing of Families*. Translated by Robert Hurley. New York: Pantheon, 1979.

Dutton, Richard. *Mastering the Revels: The Regulation and Censorship of English Renaissance Drama*. Iowa City: University of Iowa Press, 1994.

Earle, John. *Microcosmography*. Edited by Harold Osborne. London: University Tutorial Press, 1933.

Ellrodt, Robert. "George Herbert and the Religious Lyric." In *English Poetry and Prose, 1540–1674*. Edited by Christopher Ricks London: Barrie & Jenkins, 1970.

———. *L'Inspiration Personnelle et L'Esprit du Temps chez Les Poètes Métaphysiques Anglais*. 2 vols. Paris: Librairie Jose Corti, 1960.

Estienne, Robert. *Dictionariolum Puerorum Tribus Linguis Latina Anglica & Gallica*. London, 1552. Reprint, Amsterdam: Da Capo Press, 1971.

Ezell, Margaret J. M. *The Patriarch's Wife: Literary Evidence and the History of the Family*. Chapel Hill: University of North Carolina Press, 1987.

Ferrar, John. *The Ferrar Papers: Containing A Life of Nicholas Ferrar*. Edited by Bernard Blackstone. Cambridge: Cambridge University Press, 1938.

Ferrar, Nicholas. *Sir Thomas Smith's Misgovernment of the Virginia Company*. Edited by David R. Ransome. Cambridge: Roxburghe Club, 1990.

Ferry, Anne. *The Title to the Poem*. Stanford: Stanford University Press, 1996.

———. "Titles in George Herbert's 'little Book.'" *English Literary Renaissance* 23 (Spring 1993): 314–44.

Fish, Stanley. *The Living Temple: George Herbert and Catechizing*. Berkeley: University of California Press, 1978.

Flandrin, Jean-Louis. *Families in Former Times: Kinship, Household, and Sexuality*. New York: Cambridge University Press, 1979.

Flesch, William. *Generosity and the Limits of Authority: Shakespeare, Herbert, and Milton*. Ithaca: Cornell University Press, 1992.

Fletcher, Anthony, and Peter Roberts, eds. *Religion, Culture, and Society in Early Modern Britain: Essays in Honour of Patrick Collinson*. Cambridge: Cambridge University Press, 1994.

Foster, Joseph, ed. *Alumni Oxonienses*. 2 vols. Oxford: John Parker & Co., 1891–1892.

Franklin, Ben. *The Complete Poor Richard Almanacks, 1748–1758*. Introduction by Whitfield J. Bell, Jr. Barre, Mass.: Imprint Society, 1970.

Fraser, Antonia. *The Weaker Vessel: Woman's Lot in Seventeenth-Century England*. London: Weidenfeld and Nicolson, 1984.

Fraser, Russell. "George Herbert's Poetry." *Sewannee Review* 95 (1987): 560–85.

Freud, Sigmund. *The Complete Psychological Works of Sigmund Freud: Volume 9 (1906–1908)*. Edited by James Strachey and Anna Freud. London: Hogarth Press, 1959.

Friedman, Alice T. *House and Household in Elizabethan England: Wollaton Hall and the Willoughby Family*. Chicago: University of Chicago Press, 1989.

Friedman, Donald M. "Donne, Herbert, and Vocation." *George Herbert Journal* 18, nos. 1 and 2 (Fall 1994/Spring 1995): 135–58.

Fuller [Ossoli], S. Margaret. "The Two Herberts." In *Papers on Literature and Art, Part 1*, 15–34. London: Wiley and Putnam, 1846.

Fuller, Thomas. *Feare of Losing the Old Light. Or, a Sermon Preached in Exeter*. London: Printed by T. H. for John Williams, 1646. Wing STC F2424.

———. *The History of the Worthies of England*. London: J.G., W.L., and W.G., 1662. Wing STC F2440.

Fumerton, Patricia. "'Secret' Arts: Elizabethan Miniatures and Sonnets." *Representations* 15 (Summer 1986): 57–97.

Gardiner, Samuel R. *History of England from the Accession of James I to the Outbreak of the Civil War, 1603–1642*. 10 vols. London: Longman's, 1894–1896.

———. "The Political Element in Massinger." *The Contemporary Review* 28 (Aug. 1878): 495–507.

George, Charles H., and Katherine George. *The Protestant Mind of the English Reformation, 1570–1640*. Princeton: Princeton University Press, 1961.

Glare, P. G. W. *Oxford Latin Dictionary*. Oxford: Oxford University Press, 1983.

Goldberg, Jonathan. "Fatherly Authority: The Politics of Stuart

Family Images." *Rewriting the Renaissance: The Discourses of Sexual Difference in Early Modern Europe.* Edited by Margaret W. Ferguson, Maureen Quilligan, and Nancy J. Vickers, 3–32. Chicago: University of Chicago Press, 1986.

Gottlieb, Beatrice. *The Family in the Western World from the Black Death to the Industrial Age.* Oxford: Oxford University Press, 1993.

Gottlieb, Sidney. "From 'Content' to 'Affliction (III)': Herbert's Anti-Court Sequence." *English Literary Renaissance* 23 (1993): 472–89.

——. "Herbert's Political Allegory of 'Humlitie.'" *Huntington Library Quarterly* 52 (1989): 469–80.

Grazebrook, George, and John Paul Rylands, eds. *The Visitation of Shropshire, Taken in the Year 1623, by Robert Tresswell, Somerset Herald, and Augustine Vincent.* Part 2. Harleian Society Publications, vol. 29. London: Harleian Society, 1889.

Greer, Germaine, Jeslyn Medoff, Melinda Sansone, and Susan Hastings, eds. *Kissing the Rod: An Anthology of 17th Century Women's Verse.* London: Virago, 1988.

Guazzo, Stefano. *The Civile Conversation of M. Steeven Guazzo.* Translated by George Pettie and Bartholomew Young. Intro. Sir Edward Sullivan. 2 vols. London: Constable & Co., 1925.

Guiney, Louise Imogen. *A Little English Gallery.* New York: Harper and Brothers, 1894.

Hall, Joseph. *The Works of the Right Reverend Joseph Hall.* 10 vols. Vol. 6, *Characters of Virtues and Vices.* Edited by Philip Wynter. Oxford, 1863. Reprint, New York: AMS Press, 1969.

Halpern, Richard. *The Poetics of Primitive Accumulation: English Renaissance Culture and the Genealogy of Capital.* Ithaca. Cornell University Press, 1991.

Hamilton, Donna B., and Richard Strier, eds. *Religion, Literature, and Politics in Post- Reformation England, 1540–1688.* Cambridge: Cambridge University Press, 1996.

Harris, Barbara J. "Property, Power, and Personal Relations: Elite Mothers and Sons in Yorkist and Early Tudor England." *Signs* 15 (Spring 1990): 606–32.

——. "Women and Politics in Early Tudor England." *The Historical Journal* 33 (1990): 259-81.

Heal, Felicity. *Hospitality in Early Modern England*. Oxford: Oxford University Press, 1990.

Held, George. "Brother Poets: The Relationship Between Edward and George Herbert." In *Like Season'd Timber: New Essays on George Herbert*. Edited by Edmund Miller and Robert Di Yanni, 19–35. New York: Peter Lang, 1987.

Lord Herbert of Cherbury, Edward. *The Antient Religion of the Gentiles and the Causes of their Errors Considered* [translation of *De Religione Gentilium*]. Translated by William Lewis. London: Printed for John Nutt, 1705.

———. *The Autobiography of Edward, Lord Herbert of Cherbury*. 2d ed. Edited by Sidney Lee. London: Routledge, 1906. Reprint, Westport, Conn.: Greenwood, 1970.

———. *De Veritate*. Edited by Meyrick H. Carré. University of Bristol Studies, No. 6. Bristol: J. W. Arrowsmith, 1937.

———. *A Dialogue Between a Tutor and his Pupil*. New York: Garland, 1979.

———. *The Life of Edward, First Lord Herbert of Cherbury, Written by Himself*. Edited by J. M. Shuttleworth. Oxford: Oxford University Press, 1976.

———. *Lord Herbert of Cherbury's De Religione Laici*. Edited by Harold R. Hutcheson. New Haven: Yale University Press, 1944.

———. *Pagan Religion: A Translation of De Religione Gentilium*. Edited by John Anthony Butler. Binghamton: Medieval & Renaissance Texts and Studies, 1996.

———. *The Poems, English and Latin, of Edward Lord Herbert of Cherbury*. Edited by G. C. Moore Smith. Oxford: Clarendon, 1923.

Herbert, George. *The Bodleian Manuscript of George Herbert's Poems. A Facsimile of Tanner 307*. Edited by Amy M. Charles and Mario A. Di Cesare. Delmar, N.Y.: Scholars' Facsimiles, 1984.

———. *The Complete Works of George Herbert*. Edited by Alexander B. Grosart. 3 vols. London: Fuller Worthies' Library, 1874.

———. *George Herbert, The Temple: A Diplomatic Edition of the Bodleian Manuscript (Tanner 307)*. Binghamton, N.Y.: Medieval & Renaissance Texts & Studies, 1995.

———. *The Latin Poetry of George Herbert: A Bilingual Edition*. Translated by Mark McCloskey and Paul R. Murphy. Athens: Ohio University Press, 1965.

———. *The Williams Manuscript of George Herbert's Poems.* Edited by Amy M. Charles. Delmar, NY: Scholars' Facsimiles, 1977.

———. *The Works of George Herbert.* Edited by F. E. Hutchinson, Oxford: Oxford University Press, 1945.

Herbert, Henry. *Herbert's Golden Harpe or His Heavenly Hymne: A Transcription of Huntington Library Manuscript HM 85.* Edited by Chauncey Wood. *George Herbert Journal* 20, nos. 1–2 (Fall 1996/Spring 1997): 1–105.

Herbert, Sir Henry. *The Control and Censorship of Caroline Drama: The Records of Sir Henry Herbert, Master of the Revels, 1623–1673.* Edited by N. W. Bawcutt. Oxford: Oxford University Press, 1996.

———, trans. *The Minister of State,* by Jean de Silhon. London: Printed for Thomas Dring, 1658. Wing STC S3781.

———, trans. *The Second Part of the Minister of State,* by Jean de Silhon. London: Printed for Thomas Dring, 1663. Wing STC S378.

Herbert, Thomas, verse writer. *An Answer to the most Envious, Scandalous, and Libellous Pamphlet, Entituled Mercuries Message.* London: 1641. Wing STC H1527.

Herbert, Sir Thomas. *A Relation of Some Yeares Travaile, Begvnne Anno 1626.* London: William Stansby and Jacob Bloome, 1634. STC 13190.

———. *Some Yeares Travels into Divers Parts of Asia and Afrique.* Revised and Enlarged. London: Richard Bishop and Jacob Bloome, 1638. STC 13191.

Hill, Christopher. "Protestantism and Capitalism." In *Essays in the Economic and Social History of Tudor and Stuart England.* Edited by E. J. Fisher. Cambridge: Cambridge University Press, 1961.

Hill, Eugene D. *Edward Lord Herbert of Cherbury.* Boston: Twayne, 1987.

Hinman, Robert B. "The 'Verser' at *The Temple* Door: Herbert's 'The Church-porch.'" In *"Too Rich to Clothe the Sunne": Essays on George Herbert.* Edited by Claude J. Summers and Ted-Larry Pebworth. Pittsburgh: University of Pittsburgh Press, 1980.

Hodgkins, Christopher. *Authority, Church, and Society in George Herbert: Return to the Middle Way.* Columbia: University of Missouri Press, 1993.

Hoey, John. "A Study of Lord Herbert of Cherbury's Poetry." *Renaissance and Modern Studies* 14 (1971): 68–89.

Holy Bible. Authorized King James Version. Edited by C. I. Scofield. New York: Oxford University Press, 1967.

Houlbrooke, Ralph A. *The English Family, 1450–1700.* Themes in British Social History Series. London: Longman, 1984.

———. ed. *English Family Life, 1576–1716: An Anthology from Diaries.* London: Basil Blackwell, 1989.

Hovey, Kenneth Alan. "'*Inventa Bellica*'/'*Triumphus Mortis*': Herbert's Parody of Human Progress and Dialogue with Divine Grace." *Studies in Philology* 78 (1981): 275–304.

———. "'Wheel'd about . . . into Amen': 'The Church Militant' on Its Own Terms." *George Herbert Journal* 10 (1986): 71–84.

Howard-Hill, T. H. "The Origins of Middleton's *A Game at Chess.*" *Research Opportunities in Renaissance Drama* 28 (1985): 3–13.

Huxley, Aldous. *Texts and Pretexts.* New York: Harper, 1933.

James I. *The Political Works of James I.* Edited by Charles Howard McIlwain. Cambridge: Harvard University Press, 1918.

Jasper, David, ed. *Images of Belief in Literature.* New York: St. Martin's Press, 1984.

Jester, Annie L., and Marth W. Hiden. *Adventurers of Purse and Person, Virginia 1607–1624/25.* 3d ed. Edited by Virginia M. Meyer and John F. Dorman. Richmond: Order of First Families of Virginia, 1987.

Johnson, George W., ed. *The Fairfax Correspondence.* 2 vols. London: Richard Bentley, 1848.

Johnson, Lee Ann. "The Relationship of 'The Church Militant' to *The Temple.*" *Studies in Philology* 68 (1971): 200–206.

Johnson, Robert. *The New Life of Virginea.* London: Felix Kyngston for William Welby, 1612. STC 14700.

Johnson, Roger A. "Natural Religion, Common Notions, and the Study of Religions: Lord Herbert of Cherbury (1583–1648)." *Religion* 24 (1994): 213–24.

Johnson, Stanley. "John Donne and the Virginia Company." *English Literary History* 14 (1947): 127–38.

Jonson, Ben. *Ben Jonson: The Complete Poems.* Edited by George

Parfitt. English Poets Series. New Haven: Yale University Press, 1982.

Keeble, N. H., ed. *The Cultural Identity of Seventeenth-Century Woman: A Reader*. London: Routledge, 1994.

Keizer, Garret. "Fragrance, 'Marie Magdalene,' and Herbert's The Temple," *George Herbert Journal* 4 (1980): 29–50.

Kempe, Alfred John, ed. *The Loseley Manuscripts, and Other Rare Documents . . . Preserved in the Muniment Room of James More Molyneux, Esq. At Loseley House, in Surrey*. London: John Murray, 1836.

Kerrigan, John, ed. Introduction to *The Sonnets, and A Lover's Complaint*, by William Shakespeare, 7–63. Harmondsworth: Penguin, 1986.

Kerrigan, William. "Ritual Man: On the Outside of Herbert's Poetry." *Psychiatry* 48, no. 1 (1985): 68–82.

King, Henry. *The Poems of Henry King, Bishop of Chichester*. Edited by Margaret Crum. Oxford: Oxford University Press, 1965.

Kingsbury, Susan Myra, ed. *The Records of the Virginia Company of London*. 4 vols. Washington, D.C.: Government Printing Office, 1906–1935.

Kitto, J. V., ed. *The Registers of St. Martin-in-the-Fields, London, 1619–1636*. Harleian Society Publications, vol. 66. London: John Whitehead & Sons, 1936.

Klein, Joan Larsen, ed. *Daughters, Wives, and Widows: Writings by Men about Women and Marriage in England, 1500–1640*. Urbana: University of Illinois Press, 1992.

Kupperman, Karen Ordahl. "The Founding Years of Virginia and the United States." *The Virginia Magazine of History and Biography* 104 (Winter 1996): 103–12.

Lamb, Mary Ellen. *Gender and Authorship in the Sidney Circle*. Madison: University of Wisconsin Press, 1990.

Larminie, Vivienne. *Wealth, Kinship, and Culture: The Seventeenth-Century Newdigates of Arbury and their World*. Woodbridge, Suffolk: Boydell Press, 1995.

Laslett, Peter. *Family Life and Illicit Love in Earlier Generations: Essays in Historical Sociology*. Cambridge: Cambridge University Press, 1977.

————. *The World We Have Lost.* New York: Scribner's, 1965.

Lever, Sir Tresham. *The Herberts of Wilton.* London: John Murray, 1967.

Lewalski, Barbara Kiefer. *Protestant Poetics and the Seventeenth-Century Religious Lyric.* Princeton: Princeton, University Press, 1979.

————. *Writing Women in Jacobean England.* Cambridge: Harvard University Press, 1993.

Lievsay, John Leon. *Stefano Guazzo and the English Renaissance, 1575–1675.* Chapel Hill: University of North Carolina Press, 1961.

Lloyd, Christopher. *The Nation and the Navy; A History of Naval Life and Policy.* London: Cresset Press, 1954. Reprint, Westport, Conn.: Greenwood, 1974.

Lloyd, J. D. K. "A Guidebook to the Parish Church of Saint Nicholas Montgomery." Pamphlet. Welshpool: Welshpool Printing Company, 1984.

————. "The Herbert Tomb in Montgomery Church." *Montgomeryshire Collections* 51 (1949–1950): 98–115.

Lull, Janis. *The Poem in Time: Reading George Herbert's Revisions of The Church.* Newark: University of Delaware Press, 1990.

Luther, Martin. *Martin Luther: Selections from his Writing.* Edited by John Dillenberger. Garden City, NY: Doubleday, 1961.

————. *Table Talk.* Translated by William Hazlitt. London: Fount, 1995.

Macfarlane, Alan. *Marriage and Love in England: Modes of Reproduction, 1300–1840.* London: Basil Blackwell, 1986.

Mahood, M. M. *Poetry and Humanism.* New Haven: Yale University Press, 1950.

Mainwaring, Henry. *The Life and Works of Sir Henry Mainwaring.* Edited by G. E. Manwaring and W. G. Perrin. 2 vols. London: Navy Records Society, 1922.

Malcolm, Noel. "Hobbes, Sandys, and the Virginia Company." *Historical Journal* 24 (1981): 297–321.

Malcolmson, Cristina. "George Herbert and Coterie Verse." *George Herbert Journal* 18, nos. 1 and 2 (Fall 1994/Spring 1995): 159–84.

————. "George Herbert: Country Parson and the Character of Social Identity." *Studies in Philology* 85 (1988): 245–266.

————. *Heartwork: George Herbert and the Protestant Ethic.* Stanford: Stanford University Press, 1999.

Malesky, Mary A., ed. *A Fine Tuning: Studies of the Religious Poetry of Herbert and Milton.* Binghamton, NY: Medieval & Renaissance Texts and Studies, 1989.

Marcus, Leah. *Childhood and Cultural Despair: A Theme and Variations in Seveteenth-Century Literature.* Pittsburgh: University of Pittsburgh Press, 1978.

Marotti, Arthur F. *John Donne, Coterie Poet.* Madison: University of Wisconsin Press, 1986.

————. *Manuscript, Print, and the English Renaissance Lyric.* Ithaca: Cornell University Press, 1995.

Martz, Louis L. *From Renaissance to Baroque: Essays on Literature and Art.* Columbia: University of Missouri Press, 1991.

————. *The Poetry of Meditation: A Study of English Religious Literature of the Seventeenth Century.* New Haven, Conn : Yale University Press, 1954.

Mascuch, Michael. "Continuity and Change in a Patronage Society: the Social Mobility of British autobiographers, 1600–1750." *Journal of Historical Sociology* 7 (June 1994): 177–97.

Mason, John E. *Gentlefolk in the Making: Studies in the History of English Courtesy Literature and Related Topics from 1531 to 1774.* University of Pennsylvania Press, 1935. Reprint, New York: Octagon Books, 1971.

Maycock, A. L. *Nicholas Ferrar of Little Gidding.* London, 1938. Reprint, Grand Rapids, Mich.: William B. Eerdmans, 1980.

McCarron, William and Robert Shenk. *Lesser Metaphysical Poets: A Bibliography, 1961–1980.* San Antonio: Trinity University Press, 1983.

McCloskey, Mark and Paul R. Murphy, trans. *The Latin Poetry of George Herbert: A Bilingual Edition.* Athens, Ohio: Ohio University Press, 1985.

Merchant, W. Moelwyn. "Donne's Sermon to the Virginia Company, 13 November 1622." In *John Donne: Essays in Celebration.* Edited by A. J. Smith. London: Methuen, 1972.

Mercurius [psued.]. *Mercuries Message Defended, Against the vain, foolish, simple, and absurd cavils of Thomas Herbert a ridiculous Ballad-maker.* London, 1641. Wing STC M1747.

Meyrick, Sir Samuel Rush, ed. *Heraldic Visitations of Wales . . . Between the Years 1586 and 1613 . . . By Lewys Dwnn.* 2 vols. Llandovery: Welsh Mss. Society, 1846.

Miller, Edmund. *George Herbert's Kinships: An Ahnentafel With Annotations.* Bowie, MD: Heritage, 1993.

——— and Robert DiYanni, eds. *Like Season'd Timber: New Essays on George Herbert.* New York: Peter Lang, 1987.

Miller, Naomi J., and Gary Waller, eds. *Reading Mary Wroth: Representing Alternatives in Early Modern England.* Knoxville: University of Tennessee Press, 1991.

Miller, Perry. "The Religious Impulse in the Founding of Virginia: Religion and Society in the Early Literature." *William & Mary Quarterly*, 3d series, 5 (1954): 492–522.

Milton, John. *The Complete Poems and Major Prose.* Edited by Merritt Y. Hughes. Indianapolis: Bobbs-Merrill, 1984.

Mount, Ferdinand. *The Subversive Family: An Alternative History of Love and Marriage.* New York: Free Press, 1992.

Nardo, Anna K. *The Ludic Self in Seventeenth-Century English Literature.* Albany: SUNY Press, 1991.

Neill, Edward D. *History of the Virginia Company of London.* Albany, New York, 1869. Reprint, New York: Burt Franklin, 1968.

Newman, Karen. *Fashioning Femininity and English Renaissance Drama.* Women in Culture and Society Series. Chicago: University of Chicago Press, 1991.

Noakes, Aubrey. "The Mother of George Herbert." *Contemporary Review* 183 (1953): 39–45.

Norton, Mary. "Edward, Lord Herbert of Cherbury (3 March 1583–1? August 1648)." *Dictionary of Literary Biography: Seventeenth-Century British Nondramatic Poets.* Edited by M. Thomas Hester. 1st ser., vol. 121. Detroit: Gale, 1992.

Novarr, David. *The Making of Walton's "Lives".* Ithaca: Cornell University Press, 1958.

O'Day, Rosemary. *The Family and Family Relationships, 1500–1900: England, France & the United States of America.* New York: St. Martin's Press, 1994.

Olin, John C., ed. *John Calvin & Jacopo Sadoleto: A Reformation Debate*. Grand Rapids, Mich.: Baker Book House, 1976.

Orlin, Lena Cowen. *Private Matters and Public Culture in Post-Reformation England*. Ithaca: Cornell University Press, 1994.

Overbury, Sir Thomas. *The Overburian Characters, to Which is Added, A Wife*. Edited by W. J. Paylor. Oxford: Blackwell, 1936. Reprint, New York: AMS, 1977.

Palmer, George Herbert, ed. *The English Works of George Herbert*. 3 vols. Boston: Houghton Mifflin, 1905.

Parry, Graham. *The Golden Age Restor'd: The Culture of the Stuart Court, 1603–42*. New York: St. Martin's Press, 1981.

Patrides, C. A., ed. "A Crown of Praise: The Poetry of Herbert." In *The English Poems of George Herbert*, 6–25. London: J. M. Dent, 1974.

————, ed. *George Herbert: The Critical Heritage*. London: Routledge, 1983.

Peacham, Henry. *The Complete Gentleman, The Truth of Our Times, and The Art of Living in London*. Edited by Virgil B. Heltzel. Ithaca, NY: Cornell University Press for the Folger Shakespeare Library, 1962.

Pearlman, E. "George Herbert's God." *English Literary Renaissance* 13 (1983): 88–112.

Pebworth, Ted-Larry. "George Herbert's Poems to the Queen of Bohemia: A Rediscovered Text and a New Edition." *English Literary Renaissance* 9 (1979): 108–20.

————, and Claude J Summers. "Recovering an Important Seventeenth-Century Poetical Miscellany: Cambridge ADD. MS 4138." *Transactions of the Cambridge Bibliographical Society* 7 (1978): 156–69.

Perkins, William. *A Treatise of the Vocations*, vol. 1. In *The Workes of that Famovs and Worthy Minister of Christ . . ., Mr. William Perkins*. London: John Legatt, 1612. STC 19650.

Perry, James R. *The Formation of a Society on Virginia's Eastern Shore, 1615–1655*. Chapel Hill: Institute for Early American History and Culture, 1990.

Piret, Michael. "Herbert and Proverbs." *The Cambridge Quarterly* 17 (1988): 222–43.

Pollard, Alfred W. and G. R. Redgrave. *A Short-Title Catalogue of*

Books Printed in England, Scotland, & Ireland . . ., 1475–1640.
2d ed. London: Bibliographical Society, 1976–1991.

Pollock, Linda A. *Forgotten Children: Parent-Child Relations from 1500 to 1900.* Cambridge: Cambridge University Press, 1983.

———. "'Teach Her to Live Under Obedience': the Making of Women in the Upper Ranks of Early Modern England." *Continuity and Change* 4 (1989): 231–58.

———. "Younger Sons in Tudor and Stuart England." *History Today* 39 (June 1989): 23–29.

Poole, Kristen. "'The fittest closet for all goodness': Authorial Strategies of Jacobean Mothers' Manuals." *Studies in English Literature* 35 (1995): 69–88.

Pope, Alexander. *The Poetry and Prose of Alexander Pope.* Edited by Aubrey Williams. Boston: Houghton Mifflin, 1969.

Powers-Beck, Jeffrey. "Conquering Laurels and Creeping Ivy: The Tangled Politics of Herbert's *Reditum Caroli.*" *George Herbert Journal* 17 (Fall 1993): 1–23.

———. "'Not Onely a Pastour, but a Lawyer Also: George Herbert's Vision of Stuart Magistracy." *Early Modern Literary Studies* 1 (August 1995), World Wide Web.

Pritchard, Allan. "Additional Seventeenth-Century Allusions to George Herbert." *George Herbert Journal* 11 (Spring 1988): 37–48.

Prophecys Concerning the return of Popery into England, Scotland and Ireland by Arch-bishop Vsher, Mr. Herbert, et al. London: for A. Bancks, 1682.

Prynne, William. *Canterburies Doome. Or the First Part of a Compleat History of the Commitment, Charge, Tryall, Condemnation, Execution of William Lavd Late Arch-Bishop of Canterbury.* London: John Maycock for Michael Spark, 1646. Wing STC P3917.

Purchas, Samuel. *Hakluytus Posthumus or Purchas His Pilgrimes.* 20 vols. Glasgow: J. MacLehose and Sons, 1905–1907. Reprint, New York: AMS Press, 1965.

Quinones, Ricardo J. *The Renaissance Discovery of Time.* Cambridge: Harvard University Press, 1972.

Quixley, R. C. E., ed. *Antique Maps of Cornwall and the Isles of Scilly.* Cornwall: J. H. Lake and Company, 1966.

Ransome, David R., ed. *Ferrar Papers, 1590–1790.* Wakefield, England: Microform Academic Publishers, 1992.

———. "Pocahontas and the Mission to the Indians." *The Virginia Magazine of History and Biography* 99 (January 1991): 81–94.

———. "'Shipt for Virginia': The Beginnings in 1619–1622 of the Great Migration to the Chesapeake." *The Virgnia Magazine of History and Biography* 103 (October 1995): 443–58.

———. "Wives for Virginia." *The William and Mary Quarterly.* 3d series. 48 (January 1991): 3–18.

Ray, Robert H. "The Herbert Allusion Book," *Studies in Philology* 83 (1996): 1–160.

———. "Herbert's Seventeenth-Century Reputation: A Summary and New Considerations." *George Herbert Journal* Vol. 9 (Spring 1986): 1–15.

Razi, Zvi. "The Myth of the Immutable English Family." *Past & Present* no. 140 (August 1993): 3–44.

Rickey, Mary Ellen. "Rhymecraft in Edward and George Herbert." *Journal of English and Germanic Philology* 57 (1958): 502–11.

———. *Utmost Art: Complexity in the Verse of George Herbert.* Lexington: University of Kentucky Press, 1966.

Roberts, John R. *George Herbert: An Annotated Bibliography of Modern Criticism, 1905–1974.* Columbia: University of Missouri Press, 1978.

———. "'Me Thoughts I Heard One Calling, Child': Herbert's 'The Collar,'" *Renascence* 45 (Spring 1993): 197–204.

———, ed. *New Perspectives on the Seventeenth-Century English Religious Lyric.* Columbia: University of Missouri Press, 1994.

Rossi, Mario M. *La vita, le opere, i tempi di Edoardo Herbert di Chirbury.* 3 vols. Florence: G. C. Sansoni, 1947.

Rubin, Deborah. "'Let your death be my *Iliad:*' Classical Allusion and Latin in George Herbert's *Memoriae Matris Sacrum.*" In *Reconsidering the Renaissance: Papers from the Twenty-First Annual Conference.* Edited by Mario A. Di Cesare. Binghamton, NY: Medieval & Renaissance Texts & Studies, 1992.

———. "The Mourner in the Flesh: George Herbert's Commemoration of Magdalen Herbert in *Memoriae Matis Sacrum.*" In *Men*

Writing the Feminine: Literature, Theory and the Question of Genders. Edited by Thais E. Morgan. Albany: State University of New York Press, 1994.

Ryley, George. *Mr. Herbert's Temple and Church Militant Explained and Improved (Bodleian MS Rawl. D. 199).* Edited by Maureen Boyd and Cedric C. Brown. New York: Garland, 1987.

Saintsbury, W. N., ed. *Calendar of State Papers, Colonial Series, 1574–1660.* London: Longman, 1860.

——— , and F. W. Fortescue., eds. *Calendar of State Papers, Colonial Series, 1617–1621.* London: Longman, 1887.

Schoenfeldt, Michael C. "George Herbert's Consuming Subject." *George Herbert Journal* 18, nos. 1 and 2 (Fall 1994/ Spring 1995): 105–32.

———. *Prayer and Power: George Herbert and Renaissance Courtship.* Chicago: University of Chicago Press, 1991.

Schochet, Gordon J. *The Authoritarian Family and Political Attitudes in 17th Century England: Patriarchalism in Political Thought.* New Brunswick: Transaction, 1988.

Shakespeare, William. *The Complete Works of Shakespeare.* 3d ed. Edited by David Bevington. Glenview, Ill.: Scott, Foresman and Co., 1980.

Shammas, Carole. "Anglo-American Household Government in Perspective." *William and Mary Quarterly.* 3d ser. 52 (January 1995): 104–144.

Sharpe, Kevin. *The Personal Rule of Charles I.* New Haven: Yale University Press, 1992.

Shuger, Debora K. *Habits of Thought in the English Renaissance.* Berkeley: University of California Press, 1990.

Sidney, Sir Philip. *The Poems of Sir Philip Sidney.* Edited by W. A. Ringler. Oxford: Oxford University Press, 1962.

Simpson, J. A., and E. S. C. Weimer, eds. *The Oxford English Dictionary.* 2d. ed. 20 vols. Oxford: Oxford University Press, 1989.

Singleton, Marion White. *God's Courtier: Configuring a Different Grace in George Herbert's Temple.* Cambridge: Cambridge University Press, 1987.

Sizemore, Christine W. "Early Seventeenth-Century Advice Books: The Female Perspective." *South Atlantic Bulletin* 41 (January 1976): 41–48.

Slater, Miriam. *Family Life in the Seventeenth Century: The Verneys of Claydon House.* London: Routledge, 1984.

Smith, A. J., ed. *John Donne: Essays in Celebration.* London: Metheun, 1972.

Smith, W. J., ed. *Herbert Correspondence: The Sixteenth and Seventeenth Century Letters of the Herberts of Chirbury, Powis Castle and Dolguog.* Cardiff: University of Wales Press, 1963.

Stanhope, Philip Dormer, Earl of Chesterfield. *Lord Chesterfield's Letters to his Sons and Others.* Introduction by R. K. Root. London: Dent, 1969.

Stein, Arnold. *George Herbert's Lyrics.* Baltimore: Johns Hopkins Press, 1968.

Stephen, Sir Leslie, and Sir Sidney Lee. *Dictionary of Literary Biography.* 21 vols. Oxford: Oxford University Press, 1917.

Stewart, Stanley. *George Herbert.* Twayne English Author Series. Boston: Twayne, 1986.

———. "Time and *The Temple*." *Studies in English Literature* 6 (1966): 97–110.

Stone, Lawrence. *The Crisis of the Aristocracy, 1558–1641.* Oxford: Oxford University Press, 1965.

———. *The Family, Sex, and Marriage in England, 1500–1800.* New York: Harper & Row, 1977.

Strier, Richard. "George Herbert and the World." *Journal of Medieval and Renaissance Studies* 11 (Fall 1981): 347–52.

———. *Love Known: Theology and Experience in George Herbert's Poetry.* Chicago: University of Chicago Press, 1983.

———. "Radical Donne: 'Satire III.'" *English Literary History* 60 (1993): 283–322.

———. *Resistant Structures: Particularity, Radicalism, and Renaissance Texts.* Berkeley: University of California Press, 1995.

———. "Sanctifying the Aristocracy: 'Devout Humanism' in Francois de Sales, John Donne, and George Herbert." *Journal of Religion* 69 (1989): 36–58.

Summers, Claude J., and Ted-Larry Pebworth. "The Politics of *The Temple*: 'The British Church' and 'The Familie.'" *George Herbert Journal* 8 (Fall 1984): 1–15.

———, eds. *"The Muses Common-Weale": Poetry and Politics in the Seventeenth Century.* Columbia: University of Missouri Press, 1988.

Summers, Joseph H. *George Herbert: His Religion and Art.* Cambridge: Harvard University Press, 1954.

———. *The Heirs of Donne and Jonson.* Oxford: Oxford University Press, 1970.

Swartz, Douglas J. "Discourse and Direction: *A Priest to the Temple,* or the *Country Parson* and the Elaboration of Sovereign Rule." *Criticism* 36 (Spring 1994): 189–212.

———. *Priestly Poetics: George Herbert and the State-Ecclesiastical.* Ph.D. diss., Loyola University, 1991. Ann Arbor: UMI, 1992.

Swiss, Margo. "Donne's Medieval Magdalene: Apostalic Authority in 'To the Lady Magdalen Herbert, of St. Mary Magdalen.'" *English Studies in Canada* 18 (June 1992): 143–56.

Thane, John. *British Autography. A Collection of Fac-similes of Hand Writing of Royal and Illustrious Personages with their authentic Portraits.* 2 vols. London: J. Thane, 1838.

Thirsk, Joan. "Younger Songs in the Seventeenth Century." *History* 54 (1969): 358–77.

Thorpe, James. "Reflections and Self-Reflections: *Outlandish Proverbs* as a Context for George Herbert's Other Writings." In *Illustrious Evidence: Approaches to English Literature of the Early Seventeenth Century,* 23–37. Edited by Earl Miner. Berkeley: University of California Press, 1975.

Toliver, Harold. *George Herbert's Christian Narrative.* University Park: Pennsylvania State University Press, 1993.

Travitsky, Betty S., and Adele F. Seeff, eds. *Attending to Women in Early Modern England.* Newark: University of Delaware Press, 1994.

Tuve, Rosemond. *A Reading of George Herbert.* Chicago: University of Chicago Press, 1952.

Tuveson, Ernest Lee. *Millenium and Utopia: A Study in the Background of the Idea of Progress.* New York: Harper & Row, 1964.

Ustick, W. Lee. "Advice to a Son: A Type of Seventeenth-Century Conduct Book." *Studies in Philology* 29 (1932): 409–41.

Vaughan, Henry. *The Works of Henry Vaughan.* 2d ed. Edited by L. C. Martin. Oxford: Oxford University Press, 1957.

Veith, Gene Edward, Jr. *Reformation Spirituality: The Religion of George Herbert*. Lewisburg: Bucknell University Press, 1985.

———. "The Religious Wars in George Herbert Criticism: Reinterpreting Seventeenth-Century Anglicanism." *George Herbert Journal* 11 (Spring 1988): 19–35.

Vendler, Helen. *The Poetry of George Herbert*. Cambridge, Mass.: Harvard University Press, 1975.

Venn, John, and J. A. Venn, eds. *The Book of Matriculations and Degrees . . . in the University of Cambridge from 1544 to 1659*. Cambridge: Cambridge University Press, 1913.

Wall, John N. *Transformations of the Word: Spenser, Herbert, Vaughan*. Athens: University of Georgia Press, 1988.

Waller, Gary. *The Sidney Family Romance: Mary Wroth, William Herbert, and the Early Modern Construction of Gender*. Detroit: Wayne State University Press, 1993.

Walter, Alice Granbery. *Herbert in England & Virginia, 1399–1900s*. Virginia Beach, Va.: Alice Granbery Walter, 1977.

Walton, Izaak. *The Life of Mr. George Herbert*. London: Thomas Newcomb for Richard Marriott, 1670. Wing STC W669.

———. *The Lives of John Donne, Sir Henry Wotton, Richard Hooker, George Herbert, and Robert Sanderson*. Edited by George Saintsbury. London: Oxford University Press, 1927.

Wanley, Nathaniel. *The Poems of Nathaniel Wanley*. Edited by L. C. Martin. Oxford: Oxford University Press, 1928.

Warner, Rebecca, ed. *Epistolary Curiosities*. First Series. Bath: Richard Cruttwell, 1818.

Waterhouse, Edward. *A Declaration of the State of the Colony in Virginia*. London: 1622. Reprint, New York: De Capo Press, 1970.

Watson, Robert N. *The Rest is Silence. Death as Annihilation in the English Renaissance*. Berkeley: University of California Press, 1994.

Weber, Max. *The Protestant Ethic and the Spirit of Capitalism*. Translated by Talcott Parsons. London: Routledge, 1992.

Whitaker, Alexander. *Good Newes from Virginia*. London: Felix Kynston for William Welby, 1613. STC 25354.

White, Helen C. *English Devotional Literature (Prose), 1600–1640*. Madison: University of Wisconsin Press, 1930. Reprint: New York: Haskell House, 1966.

White, James Boyd. *"This Book of Starres": Learning to Read George Herbert.* Ann Arbor: University of Michigan Press, 1994.

Wilcox, Helen, and Richard Todd, eds. *George Herbert: Sacred and Profane.* Amsterdam: V.U. University Press, 1995.

Wilkinson, Henry C. *The Adventures of Bermuda: A History of the Island from its Discovery until the Dissolution of the Somers Island Company in 1684.* 2d ed. London: Oxford University Press, 1958.

Willet, Andrew. *Sacrorum Emblematum Centuria Una.* Cambridge, 1592 (?). Reprint, Delmar, NY: Scholars' Facsimiles, 1984.

Williams, Raymond. *Keywords: A Vocabulary of Culture and Society.* Rev. ed. New York: Oxford University Press, 1983.

Wing, Donald G. *Short-Title Catalogue of Books Printed in England, Scotland, Ireland, Wales, and British America . . ., 1641–1700.* 2d ed. New York: Modern Language Association, 1972–1988.

Winter, Ernest F., ed. *Erasmus-Luther: Discourse on Free Will.* New York: Ungar, 1961.

Wood, Anthony. *Athenae Oxoniensis.* Edited by Philip Bliss. 4 vols. Oxford: 1848.

Wood, Chauncey. "George and Henry Herbert on Redemption." *The Huntington Library Quarterly* 46 (1983): 298–309.

Woodnoth, Arthur. *A Short Collection of the Most Remarkable Passages from the originall to the dissolution of the Virginia Company.* London: Richard Cotes for Edward Husband, 1651. Wing STC W3243.

Woolf, Virginia. "The Art of Biography." In *The Death of the Moth and Other Essays,* 119–26. London: Hogarth Press, 1942.

———. *A Room of One's Own.* 1929. Reprint, San Diego: HBJ, 1957.

Wright, Herbert G. "Was George Herbert the Author of *Jacula Prudentum.*" *Review of English Studies* 11 (1935): 139–44.

Wright, Louis B., ed. *Advice to a Son: Precepts of Lord Burghley, Sir Walter Raleigh, and Francis Osborne.* Ithaca: Folger Shakespeare Library, 1962.

Wrightson, Keith. *English Society, 1580–1680.* New Brunswick: Rutgers University Press, 1982.

Zouch, Richard. *The Dove: or Passages of Cosmography.* London: Printed for George Norton, 1613. STC 26130.

Index

About the Author

Jeffrey Powers-Beck is associate professor of English at East Tennessee State University. With the assistance of grants from the National Endowment for the Humanities and the ETSU Research Development Committee, he has performed extensive archival research on Herbert family manuscripts in England and Wales. His articles have appeared in *English Literary Renaissance, South Atlantic Review, English Language Notes* and other journals.